INTRODUCTION TO COMPUTER SCIENCE
using the
TURING PROGRAMMING LANGUAGE

R.C. Holt

J.N.P. Hume

Department of Computer Science
University of Toronto

RESTON PUBLISHING COMPANY, INC., Reston, Virginia
A Prentice-Hall Company

ISBN 0-8359-3168-4
ISBN 0-8359-3167-6 pbk.

10   9   8   7   6   5   4   3   2

Printed in the United States of America

CONTENTS

PREFACE

This book introduces Computer Science using the Turing programming language. Computer Science encompasses a wide range of topics, including programming languages, computer systems, numerical computation, theory of computation, discrete mathematics, artificial intelligence, computer graphics, and information systems. No serious study of this science is viable without a solid underpinning in programming, in algorithms, and in basic data structures. It is the aim of this book to provide this underpinning, and while doing so to give interesting examples that serve to motivate further study in the various subjects within the science.

Programming and algorithms are taught most effectively in terms of good notation, namely an appropriate programming language. This book uses the Turing programming language. Turing can be thought of as the latest in a series of languages that has included Fortran, Algol, PL/1, and Pascal. Each of these languages has helped us to program and to teach programming with increased confidence and precision.

The Turing language is a general purpose programming language that is well suited for teaching programming. It is designed to support the development of reliable, efficient programs. It incorporates features that decrease the cost of program maintenance, and that support formal verification.

The Turing language has been implemented by a portable user-friendly compiler on the Digital Equipment Vax, on the IBM370, and (likely soon to be) on various microprocessors such as the MC68000 and NS16000. This compiler is available from the Turing Distribution Manager, Room 2002G, Sanford Fleming Building, University of Toronto, Toronto, Canada, M5S 1A4 (phone 416-978-6985). Turing is a Pascal-like language and incorporates almost all of Pascal's features. Turing alleviates many difficulties with Pascal. For example, Turing provides convenient string handling; it provides modules; its variant records are type safe, and it has dynamic parameters and arrays.

From the point of view of the teacher and student, perhaps the most pleasant aspect of Turing is its unobtrusive nature. It has a simple, unwordy syntax, allowing concentration on what is being programmed rather than on language details. As a result, although Turing is a more general language than Pascal, its basic features have an expressiveness that is characteristic of more modest languages such as Basic and Logo.

Acknowledgements. The Turing language was designed by R.C. Holt and J.R. Cordy. The Turing compiler was developed by a team consisting of J.R. Cordy, R.C. Holt, M.P. Mendell and S.G. Perelgut with assistance from P.A. Matthews and S.W.K. Tjiang. T.E. Hull, E.C.R. Hehner, J.N.P. Hume and a number of others suggested important improvements that have been incorporated into the language. I.S. Weber has carefully and promptly done the text entry and computer type setting of this book. Assistance in testing programs and indexing was given by M.N. Hume and H.A.L. Hume.

R.C. Holt
J.N.P. Hume

University of Toronto

Chapter 1

INTRODUCTION

WHAT ARE COMPUTERS?

Computers are devices consisting of electric circuits with electronic elements that act as **switches** and **gates** in the circuits. When computers were first built starting about 1945 the electronic elements were vacuum tubes. About 1959, tubes were discarded in favor of transistors. Then it was found that the electronic elements could be integrated into the circuits and produced by special "printing" techniques. By the 1980's the integrated circuits had been miniaturized to such an extent that major components of the computer could be "printed" on a chip of silicon smaller than a fingernail. Today we can obtain desk top computers for personal use that are as powerful as ones that sold for over a million dollars in the early 1960's.

As the cost of computers has dropped in the last 25 years, the uses that have been found for them have skyrocketed. There is scarcely any part of our lives that has not been changed in some way due to computers. There has been what many refer to as a **revolution** in the way things are done. With the invention of the steam engine in the nineteenth century, machines were devised to handle physical materials: to transport them and shape them into useful objects. We had what was known as the **industrial revolution**. Computers are machines that handle information and process it so that it is useful to us. We have now what is called an **information revolution**, or a **computer revolution**. The revolution has been accelerated by the concurrent advances in the technology of **telecommunications**, which includes the use of satellites for long distance communication and the transmission of digital signals.

The machines of the industrial revolution did physical work for us. The machines of the information revolution do mental work for us. That is why the early computers were referred to as **electronic brains**.

The way that a computer operates is to take in information, transform it, and then put the transformed information out. If the computer transforms information in a fixed way, we would say it is a **special purpose machine**. Computers usually are **general purpose machines**. To operate, a computer must have in it a list of instructions which specifies how the information is to be transformed. This list of instructions is called a **computer program**. The information that is to be transformed is called **data**. A computer program can itself be read into a computer and this means that you can have various programs in the machine. This is why we say that our computers are general purpose; they can run, in sequence or in parallel, a variety of programs. Any computer that you intend to use must have some programs already stored in it so that you may read in your programs and have them operate. We call programs **software**; the computer itself is the **hardware**. The software stored in the computer that allows users to enter programs and run them is called the **operating system**. Programs that transform data for you are called **applications software**.

There is a great deal of applications software available for most computer systems. This means that you may not have to write programs for yourself. You only need to know how to run the application program. Usually an attempt is made to make it as easy as possible for the user to use an applications software package. The software is designed to make the system **user friendly**. An important part of software design is to make the interface between the machine and the user as simple as possible. After all, the purpose of computers is to do as much of our work as they can for us.

WHAT IS COMPUTER SCIENCE?

Computer science is concerned with the acquisition and organization of knowledge about computers and their use. As a science it is systematic in this activity; it is concerned with generalizations, structures, abstractions, models, fundamentals, and theories. Since computer science is an emerging science we must form new concepts. Some of these are adopted from more mature sciences. As with other sciences, mathematics is the language in which ideas and facts can be most precisely expressed. But we have in computer science another kind of language which did not exist before computers existed, the language of **programming**. In mathematics the concept of a set of instructions which specifies a procedure by which certain ends can be accomplished in a finite number of steps pre-existed computers. It was called an **algorithm**. Before computers there was not much interest in devising languages to express algorithms. A computer program is an algorithm.

Perhaps one way to look at computer science is to ask what is its premise. No doubt there are as many answers to this question as there are computer scientists. One answer worth consideration is that a computer scientist is concerned not just with a tool (or machine) such as lathe, or an automobile, or a pocket calculator with limited capabilities but with a machine that is capable of almost everything that can be done mentally by a person. Many jobs presently done by people can ultimately be done equally well by machines. This does not mean that we know yet how to get the machines to do everything and perhaps this will take a very long time. Nor does it mean that we would replace people by machines that do their work.

SUBDIVISIONS OF COMPUTER SCIENCE

As our knowledge about computers grows, various parts of it split off as individual subjects to be studied. In this book we hope to introduce you to computer science as a whole but at the same time to lay the basis for future study in the field. We will be introducing many concepts, with their accompanying technical vocabulary, but will also introduce you to a specific programming language. These concepts will include:

structure of computers

structure of programs (algorithms)

design of programs

correctness of programs

efficiency of programs

complexity of programs

structure of data

structure of records and files

structure of programming languages

structure of systems software

To illustrate many of these concepts we will be giving examples in the form of programs. This means we must have a particular programming language. We will use a language called **Turing**. The Turing programming language was devised by R.C. Holt and J.R. Cordy at the University of Toronto. It was named in honor of Alan M. Turing, the Englishman who not only designed one of the first electronic digital computers but made very important fundamental contributions to the theory of computing. (It happens that his name begins with TU which can also stand for Toronto University.)

WHAT IS PROGRAMMING?

Programming is writing instructions for a computer in a language that it can understand so that it can do something for you. We will be writing programs in one particular **programming language** called Turing. When these instructions are entered into a computer directly by means of a keyboard input terminal they go into the part of the computer called its **memory** and are recorded there for as long as they are needed. The instructions could then be **executed** if they were in the language the computer understands directly, the language called **machine language**. If they are in another language such as Turing they must first be **translated**, and a program in machine language, called the **object program**, **compiled** from the original or **source program**. After compilation the program can be executed.

Computers can really only do a very small number of different basic things. The repertoire of instructions that any computer understands usually includes the ability to move numbers from one place to another in its memory, to add, subtract, multiply, and divide. They can, in short, do all kinds of **arithmetic calculations** and they can do these operations at rates that exceed a million a second. Computers are extremely fast calculating machines. But they can do more; they can also handle alphabetic information, both moving it around in their memory and comparing different pieces of information to see if they are the same. To include both numbers and alphabetic information we say that computers are **data processors** or more generally **information processors**.

When we write programs we write a sequence of instructions that we want executed one after another. But you can see that the computer could execute our programs very rapidly if each instruction were executed only once. A program of a thousand instructions might take only a thousandth of a second. One of the instructions we can include in our programs is an instruction which causes the use of other instructions to be repeated over and over. In this way the computer is capable of repetitious work; it tirelessly executes the same set of instructions again and again. Naturally the data that it is operating on must change with each repetition or it would accomplish nothing.

Perhaps you have heard also that computers can make **decisions**. In a sense they can. These so-called decisions are fairly simple. The instructions read something like this:

> if John is over 16 then place him on the hockey team
> else place him on the soccer team

Depending on the **condition** of John's age, the computer could place his name on one or other of two different sports teams. It can **decide** which one if you tell it the decision criterion, for example, over sixteen or not.

Perhaps these first few hints will give you a clue to what programming is about. The kind of programming we will present is called structured programming.

WHAT IS STRUCTURED PROGRAMMING?

The term structured programming is used to describe both a number of techniques for writing programs as well as a more general methodology. Just as programs provide a list of instructions to the computer to achieve some well-defined goal, the methodology of structured programming provides a list of instructions to persons who write programs to achieve some well-defined goals. The goals of structured programming are, first, to get the job done. This deals with **how** to get the job done and how to get it done **correctly**. The second goal is concerned with having it done so that other people can see how it is done, both for their education and in case these other people later have to make changes in the original programs.

Computer programs can be very simple and straightforward but many applications require that very large programs be written. The very size of these programs makes them complicated and difficult to understand. But if they are well-structured, then the complexity can be controlled. Controlling complexity can be accomplished in many different ways and all of these are of interest in the cause of structured programming. The philosophy of structured programming encourages us to keep track of everything that will help us to be better programmers. We will be cataloguing many of the elements of structured programming as we go along, but first we must look at the particular programming language we will be using.

WHAT IS TURING?

Turing is a language that has been developed to be independent of the particular computer on which it is run and oriented to the problems that persons might want done. We say that Turing is a **high-level language** because it was designed to be relatively easy to learn. As a problem-oriented language it is concerned with problems of numerical calculations such as occur in scientific and engineering applications as well as with alphabetic information handling required by business and humanities applications. As well, it can be used for programming systems software. It is a **procedure oriented language** which means that it was designed to express algorithms.

A high-level language lasts much longer than machine languages, which change every five years or so. This is because once an investment has been made in programs for a range of applications, you do not want to have to reprogram when a new computer is acquired. What is needed is a new compiler for the high-level language and all the old programs can be reused.

Because of the long life-span of programs in high-level languages it becomes more and more important that they can be adapted to changes in the application rather than completely reconstructed.

A high-level language has the advantage that well-constructed and well-documented programs in the language can be readily modified. Our aim is to teach you how to write such programs. To start we will present a few features of the full Turing language at a time. What we will have presented at any time is a subset of Turing. At each stage, as new concepts in computer science are introduced, new features of Turing are presented and examples are worked out to illustrate the new concepts. We will not be burdened with any more details of the programming language than we actually need to provide concrete illustrations of the concepts that we are attempting to understand.

There is no substitute for a hands-on experience in learning a new subject; submit your knowledge to the test by creating your own programs and running them on your computer.

CORRECTNESS OF PROGRAMS

One of the maddening things about computers is that they do exactly what you tell them to do rather than what you want them to do. To get correct results your program has to be correct. When an answer is displayed by a computer you must know whether or not it is correct. You cannot assume, as people often do, that because it was given by a computer it must be right. It is the right answer for the particular program and data you provided because computers now are really very reliable and rarely make mistakes. But is your program correct? Are your input data correct?

One way of checking whether any particular answer is correct is to get the answer by some other means and compare it with the displayed answer. This means that you must work out the answer by hand, perhaps using a hand calculator to help you. When you do work by hand you probably do not concentrate on exactly how you are getting the answer but you know you are correct (assuming you do not make foolish errors). But this seems rather pointless. You wanted the computer to do some work for you to save you the effort and now you must do the work anyway to test whether your computer program is correct. Where is the benefit of all this? The labor saving comes when you get the computer to use your program to work out a similar problem for you. For example, a program to compute telephone bills can be checked for correctness by comparing the results with hand computation for a number of representative customers and then it can be used on millions of others without detailed checking. What we are checking is the method of the calculation.

We must be sure that our representative sample of test cases includes all the various exceptional circumstances that can occur in practice, and this is a great difficulty. Suppose that there were five different things that could be exceptional about a telephone customer. A single customer might have any number of exceptional features simultaneously. So the number of different types of customers might be 32, ranging from those with no exceptional features to those with all five. To test all these combinations takes a lot of time, so usually, we test only a few of the combinations and hope all is well.

Because exhaustive testing of all possible cases to be handled by a program is too large a job, many programs are not thoroughly tested and ultimately give incorrect results when an unusual combination of circumstances is encountered in practice. You must try to test your programs as well as possible and at the same time realize that with large programs the job becomes very difficult. This has led many computer scientists to advocate the need to **prove** programs correct by various techniques other than exhaustive testing. These techniques rely partly on reading and studying the program to make sure it directs the computer to do the right calculation. Certainly the well-structured program will be easier to prove correct.

THE OPERATING SYSTEM

In order that a computer can accept programs in Turing and run them it must already have programs inside it. These are called **systems programs**. One of these systems programs is a Turing compiler. Another is called its **operating system**. The operating system permits you to enter your program through the keyboard, make any alterations in it that are necessary (**edit** it), store it away in the secondary memory of the computer (**file** it), initiate compilation and execution (**run** programs), initiate printed output (prepare **hardcopy**), and so on. We will describe one particular operating system, the Unix*tm* operating system devised by Bell Laboratories. This system is used on computers of various sizes even down to microcomputers. Just as we use a particular programming language, we will use a particular operating system and its command language as the vehicle for our introduction to computer science.

In order to get the Unix operating system to accept, edit, file, compile, or execute your Turing program you must give it instructions through the keyboard. These are called **system commands**. So, in addition to learning the Turing language for writing Turing programs, you must also learn the Unix **command language**. This command language, like the Turing language, is extensive and we will be introducing only as much as you will need at any time. It is a good idea to learn a few commands at a time and become confident in their use before learning more.

CHAPTER 1 SUMMARY

The purpose of this book is to introduce computer science. We have begun in this chapter by presenting the following terminology.

Computer — a device or machine consisting of electric circuits containing electronic elements and accompanied by devices by which it can communicate with its users.

Vacuum tube — an electronic element which could act in a circuit so as to produce the effect of a switch, to reroute electric signals, or a gate to selectively block signals. Tubes were used in the original computers built between 1945 and 1956.

Transistor — an electronic element which could replace vacuum tubes. It was called a solid state device and was much more reliable than a tube. Transistors started to be used about 1959.

Integrated circuit — a circuit in which the connecting wires and transistors were integrated and often produced by a form of reproduction like printing.

Silicon chip — the medium upon which the integrated circuits are now deposited. The circuits are miniaturized by photographic techniques and "printed" on the chip.

Large Scale Integration (LSI) — circuits in which thousands of electronic elements are contained on a single silicon chip often smaller than a fingernail. As more and more circuits have been placed on single chips, the term VLSI (Very Large Scale Integration) has come into use.

Personal computer — a microcomputer which can be placed on a desk and used by a single user at a time.

Information revolution — the change in society due to the advent of computers and modern telecommunications.

Special purpose machine — a machine (computer) programmed to carry out one specific task such as running a heating system.

General purpose machine — a machine (computer) into which many different programs can be read and which is thus capable of many different tasks.

Data — the information which is to be transformed by the program executing on the computer.

Software — computer programs.

Hardware — the computer itself, that is, the electronic curcuits and the input-output devices.

Applications software — programs that are written to perform specific tasks and which can be used by anyone who learns how.

User interface — what must be learned and understood by a user before use can be made of a computer system.

Computer science — the science concerned with the acquisition and organization of knowledge about computers and their use.

Algorithm — the mathematical term for a list of instructions by which some specific result can be obtained by a person or device in a finite number of steps. Programs are algorithms.

Program (or computer program) — a list of instructions for a computer to follow. We say the computer executes instructions.

Programming — writing instructions telling a computer to perform certain data manipulations.

Programming language — a language used to write programs that direct the computer to do work for us.

Turing — a high-level programming language devised by R.C. Holt and J.R. Cordy at the University of Toronto. Pascal, PL/1, Fortran, Cobol, Basic, and APL are some other high-level programming languages.

High-level language — a programming language that is designed to be convenient for writing programs. Turing is a high-level language.

Procedure oriented language — a programming language suitable for expressing algorithms.

Compiler — a systems program that translates a program written in a high-level language, such as Turing, into a language that can be executed on a computer.

Structured programming — a method of programming that helps us write correct programs that can be understood by others. The Turing language has been designed to encourage structured programming.

Correctness of programs — demonstrating that a program will necessarily accomplish its stated purpose (its specification).

Operating system — a program that is kept in the computer and which permits users to operate the computer. It lets them submit programs, edit them, file them, compile them, and execute them.

Unix*ᵗᵐ* — an operating system devised by the Bell Laboratories and used on a great variety of computer systems.

Command language — a set of commands that cause the operating system to perform certain functions for you. These are used to submit, edit, file, compile, and execute programs.

Unix command language (also called the shell language) — the particular set of commands that are used with the Unix operating system.

Chapter 2

THE STRUCTURE
OF COMPUTERS

A computer is a complex object composed of wires, silicon chips with electronic circuits on them, and so on, but we will not be trying to follow circuit diagrams and worrying about how to build a computer. What we will be interested in is the various main parts of a computer and what the function of each is. In this way your programming will be more intelligent; you will have a better idea of what is going on inside the computer.

FUNCTIONAL UNITS

We have already mentioned a number of things about computers. They have a **memory** where programs, numbers, and alphabetic information can be recorded. They can add, subtract, multiply, and divide. This means they have a part called the **arithmetic unit**. They can read information from a keyboard input and output results on a screen. They may also have a printer. The printer may output a whole line at a time or just one character at a time, like a typewriter. We say they have an **input** (for example, keyboard) and an **output** (a screen). Computers execute instructions in sequence. The part of the machine that does this is called the **control unit**. The arithmetic unit and the control unit are usually grouped together in a computer and called the **central processing unit** or **CPU**. So then the computer is thought of as having three parts, memory, input-output, and CPU.

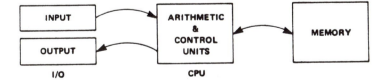

MAIN PARTS OF A COMPUTER

We will look at these different parts in turn but first we must see how numbers and alphabetic information can be represented in a computer.

CODED INFORMATION

You are probably familiar with the way that information used to travel over telegraph wires in the form of Morse Code. Perhaps you know that each letter or number is coded as a pattern of dots and dashes. For example, the letter A is a dot followed by a dash, E is one dot, V is three dots and a dash. The letters are separated from each other by a pause with no dots or dashes. The famous signal SOS is

$$\cdot\ \cdot\ \cdot\quad \_\ \_\ \_\quad \cdot\ \cdot\ \cdot$$

This is an easy one to remember in emergencies. The Morse Code was designed so that the signal could activate some noise-making device and the listener could then translate the coded message back into letters. Modern teletype machines can send messages much faster because the machines themselves can be used to decode the messages. For these, a character is represented by a pattern of pulses, each pattern being of the same length. Instead of dots and dashes, which are two different lengths of electric pulses, they use one basic time interval and in that time interval have either a pulse or a pause. Each character requires 5 basic time intervals and is represented by a sequence of pulses and pauses. We often write down a pulse as a 1 and a pause as 0, and then the pattern for *b* is 10011, *i* is 01100, *l* is 01001. The word *bill* would be transmitted as

10011011000100101001

Strings of ones and zeros like this can be associated with numbers in the **binary system**. In the decimal system the number 342 means

$$3\times 10^2 + 4\times 10^1 + 2\times 10^0$$

where 10^2 stands for 10 squared, 10^1 for 10 to the first power, that is 10, and 10^0 for 10 to the power zero, which has a value 1. In the binary system of numbers 1101 means

$$1\times 2^3 + 1\times 2^2 + 0\times 2^1 + 1\times 2^0$$

In the **decimal system** this binary number has a value $8+4+0+1 = 13$. We say that this number in the decimal system requires 2 **decimal digits** to represent it. In the binary system it requires 4 **binary digits**. We call a binary digit a **bit**. So the binary number representing the word *bill* has 20 bits, each letter requiring 5 bits. Sometimes we take the number of bits required to represent a character as a group and call it a **byte**. Then the word representing *bill* has four bytes. In a computer we must have a way of recording these bits, and usually the memory is arranged into **words**, each capable of holding a whole number of bytes.

In most computers a single letter is represented by a byte of eight bits.

Typical microcomputers have a word length of two bytes. There are many different combinations of byte length and word length in different computers. This is something the machine designer must decide.

Because information is represented as a string of bits or binary digits, we say the computers are **digital** computers. Another quite different kind of computer called an **analog computer** represents numbers as electric voltages, the bigger the voltage the bigger the number. Analog computers are rarely used today although, in the early days of digital computers, analog computers provided a highly competitive way of doing certain scientific calculations.

PULSES, CLOCKS, AND GATES

Computers are often represented by diagrams giving their logical structure. The basic speed of a computer is determined by the time of one pulse. This pulse rate is controlled by a **clock**. The clock issues pulses at a uniform rate. The clock pulse signals are used to control the sequence of activity in the computer. Changes of **state** of the machine take place only at discrete times controlled by the clock. The clocks in typical computers tick at rates of tens of megahertz (millions of ticks per second).

The **logical diagram** of a computer is built up largely of **gates** which are devices made of transistors that control combinations of signals. An **and** gate is one in which a pulse must enter simultaneously on each of its incoming lines for a pulse to appear on its output line. We represent the **and** gate by a diagram

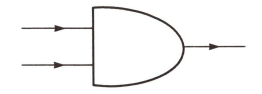

DIAGRAM OF *AND* GATE

An **or** gate is one in which a pulse appears on the output line if there a pulse on either or both of the input lines.

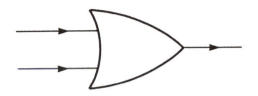

DIAGRAM OF *OR* GATE

A **not** gate is one in which there is only one incoming line and a pulse appears on the output line if in the clock interval a pulse does not appear on the input line and vice versa.

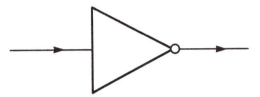

DIAGRAM OF *NOT* GATE

Groups of these basic gates can be interconnected to make a variety of other units or components which form the computer. One type of such component can act as a device for storing a binary digit. It is called a **flip-flop**. This is done by feeding the output of one **or** gate back through a **not** gate in as one input for another and vice versa. The other input to the pair of **or** gates comes from two **and** gates one of whose inputs is a pulse from the control unit, the other being a pulse that we want to store in the flip-flop.

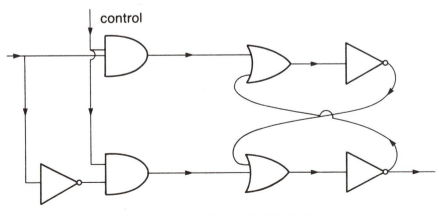

LOGICAL DIAGRAM OF FLIP-FLOP

When a pulse is given by the control, a pulse on the other incoming line to the flip-flop is passed to the output line. Because of the feedback between the **or** gates the pulse continues to be available on the output line. We say the pulse is stored. If, when the control pulse is given, there is no pulse on the incoming line then there will be no pulse on the output line and this condition too will persist. The result is a device capable of storing one bit of information. This type of storage device is volatile; the information would disappear if the power were turned off.

Flip-flops are very high-speed storage devices; they can be set and reset in a few nanoseconds (10^{-9} second). They are used in the high-speed storage registers of the computer. The main memory of the computer is more likely to be a metal oxide semiconductor (MOS) storage device. Magnetic bubble memories are also becoming possible.

MEMORY

Most machines record letters and numbers in the binary form because it is possible to have recording devices that can record, read, and hold such information. Most long term recording devices involve a non-volatile recording something like that on the tape of a magnetic tape recorder. There is a big difference, though, in the recording. On audio tape we have a magnetic recording that varies in intensity with the volume of the sound recorded. The frequency of the variations gives the pitch of the sound. For a computer, the recordings vary between two levels of intensity which you might think of as *on* and *off.* If in a particular region there is an *on* recording it could indicate the binary digit one and if *off* the digit zero. So on a strip of magnetic tape there would be designated areas that are to hold each bit of information.

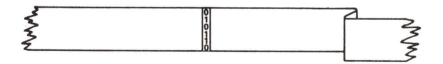

BITS RECORDED ON MAGNETIC TAPE

Binary digits can this be recorded on reels of magnetic tape. In a similar way they can be recorded on tracks of magnetic disk. To read or record information on a magnetic disk the recording-reading head moves to the correct track of the spinning disk so that the information on the track can be accessed.

Tape reels and disks can be removed from the machine and stored if you need to keep information for long periods of time. Small disk memories are often used on microcomputers where individual disks are inserted into the reader by the user. These disks are often limp and are called **floppy disks** or **diskettes**. Diskettes are kept in paper envelopes to protect them. They are **not** removed from the envelope even during use. Tape reels on regular audio-type cassettes can also be used as secondary memory.

Both tape and disk secondary memories require the movement of objects, a reel of tape, a spinning disk and sometimes read-write heads. These mechanical devices can never give really high-speed access to information. We need memory devices with no moving parts so we can perform operations at rates of the order of a million a second. The only things that move in a really high-speed memory device are the electric signals. As you know, electric signals can move very rapidly, at nearly the speed of light. A very common form of high-speed memory uses large scale integrated circuits (LSI).

The main memory of the computer is a number of bits grouped into words; to find any particular word you must know where it is located in the array of words. You need to know its **address**. Every word (which, remember, is just a group of bits) has its own address which is a number. An address may, for example, be *125*. Words that are neighbors in the array have consecutive addresses, such as *125* and *126*, just like apartments in an apartment house. The addresses themselves do not have to be stored in the computer. You can tell what address a word has from its location in the array. This is not always possible for apartments in a building because the numbering is not completely systematic.

The information that is stored in main memory is quickly accessible; any one word can be accessed as speedily as any other. We say that the memory is a **random access memory** (RAM). A disk secondary memory allows you to access any one piece of information about as fast as any other, although at a much slower rate than does main memory. For this reason we call a disk a random access device or a direct access device. Magnetic tape is not a random access device. Sometimes parts of the main memory of a computer have been arranged so that the user can read information from it but cannot write information into it. This is called a **read only memory** (ROM). The information stored in a read only memory must be placed there by the supplier. For example, a compiler program might be stored in a read only memory.

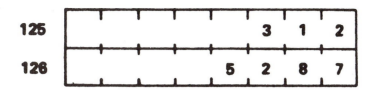

THE CONTENTS OF WORDS IN MEMORY

Since the development of microminiaturized electronic circuits on silicon chips, high-speed memory devices holding thousands of bits can be produced using as little as a single chip.

ARITHMETIC UNIT

All computers have a part where arithmetic can take place. This is the **arithmetic unit**. When a new number is written in a memory location, the old number stored there is automatically erased, just as any old recording is erased as a new recording is made on a magnetic tape recorder. Just reading a number, like playing an audio recording, does not damage the recording no matter how often you do it. If you want to combine numbers, say add them, it is usually done in one or more special locations in the arithmetic unit called **accumulators**. On some machines, the size of an accumulator is the same as the size of a word in memory. Words, or rather the information stored in memory locations, can be loaded into the accumulator. In a simple machine language, the instruction

     load 125

would cause the number recorded in location *125* to be placed in the accumulator. Whatever was recorded in the accumulator before would be erased before the load takes place. If we want to add another number we would write

     add 126

This would add the number stored in *126* to what was already in the accumulator and the sum of the two numbers would then be in the accumulator. This total could be recorded in the memory for later use by the instruction

     store 127

The result of the addition would now be in location *127* but would also remain in the accumulator.

The accumulator can also be used for subtraction, multiplication, and division. In a high-level language like Turing you never need to think about the accumulator. You merely indicate that you want numbers in two locations, say a and b, to be added and name the location, say c, where you want the answer to be stored. You write this all in one statement, namely

$c := a + b$

This Turing statement says: add the number stored in location a to the number stored in location b and place the result in location c. In the machine all location addresses are numbers. In Turing we give the locations names which are called **identifiers**. The compiler changes these names to numerical locations and changes the single Turing instruction

$c := a + b$

to the three machine instructions.

load a
add b
store c

The acccumulator is a set of storage cells, normally flip-flops, which are interconnected so that information in the form of a string of bits can on a given signal be shifted in them one position to the right or to the left. The addition of two numbers held in such shift registers can be accomplished through a combination of gates in a device called an **adder**. Multiplication is accomplished by a series of shifts and additions since shifting a number left one position is equivalent to multiplying the number by two.

CONTROL UNIT

You have just seen examples of machine language instructions. They each consist of two parts: the operation part, for example *load*, and the address part, a. Each part can be coded as a binary number, then the whole instruction will just be a string of bits. Suppose that you have a machine with a word length of 32 bits. Then an instruction might be itself stored in such a word with, say, 16 bits for the operation part and 16 bits for the address part. With 16 bits you can represent binary numbers that go from 1 up to 2 to the power 16, which is 65,536. Even though the number of memory locations is usually a power of two we often speak in terms of thousands of locations. We say the memory has 32 thousand or 64 thousand locations. This is abbreviated using the letter K to stand for thousand. We refer to $64K$ locations.

Consecutive instructions in a machine language program are stored in consecutive locations in the memory and are to be executed one after the other. The control unit does two things. It uses a special location called the **instruction pointer** to keep track of what instruction is currently being executed. It places the instruction to be executed in a special location called the **control register**. In the control register the instruction is decoded and signals are issued to the different parts of the computer so that the operation requested is actually carried out. As each instruction is executed, the instruction pointer is increased by one to give the address of the next instruction in the program. This next instruction is then fetched from the memory, placed in the control register, and executed. This process continues, with instructions being executed sequentially unless a special instruction is encountered, which resets the instruction pointer and causes a **jump** from the normal sequence to a different part of the program.

In brief, the control unit controls the sequence of execution of instructions and determines the effect that execution has on the information stored in the memory.

Computers were originally referred to as **stored program calculators** because the instructions as well as the numbers or characters they operate on are stored in the memory. They were also referred to as **sequential machines**, because normally they followed a sequence of instructions one after another unless a jump instruction directed them to do otherwise.

We have said that the memory of a computer can be contained on a single silicon chip. This is true also of the parts of the computer that make up the central processing unit. If the CPU is all on a single chip we call the computer a **microprocessor**.

INPUT AND OUTPUT

We have spoken of putting both data and instructions in the memory of the machine and changing the data by the execution of instructions. But how do we get data or instructions into the computer, and how do we get data out of the machine after it has been operated on? That is the function of the **input** and **output units**. We must have instructions that cause the machine to **read** information into its memory and to **write** information out from its memory. And we must have parts of the computer, the input and output units, that respond to these instructions. Most computer systems use individual input-output terminals at which information can be entered through a keyboard and output is produced as a display on a cathode ray tube (CRT) screen. Microcomputers often have only one terminal; we say the system is a **single-user system** or a personal computer. Larger systems have many such terminals; the system is a **multi-user system**. There is also a printer for obtaining **hardcopy** of what can be seen on the screen. Because each user enters his program and data directly into the computer and receives the results rapidly, the system is often said to be an

interactive system. If several people can simultaneously use a system interactively, we say it is a **time-sharing** computer system.

The keyboard of an input terminal is similar to that of a standard typewriter, so it helps if you can type. But hunt-and-peck methods will get you there too. In addition to the ordinary typewriter keys, there are special keys for indicating that you want the computer to take certain actions. These keys are not the same from one kind of terminal to another.

The hardcopy output units can be line-at-a-time printers or typewriters. Across a displayed page there are often positions to output 120, 132 or more characters although some printers output only 72 characters on a line. The paper is continuous but may be divided by perforations into pages, each capable of holding about 60 lines of output. Some printers form their characters out of an array of dots; these are called **matrix printers**.

PROGRAM TRANSLATION

We have said that three machine language instructions, namely,

load   a
add   b
store   c

correspond to what is written in Turing as

$c := a + b$

Instructions in the high-level language Turing are very much simpler to write than instructions in machine language. For one thing, you do not have to be aware of the accumulator; for another, the notation is very similar to the one used in simple mathematical expressions and should be easy for you to get used to. The Turing language is more powerful in that a single Turing instruction can correspond to many machine language instructions. We will see later that if you are working in a high-level language, the machine can detect when you make certain kinds of mistakes in your program.

In summary, high-level languages are designed to suit **you** rather than suit a computer. As a result, they make the job of programming less difficult.

A Turing program cannot execute directly on a computer but must be translated into the language for the particular computer you have. This is accomplished after the Turing program has been entered into the memory. The translation is performed by another program, called the compiler, that is already stored in the computer memory. The compiler scans your Turing program and produces the appropriate sequence of machine language instructions from your Turing statements. After compilation, execution of the machine language program can be initiated provided you have not made any errors in your Turing program that the compiler can detect. The kind of errors that are detectable are mostly in the **form** of the statements. If they are not proper or grammatical statements in the Turing language the compiler will report an error to you on your screen. Errors in grammar are called **syntax errors**. In English you know there is an error in the sentence,

> *The boys is walking.*

A machine can spot this kind of error but it cannot easily spot an error in meaning. It might never determine that the sentence,

> *The house is walking.*

is not a meaningful sentence; it would accept it as syntactically correct. We call an error in meaning a **semantic error**.

CHAPTER 2 SUMMARY

In this chapter we presented the main parts of a computer and showed how information is stored in the memory. We explained briefly how a high-level language such as Turing is translated, or compiled, into machine language before being executed by a computer. The following important terms were introduced.

Pulse — an electric signal which is produced by turning on an electric voltage for a certain time, the pulse time, and then turning it off.

Clock — the timing device in the computer which determines the pulse rate. Typical clock rates are tens of megahertz.

Gate — a combination of transistors and their electric connectors which has certain logical properties.

Or gate — a gate from which there is an output pulse if there is an input pulse on either or both of the two incoming lines.

And gate — a gate from which there is an output pulse if there are input pulses on both of the two incoming lines.

Not gate — a gate from which there is no output pulse if there is an input pulse and vice versa.

Flip-flop — an interconnection of *and*, *not*, and *or* gates capable of storing one bit of information.

Memory — the part of a computer that stores information, such as data or a program. Magnetic tapes and disks are called secondary memory; they require mechanical motion to access information stored on them. Main memory can be immediately accessed by the computer; main memory is usually in the form of microminiaturized circuits on a silicon chip. We say the memory is a solid state one. Other forms of memory, such as bubble memories, are being developed. The computer can transfer information between secondary memory and main memory.

RAM — random access memory, a term used for main memory since any one word may be accessed as rapidly as any other.

Random access device — a term used for a secondary memory device, such as a disk, from which any one piece of information can be obtained approximately as rapidly as any other. The access time is much longer than from main memory.

ROM — read only memory, a term used for main memory which has been produced in such a way that information can be read from it but nothing can be written there by the user. The information in a ROM is generally prerecorded by the manufacturer.

CPU (central processing unit) — composed of the arithmetic unit and the control unit. The arithmetic unit carries out operations such as addition and multiplication. The control unit directs other parts of the computer, including the arithmetic unit, to carry out a sequence of instructions that is in the main memory. If the CPU is contained on a single silicon chip we call it a microprocessor.

Accumulator — the part of the CPU where numbers can be held during the performance of arithmetic operations.

Input and output — ways of getting information into and out of a computer. An output device called a printer takes information from main memory and outputs it on paper. This is referred to as hardcopy. An input-output device suitable for use by individual users is often a keyboard and a cathode ray tube (CRT) display screen attached to the computer.

Screen — a cathode ray tube used to display the output from a computer. This is also called a video display; the terminal with screen is referred to as a video display terminal (VDT).

Keyboard — the array of keys used to enter data and instructions into a computer.

Bit — a digit in the binary system of numbers, usually written as a 0 or a 1.

Byte — a sequence of bits treated as a unit, for example, the number of bits used to represent an alphabetic character. Bytes contain 8 bits on most computers.

Word — A number of bits grouped as a unit for holding information in the memory of a computer. Each word has an address which indicates its location in the array of words in memory. A word often consists of two or four bytes.

Coded information — before information can be entered into a computer, it must be coded in a convenient form for the computer's circuitry. The circuitry recognizes *off* and *on* which we can think of as 0 and 1.

Translation (or compilation) — before a program written in a language like Turing can be executed by a computer, it must be translated into a language that can be interpreted by the computer. The program as written in Turing is called the source program. The translated program is placed in words in computer's memory and is executed by the computer's CPU.

Microprocessor — a computer in which the CPU is contained on a single silicon chip.

Syntax error — an error in the form (or grammar) of instructions.

Semantic error — an error in the meaning of a program.

Chapter 3

THE MINIMAL PROGRAM

In this chapter we will introduce the minimum number of elements of programming that you need in order to begin to program. Nothing very important will be programmed but you will be able to go through the motions of writing a complete program, entering it into a computer and having it executed. This will let you get used to the Unix command language. Also you will see what kind of output to expect. Things will happen, though what the computer is actually doing for you will not be very exciting yet. But remember you will go through the same steps as are necessary when your programs do have more content.

BASIC SYMBOLS OF THE TURING LANGUAGE

We will be presenting the programming language Turing a little bit at a time. Any language consists of words and the words are made up of **symbols** that we call **characters**. These characters are put together in **strings**. In English the word

   elephant

is a string of characters of length eight. It contains only seven different characters, the character *e* being used twice. We can tell that it is a word because it has a blank in front of it and one at the end. In a way the blank is also a character, but a **special character** for separating words. We sometimes denote the blank by *b* when we show programs in this book so that you can see how many blanks are present.

In English, we group words into sentences and we can tell the end of a sentence because of a special mark, the period. We also have a different kind of sentence that ends with a question mark, don't we? In addition to periods and question marks, we have other **punctuation marks** which serve to make sentences in the language easier to read. They also serve to remove ambiguity in a sentence. There is some doubt about the meaning of the sentence,

The student claims the teacher understands.

The doubt is removed if it is written with commas, as,

The student, claims the teacher, understands.

It is important that statements in a programming language be **unambiguous**, so punctuation is used. The comma is used to separate items in any list of similar items, quotation marks are placed around strings of characters, and parentheses are often used to enclose things that belong together.

We will have words in Turing that are made up of letters of the alphabet and might also have digits in them. When we are writing a Turing program we want it to be understandable. So we choose words like English words. We use words like *name, cost, income, tax, invoice, sum,* or words like *page1, table6, item35,* and so on. Most of these words are invented by you. You are not allowed to use words that do not at least have one letter at the beginning. If the Turing compiler sees a digit at the beginning of a word it assumes that it is a **number**. For example, *317* is taken as a number. This means that words like *3rdpage* are illegal and will not be accepted by the Turing compiler.

Before we leave characters we should perhaps list them. A **character** is a letter, or a digit, or a special character. The **letters** are

A B C D E F G H I J K L M N O P Q R S T U V W X Y Z
a b c d e f g h i j k l m n o p q r s t u v w x y z

In words in Turing, lower case letters may be used instead of upper case letters. Matching upper and lower case letters are equivalent in Turing. We will use mostly lower case letters in our programs although occasionally we will use a capital letter when it makes it more understandable.

The **digits** are

0 1 2 3 4 5 6 7 8 9

The **special characters** include

: + − * / ( ) = , . " ' [ ] < > ; { } ↑ ! ˜ |% $ _
b blank

Pairs of special characters are often used as **special symbols** in the language. For example, each of the following pairs has a fixed meaning

:=   <=   >=   ..

Various other special characters are often available on different computer systems.

NUMBERS

Computers can do arithmetic calculations and they can do them extremely rapidly. When you learned arithmetic you first learned to handle numbers that are whole numbers, or integers. You learned that $5+6=11$ and $2 \times 3 = 6$. In Turing numbers like 2, 3, 512, 809, and 46281 are called **integer constants**. Any string of digits is an integer constant. You will remember that we will be storing numbers in the computer and representing them as a string of bits in some coded representation. The largest integer we can represent will be determined by the length of the string of bits that are in a word in our computer. Word lengths vary from one computer to another, but most Turing compilers have a range of integer numbers including $-2,147,483,647$ to $2,147,483,647$.

If you have integers requiring long digit strings with a lot of zeroes at the end, for instance the population of the world, you must use the other form of numbers which is the **real** form.

If you have a large number like

635,642,000

you can write it as

6.35642×10^8

Perhaps you recognize this as what is called scientific notation. In Turing the form of a **real constant** such as our example is

$6.35642e8$

The first part is called the **significant digits**, the second part the **exponent**. The exponent follows the letter e and is the power of 10 that is to multiply the significant digits part. **Real** notation is also used for numbers that are not integers. These are either **fractions** or **mixed numbers**. We write either of these in decimal notation where a point called the decimal point separates the integer from the fraction part. Examples of fractions are

.5   .0075   .0000023

Mixed numbers are

5.27   889.6   6.0216

When we write fractions or mixed numbers in exponent notation we usually standardize the form by putting the first non-zero digit followed by a decimal point and then the remaining digits. Then the power of 10 is computed to make it right. The fraction .0000023 is written as 2.3×10^{-6}. In Turing this then is $2.3e-6$. It could also be written as $0.23e-5$, or $23.0e-7$, or even as $23e-7$.

An integer constant must **not** have a decimal point. A real constant can be written either as a mixed number for example, 9.02, or in the exponent form. In the exponent form it usually has a decimal point (with exceptions like the example $23e-7$) and **must** have an exponent part. The exponent is preceded by the letter e and consists of an optional plus or minus sign followed by one or more digits.

CHARACTER STRINGS

We have said that computers can handle both numbers and strings of characters. We have seen that there are two forms for numbers: integers and reals.

A character string can consist of any of the characters that we have specified: letters, digits, and special characters. Very often, when displaying the results of a computer calculation, we want the results labelled. What we want is to output a string of characters on the screen. In the statement that specifies what we want the computer to output, we include the actual string that we want displayed enclosed in quotation marks. These strings enclosed in quotation marks are called **explicit string constants**.

Examples of explicit string constants are

"*Bill Jones* ", "*balance in account* ", "*x = *"

EXPRESSIONS

One of the basic concepts in programming is that of an **expression**. The way that we explain what a word like expression means is to give examples and then generalize these examples. This, in fact, is how we are trying to present all the computer science concepts in this book.

First of all 32, 5, $6.1e2$ and $58.1e6$ are all expressions. So the general statement is that integer constants and real constants are expressions. So are explicit string constants like

"*This is an expression* "

Any expression may be enclosed in parentheses and still be an expression. For example (32) and ($6.1e2$) are also expressions. The expressions that are integer or real constants can be combined into compound expressions using the signs of arithmetic for adding, subtracting, multiplying, and dividing. These expressions are called **arithmetic expressions**. We use the standard signs for adding and subtracting, namely the plus and minus. For multiplication we use the asterisk (*) because there is no times sign. For division we use the slant or slash symbol (/). Examples of arithmetic expressions are

$$2 +3, 5.2e1 * 7.8e5, 6e0 / 2e0, 10 - 15$$

Integer and real values may be combined in a single expression, and when they are the result is a real value. For example, $2 +3.0e1$ has the value $3.2e1$.

If two numbers are to be divided using the slash operator, the result will be a real value even if both numbers are integers. For example, 5/2 gives the real result

2.5

Two numbers may be divided to produce an integer value using the operator **div**. For example, 5 **div** 2 would give the integer 2. The result is truncated toward zero. If you want to find the remainder in an integer division, use the operator **mod**. The result of 5 **mod** 2 is the integer 1, the remainder when 5 is divided by 2.

Numbers may be raised to a power using the operator **. For example, the value of

3 ** 2

is 9, that is, three squared. We say that ** is the operator for **exponentiation**.

Here is a very complicated arithmetic expression

$$2 * 5 +8 - 3 * 5 / 2 + 6$$

In evaluating this you have to know what to do first because the result depends on the order of evaluation. The rule is to do any exponentiations first, then the multiplications and divisions second, then the additions and subtractions. Also you start at the left-hand side of the expression and work to the right. We are using here **rules of precedence**, that exponentiation has the highest priority and the operations multiply and divide have precedence over add and subtract. Parentheses can be used to guide the sequence of evaluation. For example, you write 3 * (5 +8) instead of 3 * 5 +8 if you want the addition to take place before the multiplication. Expressions in parentheses take precedence. The operators **div** and **mod** have the same precedence as / and *.

EXAMPLES OF ARITHMETIC EXPRESSIONS

The following examples illustrate the rules for performing arithmetic in the Turing programming language.

72 + 16   Value is 88.

8 * 5 + 7   Value is 47. Note that * means multiply.

2 + 10 * 4   Value is 42. Note that multiplication is
done before addition.

(2 + 10) * 4   Value is 48. The parentheses cause the
addition to be done before the multiplication.

1 / 3   This division will produce the real value .3333333. We
can use integers and real values with / and we always
get a real value as the result.

72e0 + 16e0   Value is 88e0, which can be written in other forms such
as 8.8e1 and 8.80000e + 01.

(9.83e0 + 16.82e0)/ 2.935e0

This expression is equivalent to the following

$$\frac{9.83 + 16.82}{2.935}$$

Real numbers may be written in the exponent form or
as mixed numbers. The parentheses were used so the
division would apply to the sum of 9.83e0 and 16.82e0
(and not just to 16.82e0).

17 **div** 5   Value is 3. Note that only the integer part of the quotient
is given. The operator **div** accepts integers or real numbers
and gives an integer result.

17 **mod** 5   Value is 2. This is the remainder when 17 is divided by 5.
The operator **mod** accepts integers or real numbers and
gives an integer result.

5 ** 3   Value is 125 which is 5 raised to the power 3,
that is, five cubed.

OUTPUT

Our main purpose in this chapter is to introduce you to the elementary concepts of programming as illustrated in Turing and to get you to write your first program. The program is not going to do very much but it has to do something so that you can see that it is working. The most it can do is to output numbers or character strings on the CRT display. Then you can see that some action is taking place.

The output statement that we will use in the program is like this

put   *3, 5.1e1, "Bill"*

Output produced by the **put** statement is placed in successive fields across the output line. The output line has spaces for a certain number of characters. The items that are after the **put** are placed one to a field going from left to right and then a new line is started.

Explicit string constants are displayed, without the quotation marks, in a field the same size as the length of the string. Integers are also displayed in a field just large enough to hold the integers.

Real numbers are displayed in a variety of ways depending on the number. The size of field is always just large enough to hold what is displayed. If the real number can be displayed as an integer, it will be. If the size of the real number is less than a million and is at least a thousandth, it is printed without an exponent. Trailing zeros to the right of the decimal point are omitted. Otherwise a real is displayed in exponent form with the significant digits arranged with one digit to the left of the decimal point and the exponent displayed to the right of the significant digits as an *e* followed by the integer that is the power of 10. The output for the **put** statement we showed would be

351Bill

In this form everything may be run together. A variation on this may be obtained by specifying a minimum field size for the item that is to be output. This is done by writing a colon followed by the minimum field size right after the item to be output. For example

put *3: 10, 5.1e1: 10, "Bill": 10*

will output the same items as before but in three fields of width 10 character positions each. Integers and reals are right justified in the field size specified. If they are longer than the field size, the longer size will be used. If it is shorter than the field size the output item is padded on the left with blanks. Explicit string constants are left justified in their fields. The output for our **put** statement is *bbbbbbbbb3bbbbbbbb51Bill*

The little b is actually a blank but we have written it this way so you could count the spaces.

Since explicit string constants are normally displayed in fields whose size is the same as the length of the string, when no field size is specified it is sometimes necessary to start the constant with a blank so that a space will separate it from other items that are displayed.

A blank line can be left by using

put ""

since here the explicit string constant consists of the null string, that is no characters at all. We can leave two blank lines by writing

put skip

The **skip** keyword can be placed anywhere in a list of output items and causes a new line to be started at that point.

Expressions other than explicit integer and real constants and explicit string constants may also be placed in a **put** statement. The statement

put *2 +3: 10, 4 / 2: 14*

will result in a *5* being displayed right justified in the first field of width *10* and *2* in the second of width *14.* An interesting statement might be

put *"2 +3= ", 2 +3*

it would output

2 +3=5

Note that the quotes around the explicit string constant are not displayed. We do not specify field sizes because it is perfectly readable without them.

If you do not want to finish a displayed line in an output statement you end the **put** statement with two periods. The list of statements

put *3: 10 ..*
put *5.1e1: 14 ..*
put *"Bill"*

accomplishes exactly the same result as the single statement

put *3: 10, 5.1e1: 14, "Bill"*

The following methods of formatting can be used. Blanks are used to pad numbers on the left and strings on the right to the given width.

explicit string constant: width   Output the explicit string constant
                                          in width columns left justified

integer value: width

Output the integer value in width columns right justified

real value: width: fractional digits

Output the real value in width columns with "fractional digits" to the right of the decimal point **without** the exponent part provided that it can be displayed that way.

real value: width: fractional digits: exponent digits

Output the real value in width columns with the exponent part.

THE PROGRAM

Now that you know a statement that will give some action, you must learn what is necessary to make a complete program. Then you can try the computer for yourself. We will as a convention, not as a rule of Turing, start all programs with a line like this

   % The "opus1" program

The name *opus1* is one we made up to describe the very first complete program. (The word *opus* is Latin for "work".) You must make up an identifier you like yourself. It should not contain blanks or special characters. The first line of a program begins with a percent sign; this means that it is a **comment** to make clear what follows. It serves to indicate that it is the beginning of a program and gives the name that we will use to file the program in our Unix file.

Now comes the big moment for a complete program.

   % The "opus1" program
   put *"2 +3= ", 2+3*

There it is, our opus number one, a complete Turing program. The body of the program is a single statment, the **put** statement. In the next chapter we will describe how to try out this program on your computer.

ANOTHER EXAMPLE PROGRAM

This program illustrates the use of several **put** statements.

% The "zigzag" program
put *"z   g", "z   g"*
put *" i a": 6, "i a"*
put *" gz ": 6, "gz"*

The program causes the following pattern to be displayed.

z   gz   g
 i a i a
  gz   gz

As you can see, the top line of the pattern is displayed by the first **put** statement. This statement causes its first explicit string constant, *"z   g"*, to be displayed in the first field of the output line and its second explicit string constant, again *"z   g"*, to be displayed in the second field of the output line. The next two statements cause the output of the second and third lines of the pattern. The first output items are assigned field widths that will cause the second items to be properly placed. The last **put** statement could be replaced by the following two statements without changing the displayed pattern:

put *" gz ": 6 ..*
put *"gz"*

The first one does not end the line because the output item is followed by two dots to indicate that there is more to come.

CHAPTER 3 SUMMARY

In this chapter, we explained how to write very simple computer programs, the minimum that can be called a program and still show that it is working. The following important terms were presented.

Character — is a letter (*ABC...Z* or *abc...z*), digit (012...9) or special character +*/.;:, etc.

Integer constant — is an integer (whole number) such as 78 and 2931. There may be a plus or minus sign in front of the integer. A integer constant should not be preceded by a dollar sign and must not contain commas or a decimal point.

Real constant — is a number such as $3.14159e0$ (equal to 3.14159×10^0 or simply 3.14159). A real constant in the exponent form consists of a significant digits part (3.14159) followed by e and an exponent.

A real constant in the mixed number form contains a decimal point but not necessarily an exponent.

Explicit string constant — is a sequence of characters enclosed in quotes, such as "*Why not?*".

Arithmetic expression — composed of either a single number or a collection of numbers combined using addition, subtraction, multiplication, division, exponentiation, and **div** or **mod** (+, −, *, /, **, **div** and **mod**). Parentheses may enclose parts of the expression.

Rules of precedence — specify the order for applying +, −, *, /, **div**, **mod**, and ** to compute the value of an arithmetic expression. Parenthesized expressions are evaluated first. Proceeding from left to right, ** is applied first, * and / (or **div** and **mod**) are applied second, and then + and −.

put — means to output. The **put** statement prepares expressions (explicit string constants or arithmetic expressions) for output. A line is not actually completed if the **put** statement ends with two dots. Integers, real values, and explicit string constants such as −24, 2.7*e*3 and "*Hello*" are displayed using a statement of the form

> **put** list of expressions separated by commas

Field — **put** causes values to be output (displayed) in fields across a line. The minimum size of the field can be specified by placing a colon followed by an integer after the item to be output. If no field size is specified, values are given a field size just large enough to hold them. Integers are output right justified in the field; reals are output right justified but in a form which depends on the number. The exponent form is used as a last resort.

Formatted writing — choosing the size of the field in a **put** statement so that the output line is well spaced. For example

> −*15: 5*   produces *bb−15*
> "*Fred*": *7, 5*   produces *Fredbbb5*
> *4e1: 5: 1*   produces *b40.0*

where *b* stands for blank.

Output — display on a cathode ray tube screen, which the computer does at your request. The **put** statement produces output from the computer.

CHAPTER 3 EXERCISES

1.   What will the following program cause the computer to output?

    % The "letter" program
    put " *   * "
    put " * *   * * "
    put " *   *   * "
    put " *   * "

    Can you rearrange the lines in this program to output a different letter?

2.   What do the following cause the computer to output?

    (a) **put** *2, " plus ", 3, " is ", 2+3*
    (b) **put** *"234 +198 +362=", 234 +198 +362*
    (c) **put** *"2 formulas: ", 2 +3 * 5:10, (2 +3) * 5: 10*
    (d) **put** *"subtraction ", 20 − 10 − 5: 10, 20 − (10 − 5): 10*

3.   Write statements to calculate and output the following:

    (a) The sum of 52181 and 10032.
    (b) 9213 take away 7918.
    (c) The sum of 9213, 487, 921, 2013 and 514.
    (d) The product of 21 times the sum of 816, 5, and 203.
    (c) 343 plus 916 all multiplied by 82.
    (f) 3.14159 (π) times 8.94 divided by 2.
    (g) 3.14159 times the square of 8.94 (Note: x^2
       can be written as $x * x$ or as $x ** 2$).

Chapter 4

THE UNIX OPERATING SYSTEM

BEGINNING A SESSION AT THE COMPUTER

After your program has been composed on a piece of paper, you are ready to enter it into the computer to see how it works. You will be typing each line on the computer's keyboard just as you would on an ordinary typewriter. As you type, the letters, digits, and special characters appear on the screen.

Before you can begin entering your program you must get the terminal going and make contact with the Unix operating system. This part of the procedure varies from one computer system to another. A common procedure would be to: Turn on the power to the terminal, make connection by a telephone call to the computer system if the terminal is not permanently connected, then press the control key and at the same time the letter *d* (we call this *ctrl-d*). You will have to find out exactly what the procedure is for the particular terminal and system you are using.

When you have made contact with Unix you will see on the screen the word *login:*. A flashing symbol on the screen, called the **cursor**, shows you where the next character you type will go. The cursor is now positioned right after the prompting word *login:*. You respond by typing your name or the name of your computer account followed by pressing the return key. The system then displays the word *password:* (or some abbreviation of it). When you are given authorization to use a computer system, a password is provided to you to protect your account from having others use it. You must type in your password to authenticate your identity. As you type, the password will not be displayed on the screen. Someone looking over your shoulder would not be able to see your secret password. After you finish typing the password, again press the return key. The computer signals to you that you may proceed by displaying a single character (say $)
called a **prompt symbol**. A display of the character ? means that the computer does not understand. Try again. If the prompt symbol appears this

means that the system is ready for a **system command**.

Unix commands are given using lower case letters and are often the first few letters of the command word. Commands are usually typed starting in the first column, or in the first column after any prompt symbol.

SYSTEM COMMAND LANGUAGE

It is essential that you learn the Unix system command language if you want to enter your Turing programs, save them in a file, execute them, edit them when they have errors and run them again. The Unix command language has levels. At each level there are a certain number of different commands available; some of these commands take you to a lower level; some return you to the higher level from which you came. We say that the command language has a **hierarchical structure**. When you have logged in you are at the top level of the Unix system. This level is known as the **shell**. In the shell level there are various commands that you can give. These include the edit command, the compile command, and the execute command. As well, there are commands for finding out: who the other users of the system are, the date, and the description in the Unix manual of any system command. These will be described in detail later.

Each person using a shared computer system will be permitted to store a number of files in secondary storage. Each of these files must be given a **file name** so that it can be retrieved from storage when it is wanted. Before you begin to enter your program you must indicate what name you intend to use for the file that will contain your program. All programs in Turing must have names ending in *.t*, for example, *prog.t* could be the file name of a program. We will use the name we have already given to the Turing program and simply add the *.t*. Every file you have must have a different name. Files that are not Turing programs should not have names ending in *.t*.

ENTERING A PROGRAM

Programs are entered into the computer using an editor. There are two basic kinds of editors: **full-screen editors** and **line editors**. With a full-screen editor, insertions, deletions, and changes can be made to what is being entered anywhere on the screen. This is accomplished by moving the cursor to the point where editing is required and giving the appropriate commands. With line editors, changes take place in lines that are often referred to by line number. Full-screen editors are perhaps easier to understand, but line editors can be more efficient. We will describe the line editor of Unix which is called *ed.*

To input the program you have written, type *ed* (for edit) followed, after a space, by the file name you have chosen for your program, and then return. Now you are in the **edit level** or **mode** which is a second level of the hierarchy below the shell level. In this level there is often an * (asterisk) prompt symbol. Before you begin to type your program you must go to the next level, to the **text entry mode**, which is done by pressing *a* (for append). The characters you type in this mode will be taken to be part of your own program, rather than system commands. What you type in the text entry mode will be stored in the high speed memory of the computer in a temporary **buffer**. The text you enter must be saved in the file in secondary storage before you next return to the shell mode or it will be lost. We will say how to do this later. So now you can type your program. If you make a mistake in typing a character you can press the **backspace** and this will back up the cursor one space and you can type the correct character. (Some terminals require the use of a **rubout** key or a **left-arrow key** rather than backspace.) You could wipe out a whole line by backspacing repeatedly until the cursor is at the start of the line but instead you can delete a whole line by pressing the @ key then return, rather than pressing the backspace many times.

So your job is to type in your program, trying to make as few mistakes as possible and correcting them as soon as you detect them. When you are finished, you are ready to return to the edit mode. This is done by typing a period in the first column followed by return. This causes you to **escape** from the append mode and go back to the edit mode.

SAVING AND RUNNING THE PROGRAM

You have now entered your program and are back in the edit mode. The file that you have created in the text entry mode must be saved before you return to the shell level for program compilation and execution. To do this, type *w* (for write) followed by return. Whatever is in the temporary buffer is saved under the file name that you established when you entered the edit mode. You could write it into another file location by giving a new file name after the *w.* Files that have been just entered or modified should always be saved before you leave the edit mode to go to the shell level. To leave the edit mode and return to the shell level, type *q* (for quit) then return. If you have not remembered to save your buffer a question mark may appear on the screen. You are then given a second chance to save it before you type *q* (for quit) again.

Now you are ready to compile your program. Type the command *ttc* (for Toronto Turing compiler) which is the command which will translate your Turing program into an **object program** that can be executed. The *ttc* is followed by the file name of your program, then return. The translation now takes place. If there are no syntax errors and no detected semantic errors the object program will be stored in a file whose file name is your program name followed by *.x*. Any detected errors will be reported on the screen. If you have many errors you might just make a note of them to remind yourself when you are correcting the program. Suppose for the present that you get no error messages. You can give the command for execution of the object program which is just the file name of the object program followed by return.

For our first program, which we called *opus1*, the file name for the source program would be *opus1.t*. After it had been entered we could give the command *ttc opus1.t* which would compile the program and store the machine language program in *opus1.x*. We could then give the command

    opus1.x

to cause execution. Execution could then be obtained at any time in the future by giving the shell command

    opus1.x

When you no longer want a file you should remove it using the *rm* command. To remove the file *opus1.x* give the command

    rm opus1.x

To see a file on the screen you can give the shell level command *cat* (for catenate) followed by the file name. If the length of the file is more than the screen will hold the display will keep moving upwards with lines disappearing off the top and new lines appearing at the bottom. This is called **scrolling**. Control of scrolling varies from one system to another. Sometimes you can stop this scrolling by typing *ctrl-s ;* to start again type *ctrl-q*. If you are not interested in looking at any more output, type *ctrl-c* to escape back to the shell level. Do not try to look at files that are in code, that is, any translated programs.

You can see a list of the names of all your files in a **directory** by typing the shell command *ls* (for list). As we mentioned, when you want to remove a file, type *rm* followed by the file's name; to rename a file give the shell command *mv* (for move) followed by the old name and the new name, in that order. To create a copy of a file, rather than move it, give the shell command *cp* followed by the name of the file to be copied then the name the copy is to have.

OBTAINING PRINTED OUTPUT

If for some reason you want a hardcopy record of what you have in your file you can do this by giving the shell command

lpr file name

This activates the command called *lpr* (line printer). If you want several files printed they are just named in the order you want, after the *lpr*.

So there is no problem about getting a printed listing of your Turing program. But how do you get a printed listing of error messages, or the output from a program's execution? These things are normally displayed on the screen but not stored in a file. It is possible to redirect the output from the screen to a file instead. This is done by adding

>name of file where output is to be stored

to the compilation or execution commands. For example, the command

ttc opus1.t > opus1.error

would result in translation of the program *opus1.t* but the error messages, if any, would be stored in the file *opus1.error*. These could then be seen on the screen by giving the command

cat opus1.error

They could be printed by the command

lpr opus1.error

CORRECTING COMPILE-TIME ERRORS

As the program is being translated from a Turing program to a machine language program, as happens with the *ttc* command, the translator detects and reports errors in the statements in your program. For simple errors the translator often tries to make repairs. These may not be suitable repairs but often they permit the translation to be completed whereas it might have to stop after the first error.

You should examine any repairs to see if they are appropriate. If all errors are properly repaired you could then execute the program. These repairs are not stored in your file. Your Turing program will still have the errors. It is a good practice to fix all errors. To do this you must edit your original program. Changes are made by insertion, deletion, substitution, and movement of blocks of lines.

To modify a program: enter the edit mode with the *ed* command followed by the file name of your Turing program. You will not see your program displayed; you must give a command at the edit level to do this. The

Unix text editor that we are describing is a **line editor**. To make changes you must position the system at the line to be modified. Often you refer to the lines by number. You can display the program in the edit mode by using the *p* (for print) command. Preceding the *p* you type the line number or range of line numbers that you want to see displayed. For example, *5p* displays line 5; *3,5p* displays lines 3 to 5. At any time after a display, pressing return will result in the line following the **current line** being displayed. Pressing − (minus) before return will cause the previous line to be displayed. If you use *n* (for numbered) instead of *p* the line number will be displayed beside the line.

The **metacharacter** period stands for the current line, and the *$* for the last line of the file. Typing *.,$p* causes the lines from the current line to the last line in the file to be displayed. To find out the number of the current line you type *.=p.* You can display a line that is 10 lines on from the current line by typing *.+10p.* By using the display command you can position the system at any line you wish to modify. The current line is always the last line displayed.

To **delete the current line**: type *d* (for delete). Repeated use of the delete command will delete successive lines.

To **insert a line** (or more) just before the current line: type *i* (for insert); this puts you in the insert mode; now type the line (or lines) to be inserted; type period in the first column to return to the edit mode with the insertion completed.

To **substitute**: position the system at the line where substitution is to take place; type

     s/target string/substitute string/

If you want to see the result type a *p* after the last slash before return. The first occurrence in the current line of the target string is substituted. If you type a *g* (for global) after the last slash all occurrences in the current line are substituted.

To **change one line for another**: position at line to be changed; type *c* (for change); in the change mode enter new line; then type period followed by return to go back to the edit mode.

To **move lines to a new position**: type the number (or range of numbers) of the line (or lines) to be moved then *m* (for move) followed by the number of the line that will just precede the moved block in its new position. If you wish to copy a set of lines from one location into another use *t* (for transfer) instead of *m*.

To **incorporate another file**: if you want the other file at the end of the workfile type *r* (for read) followed by the file's name; if you want it inserted after the current line type .*r* followed by the name of the file.

To undo a substitution: if you change your mind or have made an error you can undo any substitution by typing *u* (for undo). This reverses the immediately preceding substitution.

To search for a string: the command /string/ will output the first occurrence of the string starting at the current line. The next occurrence of the same string can be found by giving the command // followed by return. All occurrences are displayed by the command *g*/string/. The search may be used to position the system at a line containing a target string for a substitution. The command that searches and substitutes is

/target string/*s*//substitute string/*p*

Applying operations to a range of lines: the operations of deletion, change, displaying, or substitution can be applied to a range of lines; the range is stated before the command by: first line, last line. The symbol *$* stands for the last line of the text so that a range *1,$* means to all lines of the text.

Special symbols (or meta symbols): the symbol *$* means the end of a line or the last line of the text; the symbol ^ means the beginning of a line; square brackets around a range of characters such as [*a-z*] means any character from *a* to *z*. An ampersand, *&*, used in the substitute string means anything mentioned in the target string. A null target string means that the string should be the same target string as mentioned in the previous command.

Examples:

  (a)   *1,$s/^[0-9]//gp*

would find all occurrences of lines starting with a digit and delete the digit. The last occurrence only would be displayed.

  (b)   *.,$-10d*

would delete lines starting at the current line and going up to 10 lines from the last line.

  (c)   *s/$/;/p*

would place a semicolon at the end of the current line and display (print) it.

  (d)   *s/round/&(/*

would add a left parenthesis after the word *round* in the current line.

  (e)   *g/proceedure/s//procedure/gp*

would search for all occurrences in the text of the target string *proceedure* and substitute the string *procedure*, each occurrence would be displayed.

Note: the target string in the substitute command can be written as //, since it is the same as the string in the global search command.

CORRECTING RUN-TIME ERRORS

When the output from your program does not agree with what you expected there are two possibilities. Either your program has an error, or your expected results are improperly calculated.

If it is the program which has an error we say that it is a **run-time error**. It does not have the meaning that we intended it to have. The compiler can detect only certain kinds of run-time errors so that you are often on your own in finding it. We will make some suggestions later about how to find semantic errors but for now just reread the program and try to see where you are going wrong. When you find the error it is corrected in the same way as you correct a compile-time error. Just go into edit mode and make the necessary changes, and then use *ttc* to re-translate the program.

OTHER UNIX COMMANDS

There are other commands that are available at the shell level.

To have the date displayed: type *date*.

To find out who is using the computer: type *who*.

To have the Unix instruction manual displayed: type *man* followed by the command that you want explained. For example, typing *man ttc* will produce a display that tells you all about the *ttc* (for Toronto Turing compiler) command.

To change your password: type *passwd*. The system responds by asking you to enter your old password. If you do this correctly the system then asks you to enter the new password. Passwords should be at least six characters long if they are all lower case letters. When choosing a password, try to pick something unusual, such as 52i4GK, and not an English word or a name. If you forget your password, only the person in charge of the system can help you. After you have entered your new password, which as usual is not displayed, the system asks you to type it again just to be sure. If they match the change is made.

To concatenate files (to join them into one file): type *cat* followed by the names of the files to be amalgamated then the > symbol followed by the name to be given to the amalgamated file.

To print a file on the printer: type *lpr* followed by the name of the file.

To log off the system: this varies from one system to another. You may type *bye*, or give a *logout* command, or type *ctrl-d*, or hang up the telephone connection. You will have to consult your own system expert.

CHAPTER 4 SUMMARY

In this chapter we explained how to put your program into the computer, how to run it, and how to correct errors. As well, we described how you could save your program for future use. In order to do all this it was necessary to become familiar with the command language of the Unix operating system. System commands are often given by typing the first few letters of the command. The command system is arranged in a hierarchy so that at each level of the hierarchy there are a number of possible commands. Except at the top level, which is called the shell level, there is always a command that causes you to return to the level above the one you are in. The following terms were presented.

Log in — the procedure that you must go through to begin a session at the computer.

Authorized user — a person who has been given permission to use a computer system. Each authorized user has a name (or number) that identifies him to the system. Files may be stored and programs executed by authorized users.

Password — most systems protect the privacy and security of users by having a password (known only to the user) required to be entered before access to the system is permitted. Passwords are requested by the system at log in time. Usually they are not displayed on the screen as they are entered so as to maintain their secrecy.

Prompt symbol — a symbol displayed on the screen to remind you of what level in the command hierarchy you are at. For example at the edit level the prompt symbol is an *; at the shell level it is usually $.

Command — an instruction given to the system to achieve certain results such as editing, running, or saving programs.

Level or mode — a stage in the hierarchy of the command language. The top level of the Unix command language is called the shell level. Other levels are the edit level or mode, the insert mode, or the execute mode. The edit mode is at the second level, one below the shell level. The insert mode is at the third level below the edit mode.

Shell mode — the top level of the command hierarchy, which is entered automatically when you log into your computer. Whenever you leave a second level to return to a higher level you are back in the shell level.

Edit mode — a second level in the command hierarchy used when you want to enter or change a program. To enter the edit mode, type the shell command *ed* (for edit) followed by the name of the file that you want to edit. If you have a file by that name then it is brought into the buffer. If not, a new file is begun. To return to the shell level type *q* (for quit) followed by return.

Line editor — a system of editing text on a screen where insertions, deletions, and changes take place on certain lines of the text at which the system is positioned. Lines can be referred to by number and the line at which the system is positioned, the current line, is the one upon which action last took place.

Full-screen editor — a system of editing on the screen where the cursor is moved anywhere on the screen, often by pressing special cursor movement keys. Insertions, deletions, and changes take place at points in the text indicated by the position of the cursor.

Insert mode — a third level, below the edit mode, in the command hierarchy. Before entering the insert mode, the current line is set to be the line before which the insertion is to occur. After pressing *i* and return, the line or lines to be inserted are typed. When you have finished typing the insertion, type a period in the first column followed by return. This returns you to the edit mode with the inserted material in place. The lines are automatically renumbered to take account of the inserted lines.

Typing errors — when entering a character, if a mistake is made, you can erase the character by pressing the backspace key (or perhaps a rubout or left-arrow key). You can delete an entire line by pressing @.

Buffer — the part of the memory used to store a program that you are editing. Before leaving the edit mode the buffer must be saved in secondary storage. This is done by typing *w* (for write). This saves the buffer as a file in secondary storage having the name that you gave after the *ed* command by which you entered the edit mode. A buffer may be stored as a file on the disk under another name. This is done by typing *w* followed by the file's desired name. If you attempt to leave the edit mode by typing *q* before you have given a write command to save the buffer, the system may question your action and give you a second chance to save your buffer. If you press *q* again without saving it, the file is lost.

File directory — a listing, by file name, of all the programs that you have stored in secondary memory. The file directory itself can be displayed by giving the shell command *ls*.

Turing compiler — a system program that translates the program in Turing into machine language so that it can be executed directly by the computer. A program is compiled by giving the command *ttc* followed by the name of the program file. The file name of a Turing program must end in *.t*. The translated program is stored in the file as *program name.x* and can be executed by giving the command *program name.x*.

Execute mode — by typing the name of a compiled program at the shell level you may execute any previously compiled program that you have in your file.

Compile-time error correction — as a program is being translated, whenever there is a syntax error, an error message is displayed. You can then correct the program by inserting, deleting, or changing lines.

Run-time error correction — errors in meaning of a program must be discovered by yourself, without the aid of the computer, by rereading your program or examining the output. Correction is handled by the same method used to correct compile-time errors.

CHAPTER 4 EXERCISES

1. Start up your terminal and see that you are in the shell mode. Begin by entering the edit mode giving the file name *opus1.t*. By going to the append mode enter into your workfile the *opus1* program from the previous chapter. When you have finished entering it, save it by writing it into the secondary storage then compile it using the *ttc* command. Run it by giving the shell command *opus1.x*.

2. Bring *opus1.t* to the workfile. Now modify the program to add 8 and 9 instead of 2 and 3. Save the modified program as *opus2.t*. Run *opus2.t* using *ttc*. Is *opus1.t* still in your file? List your directory.

3. Write a new program to output five lines listing your favorite TV stars in order of preference. Run the program then try to modify it so that your number two choice is moved into number one position.

4. Try writing a program to output a pattern like the *zigzag* program of the previous chapter. Test it.

5.   Write and test a program to output the integers 1, 2, 3, etc., five to a
     line. Go up as high as 25. Try to make the format as agreeable as
     possible. Put a title at the top of your table of integers.

Chapter 5

BASIC CONCEPTS OF PROGRAMMING

In order to read numerical information into the computer, to perform arithmetic calculations on the numbers you read in, and to output the answers we must look at the concepts of: **variable**, **data type**, **declaration**, and **assignment statement**. We will, as well, introduce the statement for **input** and the idea of **program tracing**.

VARIABLES

We have said that a computer has a memory and that in the memory there are locations where information can be stored. Each location has its own unique address. In a high-level language like Turing we do not ever refer to an actual machine address. Instead we use a name to identify a particular location. It is like referring to a house by the name of the owner rather than by its street address. We use the word **variable** to stand for the memory location. It is named by an **identifier**.

The identifier for a variable must begin with a letter and contain no blanks or special characters (except that it can contain underscore characters). If you think of the variable as the memory location and its name as the identifier then you will realize that the **value** of the variable will be the actual information that is stored in the memory location. Each location is arranged to hold only one type of information or data. We speak of the **data type** of a variable. A variable may hold integers, in which case we say it is an **integer variable**. It could also be a **real variable** or a **character string variable**. If a variable is an integer variable its value can be any integer up to a certain maximum size. The value may be changed from time to time in the program but its **type** can never change; once an integer variable, always an integer variable.

Examples of variable identifiers are

accountNumber, tax, total, mark

They are similar to the identifier we used to name a program.

It is **very** important to choose identifiers that relate to the kind of information that is stored in the corresponding locations. Well-chosen identifiers make a program easier to understand.

DECLARATIONS

We must make the names we want to use as variable identifiers known to the compiler and associate them with memory locations suitable for the particular data type they will hold. This is accomplished by means of **declarations** that are placed in the program.

We will not, at the moment, show how character string variables can be declared but will look only at integer and real variables. To declare that *sum* is to be an integer variable we write

> **var** *sum:* **int**

The identifier is after the keyword **var** and is followed by a colon and the keyword **int**. This establishes *sum* as having the type **int**. To declare *distance* to be a real variable we use

> **var** *distance:* **real**

If several integer variables are required they are all listed after the **var**, separated by commas, for example

> **var** *sum, mark, number:* **int**

If we have both **real** and **int** types we write.

> **var** *sum:* **int**
> **var** *distance, speed:* **real**

Putting declarations in a program is like phoning ahead for hotel reservations; when you need it, the space is there with the right name on it. Also the compiler can substitute the actual machine address whenever it encounters a variable in the program. It does this by keeping a directory showing variable identifiers and corresponding memory locations. This directory is set up as the declarations are read by the compiler. Declarations must precede any use that is made of the variable and are often placed at the beginning of the program just after the comment that heads it.

You should not use as variable identifiers any of the words that are Turing keywords. These are **put, var, real**, and others we have not yet encountered. When we list programs in this book we always show the keywords in bold face type. This is to make the programs easy to follow.

ASSIGNMENT STATEMENTS

In addition to declarations, in this chapter you will be learning two types of Turing statements that cause things to happen as the program is executed. We say that they are **executable statements**. The **put** statement is an executable statement; it causes output to take place. One of the two new executable statements we will have is one that **reads** input, the **get** statement, but first we will look at the **assignment statement**.

There are no keywords in an assignment statement but it has a very definite form. The form is

> *identifier := expression*

There is a colon followed by an equal sign and on the left of this is a variable identifier. This identifier must have been already declared. On the right hand of the colon and equal sign there is an expression. We have looked at expressions that contained integer or real constants; now expressions can also contain integer or real variable identifiers. We have expressions like

> 5 +10/3   (8 +9)*7

but now we can have expressions like

> *sum +1   total/ 100   sum − mark*

We will not use variable identifiers in the expression of an assignment statement to begin with but instead use a simple expression, an integer constant. For example,

> *age :=5*

is an assignment statement. It causes the number 5 to be stored in the memory location called *age*. If *age* appeared in the declaration

> **var** *age:***int**

then the number is stored as an integer and would be output by

> **put** *age*

as 5. If, on the other hand, it were declared **real** it would be stored in floating-point form. It would still be displayed as 5.

So far the expression on the right-hand side of the assignment has just been an integer constant, but we can have more complicated expressions:

> *age := 1984 − 1966*

Here we are subtracting the year of birth, *1966*, from the year *1984* to get the age in *1984*. This instruction would assign the value 18 to the variable *age*. We could get the same result as follows

birthYear := 1966
thisYear := 1984
age := thisYear − birthYear

Here we have two additional variables, *birthYear* and *thisYear*, which are given values in assignment statements and then used in an expression on the right-hand side of another assignment statement. When we have a variable identifier that is really two words we begin the second word with a capital letter to make it easier to read. Remember that in Turing a capital letter and the corresponding little letter are equivalent. This is not true of the Unix operating system; the system commands that we have mentioned must all be in little letters; capital letters will not work. If we use a capital letter in a program file name it must always be a capital letter.

Going back to our example, we could have another statement

nextAge := age + 1

which would give the age the following year to the variable *nextAge*. Remember, if we use identifiers in a program they must **all** appear in declarations. We would need the declaration

var *age, birthYear, thisYear, nextAge:* **int**

A variable may be assigned values over and over during a program. For example, we might have

sum := 2 + 3
put *sum*
sum := 3 + 4
put *sum*

and so on. Now we come to perhaps the most confusing type of assignment statement. Suppose you were making calculations year by year and needed to keep a variable *age* that held the value of the current age for the calculation. We might change the value at the end of the year by:

age := age + 1

What happens when this statement is executed is that the value stored in the variable *age* is added to the integer 1 and the result of the addition stored back in the same location.

TRACING EXECUTION

We have seen that variables are associated with locations in the memory of the computer. We can assign values to variables and, during a program, we can change the values as often as we want. The values can **vary** and that is why the locations are called variables.

Sometimes it is helpful, when getting used to writing programs, to keep track of values stored in the memory locations corresponding to each variable. This can help us to understand the effect of each statement. Some statements change a value; others do not. We call this **tracing the execution** of instructions.

We will trace now a slightly more complicated program by writing the values of all the variables involved after each instruction is executed. Here we will use some meaningless identifiers like x, y, and z because the program has no particular meaning. We just want to learn to trace execution. The labels over the right-hand side give the names of the locations; their values are listed under the names. When the value of a particular variable has not yet been assigned we write a dash.

line		x	y	z
1	% The "*trace*" program			
2	**var** *x,y,z* : **int**	—	—	—
3	% This program makes no particular sense	—	—	—
4	*x := 5*	*5*	—	—
5	*y := 7*	*5*	*7*	—
6	*z := x + y*	*5*	*7*	*12*
7	*x := x + 5*	*10*	*7*	*12*
8	*x := z*	*12*	*7*	*12*
9	*y := z*	*12*	*12*	*12*
10	*x := x + y + z*	*36*	*12*	*12*
11	*y := y*z*	*36*	*144*	*12*
12	*z := (x + y)* **div** *12*	*36*	*144*	*15*
13	*x := x* **mod** *5*	*1*	*144*	*15*
14	**put** *x : 10, y : 10, z : 10*	*1*	*144*	*15*

The lines of the program are numbered so that we can refer to them.

First notice that the variables x, y, and z do not get established until the declaration **var**. They have no values assigned at this point. All is straightforward until line 7 when x appears on both sides of the assignment statement. The values shown at the right of the program are, remember, the values after execution of the statement on that line. In line 12 note that since a division between two integers is to take place and the result assigned to an integer variable that the operator **div** must be used. When the division yields an integer the answer is exact but if there is a remainder on division the fractional part of the division is dropped. We say it is **truncated**. To get the fractional part of the result in a division we must use the operator / and store the answer in a **real** variable location. If the remainder in an integer division is desired the **mod** operator can be used.

The output statement in line 14 is different from the output statements used so far because now we can include the names of variables in the list. We have

put *x: 10, y: 10, z: 10*

The machine can tell the difference between variable identifiers and explicit string constants because identifiers have no quotes. There is no possible confusion between numbers and identifiers because an identifier may not begin with a digit. You can see now why Turing has this rule.

In this example we showed a division with truncation. Sometimes we want to round off the results of a division, say in determining costs to the nearest cent. If *cost* is the value in cents of a 2-kilogram package of soap flakes then the cost of one kilogram to the nearest cent *costKg* is produced by using the **function** *round*

costKg := round(cost/2)

The variable *costKg* has been declared to be integer so it will accept only whole number values. If you do not want to round off a positive **real** value but would rather truncate the fractional part, you should use the function *floor* as in

costKg := floor(cost/2)

Since *cost* is an integer variable, for this example we can get truncation more easily using *cost* **div** 2 instead of *floor(cost/2)*. The function *ceil* takes a value to the next nearest integer above it.

INPUT OF DATA

Now we will learn how to read data into the computer. We did not learn this at the same time as we learned to output data because the idea of a variable is essential to input. It is not essential to output because we can have numbers and explicit string constants, that is, integer and real constants and constant character strings. If we use

get *x,y,z*

we will read three numbers that are entered on the keyboard and store them in the three variables *x*, *y*, and *z*. The numbers must be separated from each other by at least one blank or return. As you type, the data is displayed on the screen. The computer will not respond to your input until you press the return key. This means that as you enter data you can backspace (or use the rubout or left-arrow key) to correct it. Here is a sample program that reads numbers in and outputs their sum.

```
% The "total" program
var  x, y, z : int
put  "Input values for x and y"
get  x, y
z := x + y
put  "sum of", x, " and", y, " is", z
```

The appearance of a sample display for this program would be:

Input values for x and y
5 7
sum of 5 and 7 is 12

The first line of the display appears on the screen and the cursor is positioned at the beginning of the second line. We will show what the computer displays in **boldface** type; what you type is in *italics*. In an actual display all the characters are the same. After the display of the first line the computer waits for you to enter the data. On input, the first number entered, namely 5, is associated with the first variable *x* and will be stored in that location. The number 7 will be stored in location *y*. The numbers are separated by at least one blank. After you have entered the 7 you must press the return key so that the numbers can be accepted by the **get** statement of the program and the sum computed. When this happens the last line, giving the sum, appears. When a program reaches the end of execution this display will remain on the screen and the system will be back in the shell level. You can tell because the shell prompt symbol will appear.

When inputting real numbers you do not have to put any more digits than necessary in either part; you need not type

2.000000e+00

You can have only *2.0e0* or *2.* If the exponent is zero, you may omit it completely. Thus numbers like

35.8   3.14159   0.025

are all acceptable as real numbers.

CONVERSION BETWEEN INTEGER AND REAL

Conversions from integer to real form will occur automatically whenever the variable that is to hold the number is of type real. If a data item is input as an integer and is read into a location defined by a variable that has been declared as **real**, then it will be converted to real. However it is not permitted to assign a real value, either in an assignment statement or by a read, to an integer variable. The reason this is not permitted is that the fraction must be rounded or truncated. The programmer can specify how to transform the real value to an integer using either the *round, floor,* or *ceil* function.

```
% The "convert" program
var x, y: int
var z: real
put "Input values for x, y, and z "
get x, y, z
put x: 10, y: 10, z: 10
put "Input values for x,y and z "
get x, y, z
put x: 10, y: 10, z: 10
```

The display for the program might be:

Input values for x,y, and z
22 36 25
      22   **36**   **25**
Input values for x,y, and z
2 181 50e4
     2   **181**   **500000**

Within a program it is often necessary to convert from a real value to an integer. For example, suppose that *averageMark* is a real variable holding the average mark in a term examination. You would like the average to the nearest mark. Declare another variable *average* as integer and write

$$average := round(averageMark)$$

average will then be an integer, the rounded average mark.

COMMENTS

One of the main aims of structured programming is that your programs be easily understood by yourself and by others. When you create useful programs you may store them for future use or share them with other users. Choosing variable names that suggest what is being stored is an excellent way to make programs readable. We have shown several programs with just *x*, *y*, and *z* as variable names. This is because these are meant to show you what happens in assignment statements and **get** and **put** statements and are not about real applications. It is not advisable to use such meaningless names. We want your programs to look more like English than like algebra when you are finished.

One other thing that you can do to make a program understandable is to include comments in English along with the program. To accomplish this, simply type a percent sign followed by the comment followed by return. For example,

> *% This is a comment*

could be placed **anywhere** in the program provided it is followed by return. Comments occur at the ends of lines or on separate lines.

We have been using a comment as a heading for our program to announce the name that we will use to file it in the Unix file. We also included another comment in the *trace* program. From now on we will be including comments in our examples.

AN EXAMPLE PROGRAM

We now give a program which illustrates the use of variables, assignment statements, **get** and **put** statements, and comments. The program reads in the length, width, and height of a box (as given in inches) and then outputs the area of the base of the box (in square centimeters) and the volume of the box (in cubic centimeters). In this example we will introduce tne declaration of **constants**.

```
1       % The "box" program
2       % Read box length, width, height in inches.
3       % Convert to centimeters and calculate
4       % the box's base area and volume.
5       const cmPerInch := 2.54
6       var len, width, height, area, volume: real
7       put "length = " ..
8       get len
9       put "width = " ..
10      get width
11      put "height = " ..
12      get height
13      len := cmPerInch*len
14      width := cmPerInch*width
15      height := cmPerInch*height
16      area := len*width
17      put "area = ", area
18      volume := height*area
19      put "volume = ", volume
```

This program will output the following:

> **length** = *2.6*
> **width** = *1.2*
> **height** = *6.92*

area = 20.128992
volume = 353.803266

where the area is in square centimeters and the volume is in cubic centimeters. The area and volume displayed depend on the three values 2.6, 1.2, and 6.92 that you enter from the keyboard for the length, width, and height. Try this program using different values for the size of the box. The data values 2.6, 1.2 and 6.92 could be replaced by the dimensions of a different box.

Lines 1, 2, 3 and 4 are comments intended for you, the reader of the program, and are ignored by the computer.

Line 5 of the program is a declaration of a constant. The constant identified by the name *cmPerInch* is given the value 2.54. (There are 2.54 centimeters in an inch.) Constants differ from variables in that they maintain the same value throughout the program's execution. As with variables, declarations of constants (**const**) must precede their use in a program. Line 6 sets up memory locations for variables called *len, width, height, area*, and *volume*. (We could not use *length* because that is a **predefined identifier** in Turing.) These variables have the **real** type, instead of the **int** type, because they have non-integer values (such as 2.6). Lines 7 to 12 cause the data values 2.6 and 1.2 and 6.92 to be read into variables *len, width* and *height*. Notice how the program prompts you to enter a value by displaying **length =**. This prompt is displayed by a **put** statement ending with two dots so that a new line is not started and you can type the value for *len* on the same line. When you have finished entering the length you type return and this then starts a new line.

Line 13 takes the value 2.6 from the *len* variable, multiplies it by the constant *cmPerInch* and then returns the result to *len*. The value of *len* will now be the length of the box in centimeters.

Line 16 takes the values in *len* and *width*, multiplies them together, and places the result in *area*. Line 17 then outputs:

area = 20.128992

As of line 17, the variable *volume* has not been used. An attempt to output *volume* in line 17 would be an error because this variable has not yet been given a value. Line 18 computes the volume and line 19 outputs the volume.

Since *area* is not used until line 16, we could delete the word *area* from the declaration on line 6, and insert this new declaration between lines 15 and 16:

var *area:* **real**

Instead of this insertion we could re-write line 16 so it both declares *area* and provides an initial value:

    var *area:* **real** *:= len * width*

Moving the declaration down means *area* cannot possibly be used above line 16, because in Turing identifiers must be declared above their use. This is called the rule of **declaration before use**.

    Since *area* never changes from its initial value, we could change this new declaration to be:

    const *area:* **real** *:= len * width*

We say *area* is a **run-time constant**, because its value never changes, and we do not know its value until the program is run (executed). The advantage of declaring an item such *area* or *volume* as **const** rather than **var** is that this makes clear an important fact: that the item's value will not change.

    When a variable is given an initial value in its declaration, we can omit the type because the initial value tells us the type. For example, we can write:

    var *area := len * width*

The type of *area* is **real** because it is being assigned a **real** value. Similarly, the type is optional in **const** declarations.

    This job would also output the same thing if we made the following change. Replace lines 7 to 12 by the three assignment statements:

    len := 2.6
    width := 1.2
    height := 6.92

Now you do not need to enter the size of the box.

    These last changes result in a program which is given the dimensions of the box by assignment statements rather than by input statements (**get** statements). The advantage of the original program, which uses **get** statements, is that the program will work for a new box simply by entering different values from the keyboard.

LABELLING OF OUTPUT

    Just as comments help to make a program more understandable, output that is properly identified by labelling is self-explanatory. What you are trying to do is to prepare a display that needs no further explanation from you when you let others see your computer output. The output data should be labelled so that there is no doubt about what the numbers are, without reading the program. Prompting words serve to label the input data.

There are two basic ways to label input or output values. If different values of the same set of variables are to be entered and displayed in columns on the screen, then a label can be placed at the top of each column. For example, the display for comparing costs of boxes of soap flakes might be

cost	weight (kg)	cost/kg
125	*1*	
		125
200	*2*	
		100
260	*3*	
		87

Here the values in the **cost** and **weight (kg)** columns are input values. You can include as many blanks as you like between input values on a line so that you can line up the entries with the column headings. You must press the return after you enter a number in the **weight (kg)** column so that the computer will know that you have finished. The output values will be on the next line but are displayed so that they line up with the **cost/kg** column heading. This is done by including in the output statement a field specification for the variable **costKg**. This places the value under the **cost/kg** heading. It would be better if you could place the result on the same line as the two input values but this is not possible.

There is no reason to use exactly the same labels as the variable names, since the labels displayed at the top of the columns can be longer and contain blanks or special symbols. They are displayed independently. The program that produces this table might be

```
% The "soap" program
% Compute and tabulate cost per kg
var cost, weight, costKg: int
% Print headings of table
put "cost": 10, "weight(kg) ": 20, "cost/kg "

% Process data for first box
get cost, weight
costKg := round(cost/weight)
put costKg: 34

% Process data for second box
get cost, weight
costKg := round(cost/weight)
```

put *costKg: 34*

% Process data for third box
get *cost, weight*
costKg := round(cost/weight)
put *costKg: 34*

You can see how comments can be inserted, how the column headings are displayed, and how each line of the table is formed. As soon as the heading of the table is displayed the program is ready to accept values for the cost and weight of the first box. Remember: after you have entered the weight, press return so that the computer will know that you have finished entering the data. After the cost per kilogram is displayed the cursor will be placed at the beginning of the next line and then you are ready to enter the data for a new box. Each **put** statement causes a new line to be started after displaying the cost per kilogram. In the program we have repeated three statements, without change, one set of three for each box. If we had 100 boxes, this would have been a little monotonous. When we want to repeat statements we do **not** do it this way; a more convenient way is possible with a Turing statement that will cause this kind of repetition. But that comes in the next chapter.

A second kind of output labelling was already used in the previous example but can be illustrated by a program segment

cost := 5
put *"cost = ", cost*

This would result in the output

cost = 5

This method is easier when just a few numbers are being displayed.

PROGRAM TESTING

It is easy to make mistakes in programming. It is a good idea to use a pencil when writing programs so you can erase your mistakes. Things that are crossed out are messy. The first thing you should do to test a program is to read over your program carefully to spot errors. It is valuable to trace the execution yourself before you enter it into the computer. Your goal should always be to produce programs that you **know** are correct without testing, but this is not always possible. You could ask someone else to read it too. If another person cannot understand your program it may show that your program is poorly written or has errors. Next you enter your program and proofread it to see that it is the same as what you wrote on the piece of paper.

If you have made errors in your program that involve the form of statements, the compiler spots these during compilation and reports them on the output. It refers to an error of a certain type and refers to the spot in the program where the error occurred. Examples of common errors of form are

1.   forgetting the colon in an assignment statement

2.   forgetting the closing quotation mark around an explicit string constant

3.   misspelling a keyword

In a way, a error in form is a good error since it is detected for you by the computer. But it is frustrating to have to correct it and recompile the job. It wastes time. Some people say that having this kind of error is a symptom of sloppy programming and a sure indication that there are other errors. If the compiler detects no errors, execution can take place right after compilation.

If answers are displayed, they should be checked against hand calculated answers. If they agree, it is possible that your program is correct. If they disagree it is possible that your hand calculations are incorrect or that your program has errors. The errors now are usually of a kind called **semantic errors**. You are asking for a calculation that you did not mean to ask for. It has a different **meaning** from your intentions. For instance, you are adding two numbers and you meant to subtract them.

To find semantic errors you must look at the program again and try to trace what it must be doing rather than what you thought it would do. To help in the tracing it is sometimes necessary to insert additional **put** instructions between other statements and output the current value of variables that are changing. In this way you can follow the machine's activity. These extra **put** instructions can be removed after the errors have been found.

Although it is good practice to place each Turing declaration or statement on a line by itself, it is not essential. No error would occur if the program were all run together into as few lines as possible. It would, however, be much harder to understand. Comments must always end a line.

COMMON ERRORS IN PROGRAMS

When you try running a program on a computer, the computer may detect **errors** in your program. As a result, **error messages** will be displayed. Since the computer does not understand the purpose of your program, its error messages are limited to describing the specific illegalities which it detects. Unfortunately, the computer's error messages usually do not tell you how to correct your program so that it will solve the problem you have in mind.

In order to help you avoid such errors, we list some of the errors which commonly occur in a beginner's programs.

Missing quotes, especially the last quote. Consider the following erroneous statement:

put *"invoice*

This statement is missing a quote after the word *invoice.*

Uninitialized variables — When a variable is declared, a memory location, or cell, is set aside, but no special value is placed in the cell. That is, the cell is not yet initialized. A variable must be given a value, either in the declaration or via an assignment statement or a **get** statement, before an attempt is made to use the value of the variable in a **put** statement or in an expression.

Undeclared variables — Before a variable is used in a statement (assignment, **get, put**) the variable must be declared. The declaration of a variable can be anywhere in the program as long as it precedes the use of that variable. Declaration of constants must precede their use.

Mistaking *o* for 0 — The characters *o* (oh) and 0 (zero) look similar, but are entirely different to the computer. The digit zero is sometimes displayed with a slash through it so that it is distinctly different from the oh.

CHAPTER 5 SUMMARY

This chapter introduced the concept of a variable, as it is used in programming languages. Essentially, a variable is a memory location, or cell, which can hold a value. Suppose x is the name of a variable; then x denotes a cell. If x is a variable having the integer type, then the cell for x can hold an integer value such as 9, 291, 0 or -11. The following important terms were discussed.

Identifier — can be used as the name of a variable or constant. An identifier must begin with a letter; this letter can be followed by additional letters or digits or the underscore character. We do not use the underscore character in identifiers in this book. We prefer to capitalize the first letter of the second word of a double-word identifier. The following are examples of identifiers: *x, i, width, incomeTax* and *a1.*

Type — each variable has a data type; in this chapter we introduced the **int** and **real** types. The type of a variable is determined by its declaration.

Variable declaration — establishes variables for use in a program. For example, the declaration

> **var** *sum:* **int**

creates a variable called *sum* which can be given integer values. Declarations of variables must occur before their use in a program.

Constant declaration — establishes named constants for use in a program. For example, the declarations

> **const** *pi* := 3.14159
> **const** *convert* := 2.54

create named constants *pi* and *convert*. Declarations of constants must occur before their use in a program.

var — the keyword instructing the computer to create variables. A declaration can be of the form:

> **var** list of identifiers separated by commas: type

The type must be **int** or **real** for the present. We sometimes express the form of the declaration of variables by writing

> **var** variable {, variable} : type

where the curly brackets indicate that what is contained in them can appear zero or more times.

Assignment — means a value is assigned to a variable. For example, the following is an assignment statement which gives the value 52 to the variable *i*:

> *i* := 52

Truncation — throwing away the fractional part of a number. When a positive real number is to be assigned to a variable with the **int** type, the variable can be given the truncated value by using the *floor* function. If *x* is real and *y* integer

> *y* := *floor(x)*

will assign the nearest integer value less than or equal to *x* to the integer variable *y*.

Rounding — changing a real number to the nearest integer. If *x* is real and *y* integer

> *y* := *round(x)*

assigns the value of *x*, rounded off, to the integer variable *y*. The function *ceil* takes a positive value to the next highest integer.

Number conversion — changing an integer number to a real number or vice versa. Conversion from real to integer can be done by either truncation or rounding of the result. Integer values are converted automatically to real when assigned to (or read into) a real variable location.

Data (or input data) — values which a program can read are typed in on the keyboard during the execution of the program. Whenever you have reached the end of the data items that you are entering you must type return.

get — means to read data. The **get** statement reads data values into a list of variables. As the data is typed, it is displayed on the screen. The **get** statement expects the data to be terminated by return. This statement is of the form:

> **get** list of variable names separated by commas

Reading will automatically proceed to the next line when the values of one line have all been read and still more values are expected.

Comments — information in a program which is intended to assist a person reading the program. The following is a comment which could appear in a Turing program:

> *% This program computes gas bills*

Comments do not affect the execution of a program. We use a standard beginning comment to indicate the name of a program.

Documentation — written explanation of a program. Comments are used in a program to document its actions.

Keyword — a word, such as **var** or **put**, which is part of the programming language. Keywords must not be used as identifiers. We always show keywords in bold face type in this book.

Syntax errors — improper parts of a program. For example, the statement

> **put** ** 4*

has a syntax error in that a number is missing to the left of the multiplication sign. If the computer detects an error in your program, it will output an error message. Sometimes the compiler attempts to repair errors.

CHAPTER 5 EXERCISES

1. Suppose that *i*, *j*, and *k* are variables with the integer type and they presently have the values 5, 7, and 10. What will be displayed as a result of the following statements?

   put *i: 3, i + 1: 3, i + j: 3, i + j*k: 3*
   k := i + j
   put *k*
   j := j + 1
   put *j*
   i := 3*i + j
   put *i*

2. Suppose that *radius, diameter, circumference,* and *area* are **real** variables. A value has been read into *radius* via a **get** statement. Write statements which do each of the following.

   (a) Give to *diameter* the product of 2 and *radius.*

   (b) Give to *circumference* the product of pi (3.14159) and *diameter.*

   (c) Give to *area* the product of pi and *radius* squared (*radius* squared can be written as *radius*radius* or as *radius**2*).

   (d) Output the values of *radius, diameter, circumference,* and *area.*

3. Suppose *i* is a variable with the **int** type. Assume that *i* has already been given a value via an assignment statement. Write statements to do the following.

   (a) Without changing *i*, output twice the value of *i*.

   (b) Increase *i* by 1.

   (c) Double the value of *i*.

   (d) Decrease *i* by 5.

4. Assume that *m*, *n* and *p* are variables with the integer type. What will the following statements cause the computer to output?

   m := 43
   n := 211
   p := m
   m := n
   n := p
   put *m: 4, n: 4*

5.   What will be displayed by the following program if 22, 247, −16 and 538 are input? What happens if they are all input on one line?

> *% The "pairs" program*
> **var** *first, second:* **int**
> **put** *"Input two integers"*
> **get** *first, second*
> **put** *first + second*
> **get** *first, second*
> **put** *first + second*

6.   What will be displayed by the following program if the grades are 81.7 and 85.9?

> *% The "combine" program*
> *% Calculate term mark*
> **var** *grade1, grade2:* **real**
> **var** *mark:* **int**
> **put** *"Input two grades"*
> **get** *grade1, grade2*
> *mark := round((grade1 + grade2)/ 2)*
> **put** *mark*

7.   Trace the execution of the following program. That is, give the values of the variables *len*, *width*, and *about* and give any output after each line of the program. Use as the two input values 9.60 and 15.9.

> *% The "area" program*
> **var** *size,len,width:* **real**
> **var** *about:* **int**
> *% Read sizes; convert feet to yards*
> **put** *"size = "* ..
> **get** *size*
> *width := size / 3*
> **put** *"size = "* ..
> **get** *size*
> *len := size / 3*
> *about := round(width*len)*
> **put** *"length and width are ", len: 14, width: 14*
> **put** *"area is:", len*width: 14,*
>   *" this is about ",about: 10, " (sq yards)"*

8.   Write a program which reads three values and outputs their average, rounded to the nearest whole number. For example, if 20, 16, and 25 are entered then your program should output 20. Make up your own data for your program.

Chapter 6

CONTROL STRUCTURE

In all programs we have examined so far the statements were executed in sequence until the last statement was reached, at which time the program was terminated. In this chapter we will learn two ways in which the order of executing statements may be altered. One involves the repetitious use of statements; the other involves a selection between alternate paths in the flow of statements. The first is called a **loop** or **repetition**, the second a **selection**. We speak of the **flow of control** since it is the control unit of the computer that determines which statement is to be executed next by the computer.

COUNTED LOOPS

The normal flow of control in a program is in a straight line. So far, in the statements of a program one statement is executed after another. We will now show the Turing construct that will cause statements to be repeated. In the last chapter, in the example where we were computing information about boxes of soap flakes, we had to write the statements over and over to get repetition. A statement that will produce repetition is the **counted loop** or **for** loop. For our example we could have written

> **for** *i: 1..3*
>   **get** *cost,weight*
>   *costKg := round(cost/weight)*
>   **put** *costKg: 34*
> **end for**

The statements that we want to repeat, called the body of the loop, are prefaced by

> **for** *i: 1..3*

and followed by **end for**.

The name *i* identifies an index. It is automatically declared as an integer, and counts the number of repetitions. First the index *i* is set to 1, then the loop body is executed. After the execution, control is sent back to the **for** from the **end for**. At this time the index *i* is increased by 1, making it 2. The loop body is again executed and, then at **end for**, back we go to the **for**. This time *i* becomes 3 and a third execution of the body in the **for** loop takes place. When control returns to the **for** this time, *i* is found to be already equal to the final value 3 so control goes out of the loop to the next statement after the **end for**.

Each time through a **for** loop, the index has a particular value that cannot be changed in the body of the loop; it cannot, for example, be assigned to. The index is actually a run-time constant, automatically re-declared with a new value at the beginning of each loop repetition. After the loop has finished executing, the index can no longer be accessed; we could output the value of the index *i* only between the two lines **for** *i: 1..3* and **end for**. Since *i* only exists inside the loop, we say it is **local** to the loop.

In a case like this example, where index *i* is not accessed in the loop, we do not need to give it a name, and we can use the simpler form:

> **for:** *1..3*

A counted or **indexed loop** is used whenever we know exactly how many repetitions we want to take place. We do not need to start the count at 1. We could have, for example:

> **for** *count: 12..24*

Here we have called the index *count* and are starting at 12 and going up to, and including 24. In both these **for** loops we have counted forward by 1. We can also count backwards by −1. If we write

> **for decreasing** *count: 10..1*
> > body
> **end for**

the body of the loop will be executed with *count* taking the values 10, 9, 8, ..., 1.

The other kind of loop is the conditional loop, but we cannot introduce it until we look at conditions. We will be exiting from the body of a conditional loop when certain conditions are true.

CONDITIONS

There are expressions in Turing that are called **conditions** or **relational expressions** and these have values that are either **true** or **false**. To illustrate we will give a list of relational expressions with their value written on the same line. The symbol > means is greater than, < means is less than, the equal sign means is equal to, and **not** $=$ means is not equal to. You can see how these work. Expressions like these whose value is **true** or **false** are called **Boolean expressions** after the logician George Boole.

relational expression	value
$5 = 2 + 3$	true
$7 > 5$	true
$2 < 6$	true
$5 + 3 < 2 + 1$	false
6 **not** $= 10$	true
$5 > 5$	false
$5 > = 5$	true

There are also **compound conditions** formed by taking two single conditions and putting either the **Boolean (logical) operator** called **and** or the Boolean operator called **or** between them. You need not have parentheses around the individual conditions since Boolean operators have lower precedence than relational operators.

With the operator **and**, both conditions must be true or else the compound condition is false. For example,

$8 > 7$ **and** $6 < 3$

is false since $6 < 3$ is false. With the operator **or**, if either or both of the single conditions is true, the compound condition is true. For example, the compound condition $8 > 7$ **or** $6 < 3$ is true since $8 > 7$ is true. It is possible to have multiple compoundings. For example,

$(8 > 7$ **and** $2 = 1 + 1)$ **and** $(6 > 7$ **or** $5 > 1)$

is true. The parentheses here show the sequence of the operations. There is a rule of precedence if there are no parentheses, namely, the **and** operator has higher precedence than the **or** operator. This means that **and** operations are done before **or** operations.

A Boolean operator that requires only one condition is the **not** operator. The condition

not $5 > 6$

is true since 5 is **not** greater than 6. The **not** has higher precedence than **and**.

BOOLEAN VARIABLES

If you want to assign a Boolean value to a variable, it must be typed by a declaration as **boolean**. The type **boolean** is a variable type just like **real** and **int**. But a Boolean variable can only have one of two values, namely **true** or **false**. Boolean variables cannot be read or output but can be assigned Boolean values. They cannot be used in numeric expressions. For example, if you want a Boolean variable *switch* assigned the value **true** you must include the declaration and the assignment.

> **var** *switch:* **boolean**
> *switch* := **true**

The variable *switch* may be used in a condition.

CONDITIONAL LOOPS

We have introduced the notion of a condition; now we will actually use it. One of the major uses of conditions is in the conditional loop. The form of this loop is

> **loop**
>
>   ...
>
>   ...
>
> **exit when** *condition*
>
>   ...
>
>   ...
>
> **end loop**

The repetition of the body of the loop is to be interrupted when the condition stated after the words **exit when** is true. As long as it is false, the control goes to the next statement after the **exit when** statement.

So far we have discussed only conditions involving integer constants. These never change values and are always true or false. The condition in the conditional loop cannot be like this, because if it were always false we would loop forever and if always true we would exit the first time we reach the **exit** statement. The condition must involve a variable whose value changes during the looping.

In the following program segment a conditional loop is used to accomplish what the counted **for** loop did for the soap flakes boxes.

```
1     var i := 1
2     loop
3         get cost, weight
4         costKg := round(cost/weight)
5         put costKg: 34
```

```
6          exit when i = 3
7             i := i + 1
8       end loop
9       next statement after loop
```

In statement 1 the value of the variable i appearing in the condition is set initially to 1, then we enter the loop. This stage is called **initialization**. In line 2 we begin the loop. Lines 3 through 5 of the loop body read the values of *cost* and *weight*, then compute and output *costKg*. The condition after the **exit when** is false since i is 1, which is less than 3. Thus the execution of the body of the loop continues. In the body, statement 7 alters the value of the variable appearing in the condition. This means that it is changing each time around the loop. During the second execution of the loop i has become 2. The condition is then examined and since it is false $(2 < 3)$, the execution of the body continues. It will be true on the third time because, i will be 3 and $(3 = 3)$ is true. At this stage, control exits to the statement following the **end loop**.

The various phases of a *conditional* loop are

Phase 1. Initialization preceding the loop, especially of the variable in the condition.

Phase 2. Begin the loop at the **loop**.

Phase 3. When **exit** is reached, if the condition following the keyword **when** is false then go to the next statement which is part of the body of the loop, if true go to the statement following the **end loop**.

Phase 4. When the **end loop** is reached transfer control back to the **loop** (that is, to Phase 2).

Phase 1 is necessary to give the variable appearing in the condition an initial value.

READING INPUT

As an example of looping we will look at reading data for student marks and computing an average mark for the class. The number of students in the class is not known at the time the program is prepared. The only real problem will be to stop reading marks after the last mark is entered and compute the average. We will give two distinct ways of doing this. One is to count the number of students and enter the count before you begin entering the marks. Then we use a counted **for** loop to read them. The second method is to enter at the end of the data a piece of data that is impossible as a real entry. We call it a **dummy entry**. Sometimes it is called an **end-of-file marker**. In a later chapter we will see how the *eof* (end of file) predefined function can be used to detect that there is no more data to read.

We will now examine the two methods in turn. Suppose, to talk specifically, that each data entry consists of a student number and a grade received in an examination. To illustrate we will have only three data entries, but you can see how it will work with more.

Method 1. Counting the number of entries

```
% The "marks1" program
var studentNumber, mark, count, sum: int
put "How many students?"..
get count
sum := 0
put "Give", count, " student numbers with marks"
put "Student no.    Mark"
for: 1..count
    get studentNumber, mark
    sum := sum + mark
end for
put "average = ", round(sum/count)
put  "count = ", count
```

The screen will display

How many students? *3*
Give 3 student numbers with marks
Student no.   Mark
1026   86
2051   90
3163   71
average = 82
count = 3

Notice that we took the trouble to label the output. The data entries you type can be placed under the column labels *Student No.* and *Mark*.

In the second method we will place a dummy entry with two zeros in it after we have finished all the valid entries. This will then trigger the calculation of the average mark.

Method 2. Testing for the dummy entry

```
% The "marks2" program
var studentNumber, mark, count, sum: int
count := 0
sum := 0
put "Give student numbers with marks"
put "Student no.    Mark"
loop
    get studentNumber, mark
    exit when studentNumber = 0
    sum := sum + mark
    count := count + 1
end loop
put "average = ", round(sum/count)
put "count = ", count
```

Here the display on the screen is

Give student numbers with marks
Student no.   Mark
1026   86
2951   90
3163   71
0   0
average = 82
count = 3

In this example you will notice that there is no initialization outside the loop since the statement which changes the variable *studentNumber* in the condition, namely the **get** statement, is the same one as you need to initialize the variable.

Methods 1 and 2 for dealing with a variable number of items are used again and again in programming. The conditional loop is more difficult to program but probably more useful, since if there are many items, it is better for the user to stick in an end-of-file item than to count items.

EXAMPLES OF LOOPS

We will now give example programs to illustrate details about loops. The examples each draw a wiggly line. Here is the first example:

```
1    % The "wiggle" program
2    % Illustrates the counted loop
3    for j :1..3
```

```
4         put "*"
5         put " *"
6         put "  *"
7         put " *"
8     end for
```

This program, called *wiggle*, outputs the following pattern:

```
*
 *
  *
 *
*
 *
  *
 *
*
 *
  *
 *
*
```

The *wiggle* program causes the body of the loop, lines 4 through 7, to be executed three times. The counter j is 1 during the time the first four stars are displayed. Then j is 2 during the time the next four stars are displayed, and j is 3 while the last four stars are displayed. After the last star is displayed, the loop is terminated because j is 3.

Notice that in this program the counter j is used for only one purpose: to see that the loop is repeated the desired number of times. Line 3 means, essentially, "Repeat this loop three times." If we replaced line 3 by the following line

for j *:9..11*

then the program would still output the same pattern. The only difference is that j would have the values 9,10, and 11 during the output of the stars. Although this replacement for line 3 does not change the pattern displayed, it should not be used because it makes the program more confusing for people to understand. This is because people more naturally think of "repeat this loop three times" as running through the loop with values 1, 2, and 3, rather than 9, 10, and 11.

Here is one more possible replacement for line 3 which does not change the displayed pattern:

for decreasing j *:3..1*

In this case, j will be 3 while the first four stars are displayed, then j will be 2 while the next four stars are displayed, and then j will be 1 while the last four stars are displayed. This illustrates the fact that if the **for** loop is **decreasing** then the loop will count backwards to smaller values. Again, for this example program, the original version of line 3 is preferable because it is easier to understand its meaning at a glance.

We will now rewrite our *wiggle* program using a conditional loop instead of a counted **for**. We will call our new program *waggle*.

```
1      % The "waggle" program
2      var j: int
3      j := 1
4      loop
5          put "*"
6          put " *"
7          put "  *"
8          put "   *"
9          exit when j = 3
10         j := j + 1
11     end loop
```

This *waggle* program works like our previous *wiggle* program. Line 3 together with lines 9 and 10 is equivalent to line 3 of *wiggle*. Since it is easier to see that line 3 of *wiggle* means, "Repeat this loop three times," the *wiggle* version is preferable.

Now let us look again at the *waggle* program. Suppose that you prepared this program for the computer and mistakenly made line 10 into

$$j := j - 1$$

The mistake is that the plus sign was changed to a minus sign. Such a small mistake! Surely the computer will understand that a plus was wanted! But it will not do so. The computer has a habit of doing what we **tell** it to do rather than what we **want** it to do. Given the *waggle* program, with the mistake, the computer will do the following. With j set to 1 it will output the first four stars. Then, as a result of the erroneous line 10, it will set j to 0 and will output another four stars. Then it will set j to -1 and output four more stars. Then it will set j to -2 and output four more stars, and so on, and so on. In theory, it will **never stop** outputting stars because the condition $j = 3$ will always be false. This is called an *infinite loop*. You will have to stop the computer from executing your program by pressing the reset key (ctrl-c).

An infinite loop can be programmed intentionally using the **loop** with no **exit when** at all. We use such a loop when we are working interactively and want to terminate the looping by an interruption from the keyboard.

SELECTION

We have learned how to change from a flow of control in a straight line, or **sequential** control, to flow in a loop, either counted or conditional. Now we must look at a different kind of structure in the sequence of control. This structure is called **selection**. The basic form of a selection statement is

> **if** *condition* **then**
>   *statements*
> **else**
>   *statements*
> **end if**

When the condition following the keyword **if** is true the statements following the keyword **then** (called the **then** clause) are executed and if the condition is false the statements following the keyword **else** (called the **else** clause) are executed. Only one of the two sets of statements is executed; we select one or the other. If no statements are to be executed after the **else** then the keyword **else** is also omitted.

After one or the other of the two sets of statements has been executed, control goes to the statement after the keywords **end if**.

Here is an example. Suppose that there is a variable called *classA* which contains the number of students in a class called *A*. Students are to be assigned to Class *A* if their mark in computer science (*csMark*) is over 80; otherwise they are to be assigned to Class *B* (*classB*). The Turing statement which decides which class to place the student in, and counts the number going into each class, is

> **if** *csMark* > 80 **then**
>   *classA := classA + 1*
> **else**
>   *classB := classB + 1*
> **end if**

The **if** statement causes control to split into two paths but it immediately comes back together again. This means that we are never in any doubt about what happens; after the execution of one or the other of the two sets of statements, the control returns to the normal sequence. The **if** statement provides two possibilities, only one of which is to be **selected**, depending on whether the condition following the **if** is true or false. After one or the other path is executed the normal control sequence is resumed.

As we said, if there is nothing that you want to do in the **else** body you can leave out the word **else** entirely. For instance, you may have the statement which would eliminate the balance in a bank account if it were less than 10 cents.

> **if** *balance* < *10* **then**
>> *balance* := *0*
>
> **end if**

Here there is no **else**; this just means that if the balance is larger than 10 cents we do **not** make it zero.

THREE-WAY SELECTION

We have presented a statement which selects between two alternatives. We will now show a statement that selects among three alternatives.

As an example, we will write a program that counts votes in an election. Suppose that there are three political parties called Conservative (right), Radicals (left), and Mugwumps (middle-roaders) and that to vote for one of these parties you enter a 1, or a 2, or a 3 respectively. Here is the program that reads the vote entries and counts each party and the total. The last vote entry is the dummy value −1.

```
% The "voting" program
const conservative := 1
const radical := 2
const mugwump := 3
var vote, right, left, middle,count: int
right := 0
left := 0
middle := 0
put "Enter votes one to a line, finish with − 1"
loop
    get vote
    exit when vote = − 1
    if  vote = conservative then
        right := right + 1
    elsif vote = radical then
        left := left + 1
    elsif vote = mugwump then
        middle := middle + 1
    end if
end loop
count := right + left + middle
put "conserv.": 10, "radical": 10, "mugwump": 10, "total"
put right: 4, left: 10, middle: 10, count: 10
```

Two different things are happening in this program. One is a three-way selection, which is accomplished by a **cascaded if** statement. A cascaded **if** statement is one that contains one or more **elsif**s. Its meaning is obvious. In our program an invalid vote does not get counted anywhere. If we wanted notification that there was an invalid vote we could have inserted the following in the program right before the words: **end if**.

> **else**
>> **put** *"invalid vote"*, *vote*

This then makes it a four-way branch. The minimum program needed for a three-way branch would be an **if** statement with one **elsif**.

> **if** *vote = conservative* **then**
>> *right := right + 1*
>
> **elsif** *vote = radical* **then**
>> *left := left + 1*
>
> **else**
>> *middle := middle + 1*
>
> **end if**

If there are any invalid votes, they are given to the *mugwump* party. Notice that we put the **else** or **elsif** that goes with an **if** vertically beneath it so that the structure is clear. In the next section we will show how three-way and higher selection might be handled using a **case** statement.

CASE STATEMENTS

If there are more than two alternatives in a selection process where the alternative selected depends on an integer we can use a **case** statement. The basic form of this statement is

> **case** *expression* **of**
>> **label** *case— label1: statements1*
>> **label** *case— label2: statements2*
>>
>> ...
>> **label** *case— labelN: statementsN*
>
> **end case**

Instead of the cascaded **if** statement in the *voting* program we could have this **case** statement

> **case** *vote* **of**
>> **label** *conservative: right := right + 1*
>> **label** *radical: left := left + 1*
>> **label** *mugwump: middle := middle + 1*
>
> **end case**

The value of the variable *vote* should be the same as one of the three named constants: *conservative, radical*, or *mugwump*, and depending on its value the correspondingly labelled statement is executed. For example, if *vote*=2 (*radical*) then we execute *left := left + 1*. The label of a statement is separated from the statement itself by a colon. Each label must be an integer constant, for example 3 or *mugwump*, otherwise we cannot use a **case** statement. Notice that there is an **end case** terminating the **case** statement.

The **case** statement expects to select exactly one of the labelled set of statements, so the selecting value, *vote* in this example, must have one of the values of the case labels. If we are not sure that *vote* is 1, 2 or 3, we can expand the program to

> **if** *vote* has the value 1, 2, or 3 **then**
> > **case** *vote* **of**
> > > (Same as in previous *case* statement)
> > **end case**
> **else**
> > **put** "*invalid vote* ", *vote*
> **end if**

The only thing missing is that we have not written "*vote* has the value of 1,2 or 3" in Turing. We will see how this can be done using **and** and **or** in the next chapter. If you want to allow invalid votes to be counted you can have a **label** with no value specified as in this example

> **case** *vote* **of**
> > **label** *conservative: right := right + 1*
> > **label** *radical: left := left + 1*
> > **label** *mugwump: middle := middle + 1*
> > **label** *:* **put** "*invalid vote* ", *vote*
> **end case**

The **label** with no specified values is like the **else** part of an **if** statement; this must be the last **label** in the **case** statement.

A particular alternative in a **case** statement can have more than one label. Suppose the Conservative and Mugwump parties form a coalition and we wish to count their votes together in the variable *coalition*. We could use this *case* statement.

> **case** *vote* **of**
> > **label** *conservative,mugwump: coalition := coalition + 1*
> > **label** *radical: left := left + 1*
> **end case**

Of course we would need to declare *coalition* as an integer variable.

INITIALIZATION OF VARIABLES IN DECLARATIONS

In Turing it is possible to set the initial values of variables when they are declared. For example, the declaration

var *i:* **int** *:= 0*

not only declares that *i* is to be a variable of type **int** but that its value is to be set equal to zero.

A number of variables of the same type maybe initialized to the same value in a single declaration. For example, for the *voting* program the declarations might be

var *right,left,middle:* **int** *:= 0*
var *vote,count:* **int**

We have used two declarations because although *vote* and *count* are of type **int** they are not to be given a value 0 as *right, left,* and *middle* are.

EXAMPLE IF STATEMENTS

We will now give a series of examples of **if** statements which might be used in a government program for handling income tax. Let us suppose that the program is to write notices to people telling them whether they owe tax or they are to receive a tax refund. The amount of tax is calculated and then the following is executed.

```
if tax > 0 then
    put "Tax due is ", tax, " dollars "
else
    put "Refund is ", − tax, " dollars "
end if
```

Notice that it was necessary to change the sign of *tax* when we output the refund. Unfortunately, our program, like too many programs, is not quite right. If the calculated tax is exactly zero, then the program will output *Refund is 0 dollars.* We could fix this problem this way.

```
if tax > 0 then
    put "Tax due is ", tax, " dollars "
elsif tax = 0 then
    put "You owe nothing "
else
    put "Refund is ", − tax, " dollars "
```

end if

We have used a cascaded **if** statement to solve the problem, that is, an **if** statement which contains one or more **elsif**s.

Now suppose that when the tax is due we wish to tell the taxpayer where to send his check. We can expand the program as follows:

```
if tax > 0 then
    put "Tax due is ", tax, " dollars "
    put "Send check to district office "
elsif tax = 0 then
    put "You owe nothing "
else
    put "Refund is ", − tax, " dollars "
end if
```

PARAGRAPHING THE PROGRAM

In order to follow the **structure** of the **if** statements we have indented the program so that the **if** and **else** or **elsif** that belong to each other are lined up vertically. The statements following the **then** and the **else** are indented. This is called **paragraphing** the program, and is analogous to the way we indent paragraphs of prose to indicate grouping of thoughts. Paragraphing makes a valuable contribution to understandability and is a **must** in structured programming.

Also, if you examine the programs with **for** loops, you will see that the loop body has been indented starting right after the **for**. In the next chapter we will be examining the situation where **for** loops are nested, and then we will use two levels of indentation.

There are no set rules about how much indentation you should use, or how an **if**...**then**...**else** statement should be indented; but it is clear that being systematic is an enormous help.

If you have entered a Turing program, say *prog.t*, without indentation you can have it paragraphed for you by giving the shell command

    ttp prog.t

The paragraphed program will be stored back in file *prog.t*.

CHAPTER 6 SUMMARY

In this chapter we introduced statements which allow for the repetition of statements and for the selection between different possibilities. We introduced conditions which are used to terminate the repetition of statements and to choose between different possibilities. Comparisons and Boolean operators are used in specifying conditions. The following important terms were discussed in this chapter.

Loop — a programming language construct which causes repeated execution of statements. In Turing, loops are either counted **for** loops or conditional loops.

Counted **for** loop — has the following form:

> **for** *variable: start..limit*
>   *statements*
> **end for**

The variable, called the counting variable or index, is automatically declared as an **int** type. Each of *start*, and *limit* can be expressions; these expressions are evaluated before the repetition starts and are not affected by the statements of the loop body. Counting proceeds by ones from the *start* up to and including the *limit*. If *start* is not less than or equal to *limit* no execution of the loop body will take place. Counting backwards by −1 is accomplished by using the form

> **for decreasing** *variable: start..limit*
>   *statements*
> **end for**

Conditional loop — has the following form:

> **loop**
>
>   ...
>
>   **exit when** *condition*
>
>   ...
>
> **end loop**

The condition is tested when control reaches the **exit** statement each pass through the loop. If it is found to be false, the next statement of the loop body is executed. When the condition finally is found to be true, control is passed to the statement which follows the **end loop**, terminating the loop body. Any variables which appear in the condition must be given values before the **exit** statement. The part of the body up to the **exit** is executed at least once. The part of the loop body following the **exit** is executed zero or more times.

Loop body — the statements that appear inside a loop between the keyword **loop** and the keywords **end loop**.

Comparisons — used in conditions. For example, comparisons can be used in a condition to determine how many times to execute a loop body. The following are used to specify comparisons.

<	less than
>	greater than
<=	less than or equal
>=	greater than or equal
=	equal
not =	not equal

Conditions — are either true or false. Conditions can be made up of comparisons and the three Boolean operators:

and

or

not

End-of-file (or end-of-data) detection — When a loop is reading a series of data items, it must determine when the last data item has been read. This can be accomplished by first reading in the number of items to be read and then counting the items in the series as they are read. It can also be accomplished by following the last data item by a special dummy entry which contains special, or dummy data. The program knows to stop when it reads the dummy data.

if statement ¬ has the following form:

> **if** *condition* **then**
>> *statements*
>
> {**elsif** *condition* **then**
>> *statements*}
>
> [**else**
>> *statements*]
>
> **end if**

The square brackets are shown around the **else** clause to show that it can be omitted. If the condition is true, the statements after the **then** are executed. If the condition is false, the statements after the **elsif** if present, or the **else** if not, are executed. We have shown the **elsif** and its statements in curly brackets to indicate that you can have zero or more repetitions of this part. In any case, control then goes to next statement after the **end if** when the selection is complete. Note the only one of the sets of statements is selected.

Cascaded **if** statement — an **if** statement with one or more **elsif**s.

case statement — when an integer value is used to choose among more than two alternatives in a selection statement, a **case** statement can be more direct than a cascaded **if** statement. It has the form

> **case** *expression* **of**
> > **label** *case-label1: statements1*
> > **label** *case-label2: statements2*
> >   ...
> > **label** *case-labelN: statementsN*
> **end case**

When the **case** statement is encountered in a program the expression is evaluated and the statements executed whose case label matches that value. The expression must match one of the labels or the meaning of the **case** statement is undefined unless there is one **label** with no case-label value specified. This alternative must be last in the list. Each case label is an integer constant. Several case labels separated by commas can label a single choice.

Paragraphing — indenting a program so that its structure is easily seen by a reader. The statements inside loops and inside **if** statements are indented to make the overall program organization obvious. The computer ignores paragraphing when translating and executing programs.

CHAPTER 6 EXERCISES

1.   Suppose *i* and *j* are variables with values 6 and 12. Which of the following conditions are true?

> (a) $2*i <= j$
> (b) $2*i - 1 < j$
> (c) $i <= 6$ **and** $j <= 6$
> (d) $i <= 6$ **or** $j <= 6$
> (e) $i > 0$ **and** $i <= 10$
> (f) $i <= 12$ **or** $j <= 12$
> (g) $i > 25$ **or** $i < 50$ **and** $j < 50$
> (h) i **not** $= 4$ **and** i **not** $= 5$
> (i) $i < 4$ **or** $i > 5$
> (j)   **not** $i > 6$

2. The following program predicts the population of a family of wallalumps over a 2-year period, based on the assumption of an initial population of 2 and a doubling of population each month. What does the program output?

```
% The "explode" program
var population: int
population := 2
put "    month ", " population "
for month: 0..24
    put month: 10, population: 10
    population := 2*population
end for
```

3. Suppose you have hidden away 50 dollars to be used for some future emergency. Assuming an inflation rate of 12 per cent per year, write a program to compute how much money, to the nearest dollar, you would need at the end of each of the next 15 years to be equivalent to the buying power of 50 dollars at the time you hid it.

4. Trace the following program. That is, give the values of the variables together with any output after the execution of each statement. Use as data entries 95 110 85 −1.

```
1   % The "class" program
2   var number, sum: int := 0
3   var grade: int
4   put "Enter grades, one to a line − 1 at end"
5   % Read grades and sum valid grades
6   loop
7       get grade
8       exit when grade = − 1
9       if grade > 0 and grade < = 100 then
10          sum := sum + grade
11          number := number + 1
12      else
13          put " **error: grade = ", grade
14      end if
15  end loop
16  put "Average is ", sum/number
```

5. Write a program that reads the following lines of data and calculates the average of (a) each of the two columns of data, and (b) each row of the data. You should either precede the data with a number giving

the count of the following data items or add a dummy entry following these data items.

92	88
75	62
81	75
80	80
55	60
64	60
81	80

6.   Write a program which reads in a sequence of grades (0 to 100) and outputs the average grade (rounded to the nearest whole number), the number of grades and the number of failing grades (failing is less than 50). Assume that a dummy grade of 999 will follow the last grade. See that your output is clearly labelled. Answer the following questions:

(a)   What will happen if the grade 74 is misentered as 7 4?

(b)   What will happen if the dummy grade 999 is left off? (You can try this.)

(c)   What will your program do if there are no grades, that is, if 999 is the only data item?

(d)   What will happen if the two grades 62 and 93 are misentered as 6293?

Test your program using the following data:

85	74	44	62	93
41	69	73	999	

7.   Write a program which determines the unit price (cents per ounce) of different boxes of laundry soap. Round the unit price to the nearest cent. Each box will be described by an entry of the form:

pounds	ounces	price
5	0	125

This box of soap has a rounded unit price of 2 cents per ounce. Make up about 10 data entries describing soap boxes; if you like, use real examples from a supermarket. You are to precede these entries with one data entry containing a single integer giving the number of soap box entries. Do not use a dummy entry to mark the end of the data. Arrange your display so that it results in a nicely labelled table giving weights, prices in cents, and unit costs. Answer the following questions:

(a) What would your program do if the above example data entry were mistyped as

50   125

(b) Would it be possible to make your program smart enough to detect some kinds of improper data? How or why not?

Chapter 7

COMPLEX CONTROL STRUCTURES

In the last chapter we introduced the two kinds of statements that cause an alteration from the linear flow of control in a program. One kind caused repetition or looping, the counted **for** and the conditional **loop**. The other caused selective execution, the **if** and the **case** statement. Learning to handle these two kinds of instructions is essential to programming. And learning to handle them in a systematic way is essential to structured programming. In this way we can control the complexity of a program's structure. We will see that all programs can be formed from the three basic control structures and that, no matter how complicated the program is the structure can be understood.

BASIC STRUCTURE OF LOOPS

It is hard to appreciate, when you first learn a concept like loops, that all loops are basically the same. They consist of a sequence of statements in the program that:

1. Initialize the values of certain variables that are to be used in the loop. These may consist of assigning starting values to

    (a) variables that appear in the condition of an **exit when**.

    (b) variables that appear in the body of the loop on the right-hand side of assignment statements.

2. Indicate that a loop is to commence. If it is a conditional loop (or an infinite loop), it begins with the keyword **loop**. If it is a **for** loop give the number of repetitions. Each loop has a control phrase that determines the number of repetitions.

    (a) A counted loop's repetition is controlled by the range of values after the **for**, for example

    > **for** $i : 1..20$

(b)   In the conditional loop, the control phrase is placed inside the loop, for example

exit when $i > 20$

The condition should contain at least one variable.

3.   Give the list of statements, called the body of the loop, that are to be executed each time the loop is repeated. If the loop is a conditional loop, then within the body of the loop before the **exit when** statement there must be some statements that assign new values to the variables appearing in the condition. Commonly there is only one variable and its value may be changed by either

(a)   an assignment statement or

(b)   a **get** statement.

4.   The end of the loop is indicated by either **end for**, in the case of a **for** loop, or **end loop** with the **loop**.

5.   Give the next statement to be executed once the looping has been carried out the required number of times. Control goes from the **exit when** or the beginning of the **for** loop to this statement when

(a)   the condition after the **exit when** is true

(b)   the value of the index controlling the counted **for** loop has already reached the limit value.

In the loops we have programmed there is no exit from the loop, except from one fixed location (either the beginning or from the **exit when** depending on the kind of loop it is), and this exit **always** goes to the statement immediately after the end of the loop. It is never possible to go somewhere else in a program.

Many high-level languages offer a statement for altering the path of control called the **goto** statement. It permits you to send control to statements with **labels** in your program. Since computer scientists came to recognize the importance of proper structuring in a program, the freedom offered by the **goto** statement has been recognized as not in keeping with the idea of structured control flow. For this reason it is **not** in the Turing language.

It is possible in Turing to use multiple **exit when** statements or even an unconditional **exit** inside a loop. We will try to limit outselves to a single **exit** statement in a loop body.

FLOW CHARTS

A flow chart is a diagram made up of boxes of various shapes, rectangular, circular, diamond, and so on, connected by lines with directional arrows on the lines. The boxes contain a description of the actions of a program and the directed lines indicate the flow of control among the statements. The main purpose of drawing a flow chart is to exhibit the flow of control clearly, so that it is evident both to the programmer and to a reader who might want to alter the program.

A method of programming that preceded the present method of structured programming found that drawing a flow chart helped in the programming process. It was suggested that a first step in writing any program was to draw a flow chart. It was a way of controlling complexity.

When we limit ourselves to the two standard forms of altering control flow, the loop and the selection constructs, there is little need to draw these flow charts. In a sense, especially if it is properly paragraphed, the program is its own flow chart; it is built of completely standard building blocks.

Perhaps it would be helpful to show what the flow charts of our basic building blocks would be like in case you wanted to draw a flow chart for your whole program. We use a diamond-shaped box when conditions are being tested. An **if** statement of the form

> **if** *condition* **then**
> > *statements1*
>
> **else**
> > *statements2*
>
> **end if**
> *next statements*

has this flow chart:

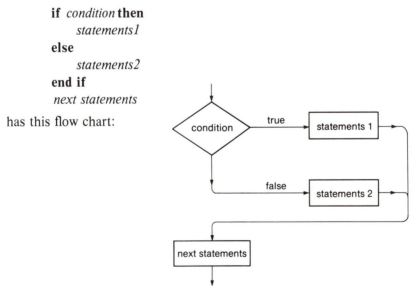

FLOW CHART FOR **if**...**then**...**else**...**end if** STATEMENT

The cascaded **if** statement has several parts:

> **if** *condition1* **then**
>> *statements1*
>
> **elsif** *condition2* **then**
>> *statements2*
>
> ...
>
> **elsif** *conditionN* **then**
>> *statementsN*
>
> **else**
>> *statementsForElse*
>
> **end** **if**
>> *next statements*

Here is the flow chart for a cascaded **if** statement.

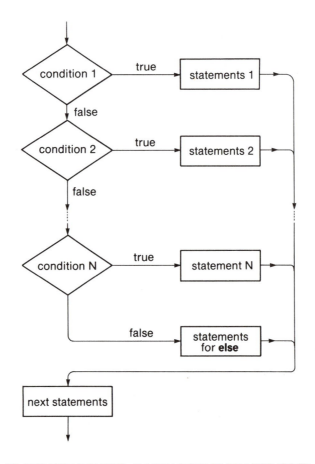

FLOW CHART FOR CASCADED **if** STATEMENT

The flow chart for a **case** statement would be similar except that the alternative paths are chosen on the basis of an index.

A simple conditional loop of the form:

loop
      statements1
      exit when *condition*
      statements2
end loop
   next statements

has this flow chart:

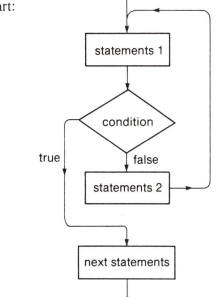

FLOW CHART FOR SIMPLE CONDITIONAL LOOP

The flow chart for the counted **for** would be similar except that it would initialize the index to its first value, increment it by the required amount, and then test to see if the loop has been executed the specified number of times.

With these basic diagrams and the ordinary straight line sequence, flow charts for all Turing programs can be built. In a way, because they are so obviously related to the program, they do not really need to be drawn. Any one of the rectangular boxes in these diagrams may be replaced by a sequence of rectangular boxes, or else one of the two basic diagrams themselves.

NESTED LOOPS

We will now look at more complicated loops. We will examine a program that sums the marks of students in 4 subjects and outputs these with the average, to the nearest mark. There are a number of lines of data, two for each student. One line contains the input data, the next the output. An entry with the total number of students precedes the mark entries. We will test the program first using only three students to see if it is working.

```
% The "class" program
% A sample program with nested loops
var numberOfStudents, sum, average, mark, studentNumber: int
put "number of students = " ..
get numberOfStudents
put "student":10, " mark1  mark2  mark3  mark4":32, " average"
for i :1..numberOfStudents
    sum := 0
    get studentNumber
    for j :1..4
        get mark
        sum := sum + mark
    end for
    average := round(sum/4)
    put average: 44
end for
```

Here is the display:

number of students = *3*

student	mark1	mark2	mark3	mark4	average
205	*55*	*60*	*65*	*70*	
					62
208	*83*	*81*	*96*	*90*	
					88
209	*72*	*68*	*78*	*81*	
					75

You will notice that when we have one **for** loop nested inside another, we use two levels of indentation to indicate the control structure. As the student number and marks are entered there is no execution of the program until the return is pressed after entering the 4th mark. Then the **get** statement is executed 5 times, once outside and 4 times inside the loop. The output of the average mark must be spaced over to the right by 42 spaces to align it with the table heading. The average will be on the next line after the mark entries. Again the part of the display produced by the program is shown in bold face type; the data you enter is in italic type.

We will illustrate some details about nested loops with another program. Like some of our previous examples, this program outputs a zigzag. However, our new program is more versatile than the old ones in that it can output different sizes of and numbers of zigs and zags, depending on the input.

```
% The "pickzig" program
var howMany, howBig: int
put "How many?"
get howMany
put "How big?"
get howBig
for major :1..howMany
    put "****"
    for minor :1..howBig
        put "*"
    end for
    put "****"
    for minor :1..howBig
        put "    *"
    end for
end for
```

This program, given the data values 3 and 2 for *howMany* and *howBig*, outputs the following pattern. We have shown in parentheses values of *major* and *minor* during the output of each of the single-star lines.

```
How many?
3
How big?
2
****                        (major, minor)
*                           (1,1)
*                           (1,2)
****
    *                       (1,1)
    *                       (1,2)
****
*                           (2,1)
*                           (2,2)
****
    *                       (2,1)
    *                       (2,2)
****
```

```
*                                    (3,1)
*                                    (3,2)
****

    *                                (3,1)
    *                                (3,2)
```

The first data value, 3, caused the sub-pattern

```
****
*
*
****
    *
    *
```

to be displayed three times. The second data value, 2, was used in determining the height of this sub-pattern.

As you can see in the program, there are two separate loops inside the main **for** loop. In both of these loops, the index is called *minor*. There is no difficulty in using the name *minor* twice; in each loop it is a new index.

We can change the pattern displayed by changing the data entries. For example, the following pattern is displayed for data values 1 and 1.

```
****                         (major,minor)
*                               (1,1)
****
    *                           (1,1)
```

In this case, the loops are each executed only once.

We can shrink the pattern down to nothing at all by using the data values 0 and 1. When the first data value is zero, then the limit value *howMany* is also zero and is less than *major*'s starting value 1. As a result, the main loop is executed zero times. Since the main loop is not executed, the second data value, 1, has no effect. We could supply data values 0 and 2 instead of 0 and 1 and would still get the same pattern, namely, no pattern at all.

Now let us switch things around so the second data value is zero, but the first is not. For data values 2 and 0, the pattern becomes

```
****
****
****
****
```

In this case the main loop is executed twice, but the two inside loops were each executed zero times.

The data values were used by this program to determine the pattern to output. You could write other programs which output different patterns for different data.

LOOPS WITH COMPOUND CONDITIONS

Sometimes we must terminate a loop if something happens that is unusual. One of the conditions controlling the loop is the standard one; the other is the unusual one. We have seen that compound conditions can be formed from two or more simple conditions using the **and** and **or** Boolean operators.

As an example, we will write a program to look for a certain number in a list of numbers that you enter. If you find it in the list, immediately output the position it occupies in the list; if it is not in the list, output *not in list.* The list will be positive integers terminated by an end-of-file marker -1.

```
% The "hunt" program
var number, listNo,i : int
put "Number you are looking for = " ..
get number
put "Start typing in list; finish with − 1 "
i := 1
loop
    get listNo
    exit when listNo = number or listNo = − 1
    i := i + 1
end loop
if listNo = number then
    put "i = ", i
else
    put "not in list"
end if
```

Here is a sample display:

Number you are looking for = *35*
Start typing in list; finish with −**1**
12
16
25
35
i =**4**

Notice that in the body of the loop the variable *listNo* in the condition of the **exit when** can be initialized and changed by the **get** *listNo* statement. Since an index *i* is required to give the position of the number in the list, it must be incremented in the statement $i := i + 1$ and initialized to 1 outside the loop. We could type the list of numbers all on one line but no action would take place until we had pressed return. This means we could type other numbers after the 35.

COUNTED LOOPS WITH CONDITIONAL EXITS

We have just considered **loop** statements with two or more reasons for exitting. We are permitted in Turing to place an **exit** statement inside the body of a **for** loop. As an example, here is a program that reads in a maximum of 10 integers but stops if the number 7 is read. It outputs the total of the integers up to the 7 that are read.

```
% The "seven" program
var number, sum: int
sum := 0
for i: 1..10
    get number
    exit when number = 7
    sum := sum + number
end for
put "total up to 7 = ", sum
```

This **for** loop may or may not execute 10 times because the number 7 may not or may be in the list.

IF STATEMENTS WITH COMPOUND CONDITIONS

Just as the conditional loop can have compound conditions, so also can **if** statements. These can be used very effectively to avoid cascaded **if** statements. Suppose you want to count people in a list who fall into a particular age group, say 18-65, as adults. The following program will count the number in the category *adult* in the list. The list of ages is terminated by a -1 followed by return.

```
% The "workers" program
var age: int
var adult: int := 0
const dummy := -1
put "Start typing list of ages; finish with - 1"
loop
```

```
        get age
        exit when age = dummy
        if age > = 18 and age < = 65 then
            adult := adult + 1
        end if
    end loop
    put "number of adults = ", adult
```

Here is a sample display:

Start typing list of ages; finish with −1
16 25 31 12 28 29 69 − 1
number of adults = 4

LOCALIZING DECLARATIONS

In Turing, declarations can appear inside loops. For example, in the *workers* program, we can move *age*'s declaration into the loop:

```
    ...same as "worker" program, but age's declaration
            is moved into the loop...
loop
    var age: int   % Declaration is moved here
    ...same as previous loop body...
end loop
put "number of adults = ', adults
```

With this arrangement, each time through the loop, the *age* variable is created at its declaration and is deleted at **end loop**.

This means the *age* cannot be referenced outside the loop; we say that the **scope** of *age* is the loop body. This is similar to the counter of a **for** loop, which can be accessed only in the loop body. In general, the scope of a declared item lasts from its declaration to the end of its enclosing construct (to **end loop, end for**, end of **then** or **else** clause, end of **case** alternative, etc.).

The advantage of moving *age*'s declaration into the loop body is that this localizes the effect of the declaration. It is easier to understand a program when you know that certain items can only be used in limited parts of the program. It might seem that the repeated creation and deletion of *age* would be inefficient, but the compiler for Turing can produce the same machine language for the program whether or not *age*'s declaration is moved into the loop.

Notice that the declaration for *adult* must appear before the loop, because *adult* must be initialized to zero before the loop begins and because its final value is used after the loop terminates.

CHAPTER 7 SUMMARY

In this chapter we have taken a closer look at loop and selection constructs. We discussed flow charts. We presented more complex examples of loops and selection constructs with compound conditions. We also looked at nested loops. The following important terms were discussed.

Flow chart — a graphic representation of a program. A flow chart consists of boxes of various shapes interconnected by arrows indicating flow of control. Turing programs can be represented by flow charts.

Exit from a loop — means stopping the execution of a loop. Exit from a conditional loop occurs at the **exit when** statement when the condition is found to be true.

Exit from within a counted loop — means including an **exit when** condition statement in the body of a counted loop. This means that the loop may not execute the number of times indicated in the control phrase after the **for**. Some programmers do not approve of this method. You can use a conditional loop with a double condition to get the same result if you prefer.

goto statement (not in Turing) — transfers control to another part of a program. The **goto** statement is available in most high-level languages and is sometimes used to exit from a loop by transferring control to the statement following the loop. The **exit when** or **exit** statement does that in Turing. Careless use of **goto** statements leads to complex program structures which are difficult to understand and to make correct. That is why **goto** does not exist in Turing.

Nested statements — means statements inside statements. For example, **for** loops can be nested inside **for** loops.

Compound conditions — conditions the **and** and **or** operators.

Scope of declaration — a declaration creates an item, for example, **var** *age:* **int**, creates the *age* variable. If the declaration is in a loop or in the clause of an **if** or **case** statement, the item is deleted at the end of that construct. The **scope** of the variable lasts from its declaration to the end of the construct.

CHAPTER 7 EXERCISES

We will base all the exercises for this chapter on the same problem, which we now describe. A meteorologist keeps records of the weather for each month as a table. The first line of the table gives the number of days in the month.

The following lines give the rainfall, low temperature, high temperature, and pollution count for each day of the month. For example, the data for a month could be as follows:

```
31
0    33   37   3
1.2  34   39   3
0    35   40   0.5
0    34   38   2
etc.
```

Each of the following exercises requires writing a program which reads one month's weather and answers some questions about the month's weather. To make things easier for you, answers for the first two exercises are given.

1. Find the first rainy day of the month. (The following program finds the required day and is a solution for this exercise.)

```
% The "wetday" program
var   rain, low, high, pollution: real
var monthLength: int
put "length of month = " ..
get monthLength
put "rain": 5, "low": 10, "high": 10, "pollution"
var day: int := 1
loop
    get rain, low, high, pollution
    exit when rain not = 0 or day = monthLength
    day := day + 1
end loop
if rain > 0 then
    put "Day", day, " was rainy "
else
    put "No rainy days "
end if
```

2. See if the data entries for the days of the month are reasonable. Verify that the rainfall does not exceed 100 and is not negative. Verify that the temperature lies between -100 and 200 and that the high is at least as large as the low. Verify that the pollution count is neither above 25 nor below zero. (The following program validates the month's data and is a solution for this exercise.)

```
% The "verify" program
var  rain, low, high, pollution: real
var monthLength: int
put "length of month = " ..
get monthLength
put "rain": 5, "low": 10, "high": 10, "pollution"
for  day: 1..monthLength
    get rain, low, high, pollution
    if rain < 0 or rain > 100 then
        put " day", day," wrong rain:", rain: 6: 2
    end if
    if low < − 100 or low > high or high > 200 then
        put " day", day, " wrong temperatures:", low: 6: 2, high: 6: 2
    end if
    if pollution < 0 or pollution > 25 then
        put " day", day, " has wrong pollution:", pollution: 6: 2
    end if
end for
```

3. What was the warmest day of the month, based on the high?

4. What was the first rainy day having a high temperature above 38?

5. What were the days of the month with more than a 5-degree difference between the high and low temperatures?

6. What were the two warmest days of the month?

7. Did the pollution count ever exceed 5 on a day when the temperature stayed above 35?

8. What three consecutive days had the most total rainfall?

9. Was it true that every rainless day following a rainy day had a lower pollution count than the rainy day?

10. Using the first 10 days' data, predict the weather for the 11th day. Compare (either by hand or within the program) the prediction with the data for the 11th day.

Chapter 8

ALPHABETIC INFORMATION HANDLING

We have said that computers can handle alphabetic information as well as perform numerical calculations. But most of the emphasis so far, except for labelling our tables of numerical output, has had very little to do with alphabetic data handling. It is true that we have been dealing with words, like identifiers, but these have been in the Turing programs rather than being handled by them as data. We have, in fact, never had anything but numbers, either **real** or **int**, that could be read by the **get** statement. In this chapter we will learn how to read in alphabetic data, how to move it from one place to another in the memory of the computer, how to join different pieces of information together, and how to separate out a part of a larger piece of information.

CHARACTER STRINGS

The term alphabetic information that we used in the last section is really not general enough to describe what we will learn to handle in this chapter. It is true that we will be able to handle what you normally mean by alphabetic information, things like people's names -

Sarah Marie Wood

but we also want to handle things like street addresses. For example, an address like

2156 Cypress Avenue

includes digits as well as letters of the alphabet. This kind of information we call **alphanumeric** or **alphameric** for short. But that is not all; we want to handle any kind of English text with words, numbers, and punctuation marks, like commas, semicolons, and question marks.

This text contains 7 words; doesn't it?

We have defined a word as being a string of one or more characters preceded and followed by a blank or a punctuation mark, other than an apostrophe. This definition makes 7 a word.

The information we want to handle is any string of characters that may be letters, digits, punctuation marks, or blanks. We tend to think of a blank as being not a character; but a string of blanks is quite different from a string with no characters at all. We call the special string with no characters at all a **null string**. We often write b for the blank character so that you can count how many blank characters are in a string.

HEREbISbAbCHARACTERbSTRINGbSHOWINGbTHEbBLANKS.

In Chapter 3 we introduced the characters in the Turing language. In that listing there are more than we have referred to so far in this chapter. The list of special characters includes symbols we need for arithmetic operations $+$, $-$, $/$, $*$, as well as for making comparisons in logical conditions $>$ and $<$. Then often we used parentheses, not to mention characters like colon (:) and percent (%).

One reason we want to be able to handle strings of any of these characters is to be able to do the important job of word processing. Another is to be able to work with Turing programs themselves as data. This is the kind of job a compiler must do, and a programming language like Turing should be suitable for writing a compiler program.

CHARACTER STRING VARIABLES

Just as we had to set aside space in the computer memory for storing integer and real numbers, we must have space for storing strings of characters. Character strings are much more changeable than numbers in that they can contain values with different lengths. For example, some people's names have many characters; others' have few.

We might declare a character string variable named *text* by

var *text*: **string** (50)

We know it is a character string variable because of the keyword **string**. The amount of memory reserved for the variable *text* is enough for a maximum of 50 character spaces. The length of the string will vary between zero characters, for the null string, and 50 characters, which is the maximum available space for this string.

READING AND OUTPUTTING STRINGS

We learned earlier how to output a string of characters that was in the form of an explicit string constant such as "Cost=", and we have been using this for outputting labels on our numeric output. We just put the constant, which is a string of characters enclosed in quotes, in the list of a **put** statement. It will be output in a field just large enough for it, unless a field size is specified by following it by a colon and the size. The string would be output, left-justified in the field specified and with the quotation marks removed. If the length of the string exceeds the field size specified after a colon it spills over to take up more space.

Now that we can have character string variables we can read information into them and output them. For example, this program reads and outputs a character string.

```
% The "getput" program
var text: string (40)
get text
put text
```

If the input data is

"Here is a sample text"

The output is

Here is a sample text

Notice that the input data has quotes around the character string and that these quotes are not output since they are not part of the string. Variables that are input must fit onto a data input line. On output the size should be limited by the length of an output line, because variables that go from line to line are difficult to manage. The compiler limits string variables to being at most 255 characters.

We do not have to specify a length for each **string**, for example, we can write

var *text:* **string**

This results in a default maximum length, which is 255 for most compilers. The advantage of giving the maximum length explicitly is that space in the computer's memory can be saved.

Character string variables may also be given values in an assignment statement. In the example

> **var** *name:* **string** *(10)*
> *name :=* "*Corley Phillips* "   % *This won't work!*
> **put** *name*

The character string to be assigned to *name* has more characters than the maximum 10 that are declared. This is an error because "*Corley Phillips*" will not fit into *name.* (You should try running this program to see what happens.) To make this program legal, we can change the maximum length of *name* from 10 to a large enough number such as 20. If we do this then the program prints

> *Corley Phillips*

TOKEN-ORIENTED STRING INPUT

We can read an explicit string constant such as "Corley Phillips" into a string variable using the **get** statement. The string constant can be preceded by *white space*, which includes blank characters, tab characters, and ends of lines. It is also possible to read strings that are not enclosed in quotes provided the string does not contain white space; for example, the following program reads a first name and then a last name that are not in quotes.

> **var** *firstName:* **string**
> **var** *lastName:* **string**
> **put** "*Type a first name and a last name* "
> **get** *firstName, lastName*
> **put** *firstName, lastName % Forgot a blank*
> **put** *firstName,* " ", *lastName % Print the blank*

If the input data is

Corley Phillips

The output is

CorleyPhillips
Corley Phillips

Since the input does not have any quotes, the string of characters starting with C then o and so on is read up to the y. Then the reading for *firstName* stops because a blank space comes next. Similarly, the string consisting of the letters in Phillips is read into *lastName.* String variables are read as follows. White space, such as blanks, is skipped, then if a quotation mark is found, an explicit string constant is read. But if a quotation mark is not found, characters are read into the string until white space or the end of the line or file is encountered. The string of characters surrounded by white space or enclosed in quotation marks is called a **token**. This kind of input reads a token such as *Phillips*, so we call it **token-oriented input**.

The first **put** statement of our example prints "CorleyPhillips". This is because we did not place a blank between the first and last names. The second **put** fixes this problem by including the needed blank character.

JOINING STRINGS TOGETHER

Character strings may be read in, stored, and output. But we can do more than that. We can perform certain operations on them. Just as all programs can be constructed using the three basic control structures; linear, repetition, and selection, all string manipulations can be accomplished using three basic operations. These are joining two strings together, selecting a part of a string (a substring), or finding the length of a string.

The first of these operations is to join two strings together to make one longer string. This operation is called **catenation** (or sometimes **con-catenation**) and the operator is the plus sign +. Here is an example of catenation:

> **var** *line:* **string**
> *line := "up" + "stairs"*
> **put** *line*

The output is *upstairs*, the two strings have been joined into one. The plus sign + used here does not mean numeric addition. For example, the string expression "23" + "15" is the string "2315" and *not* "38". It is not allowed to combined strings and numbers using +; for example 23 +15 is legal and equals 38 but "23"+15 is not allowed because "23" is a string and 15 is a number. Here is a program using catenation that has a loop in it:

> *% The "stars" program*
> **var** *stars:* **string** *:= ""   % Set to the null string*
> **for** *i: 1..15*
>   *stars := stars + "*"*
>   **put** *stars*
> **end for**

The output will be

>   *
>   **

```
* * *
* * * *
```

etc., until we have a line of 15 asterisks.

In the example the variable *stars* is initialized to the null string which is written as "". Each time the loop is executed, an asterisk is catenated on to the right end of the string and the resulting string is output. Since it is difficult to read "", we often give it a name, as in

> **const** *null* := ""
> **var** *stars:* **string** := *null*

SELECTING PARTS OF STRINGS

In addition to joining strings together, we can also take them apart by selecting parts of strings. We call a part of a string a **substring**. Suppose we have a string variable *s* which is set to the string *million:*

> **var** *s:* **string** := "*million* "
> **put** *s(2..4)*   % *This outputs* "*ill* "

In the second line *s(2..4)* means the substring of *s* from the second character through the fourth character, which is the word *ill.* In general, we can write

> *string Variable (leftChar..rightChar)*

to pick the substring running from character number *leftChar* to character number *rightChar*, where we count the characters starting with 1, then 2, then 3, and so on. The two dots *(..)* are pronounced as *to.* We can use an asterisk for *rightChar*, as is done here:

> **put** *s(4..*)*   % *This outputs* "*lion* "

This starts with the fourth character of *s* and goes to the end of *s.* This can be useful for removing the first character of a string when we do not know how long the string is, for example, *s(2..*)* is "*illion* ".

Commonly we want to pick a single character of a string, as in:

> **put** *s(5)*   % *This outputs* "*i* "

Note that *s(5)* is the same substring as *s(5..5).*

FINDING THE LENGTH OF A STRING

We can determine how long a string is by using the predefined function named *length.* For example

```
The "sensation" program
var example: string (15)
example := "sensational"
put length(example)
example := "stop"
put length(example)
```

This program outputs:

11

4

The *length* built-in function is useful in chopping letters off the ends of words. This program will output the last letters of a series of 4 words.

```
% The "ending" program
% Print last letter of each word
var word: string
put "Please type four words, one to a line"
for i : 1..4
    get word
    put word: 10, word(length(word))
end for
```

This program could be run as shown here:

Please type four words, one to a line
splash
splash   **h**
sick
sick   **k**
so
so   **o**
sloppy
sloppy   **y**

Notice that in the **put** statement we used a field width of 10; this prints the *word* at the left end of a field that consists of 10 characters. The result is that the letters h, k, o, and y form a column on the right.

AN EXAMPLE USING STRINGS

We will now give a program which gives various forms of French verbs. It cannot handle every French verb. The program works only for regular verbs of the so-called *er* variety. But you do not need to know any French to follow this example. If the program reads the verb *parler* which means *to speak*, then it outputs the following.

Je parle	(I speak)
Tu parles	(you speak)
Il parle	(he speaks)
Nous parlons	(we speak)
Vous parlez	(you speak)
Ils parlent	(they speak)

The equivalent English is shown in parentheses at the right. This is called conjugating the verb *parler.* Here is the complete program:

```
% The "bonjour " program
% Read a French "er " verb and conjugate it
var infinitive: string
put "Type a French — er verb "
get infinitive
const len := length(infinitive)
% Note: infinitive(len − 1..*) = "er "  i.e. Must end in "er "


const root := infinitive(1..len − 2)
% Note: root + "er "  = infinitive  e.g. "parl " + "er " = "parler "


put "Je " + root + "e "
put "Tu " + root + "es "
put "Il " + root + "e "
put "Nous " + root + "ons "
put "Vous " + root + "ez "
put "Ils " + root + "ent "
```

An example input could be the verb
> *parler*

After reading the infinitive, our program determines its length; if the infinitive is parler then len=6. We want to find the root of the verb, which is just the infinitive with the "er" chopped off. This is found by

> **const** *root := infinitive(1..len − 2)*

This takes the characters from the first to the third to last, whose position is *len − 2.* For example, if the verb is parler, we take characters 1 through 4, resulting in *"parl ".* In a comment we note that if our root is as we expected, if we catenate *"er "* onto its end we get the infinitive back. The comment indicates what is a necessary condition for correct results.

ASSERTIONS

The *bonjour* program provides an example where we can use a new language feature called an **assertion**. In that program we have two comments that begin with

> *% Note: ...*

Each of these comments tells the reader that a certain relationship has been established among values, for example, that *root* + *"er"* = *infinitive*. The program is intended to establish the relationship. We could replace the first of these comments by the **assert** statement:

> **assert** *infinitive(len − 1..*)* = *"er"*

and the second by:

> **assert** *root* + *"er"* = *infinitive*

The **assert** statement contains a condition (a Boolean expression) which is tested at run time. If it is true, it is ignored. If it is false, the program is halted with an error message, because something we have assumed about our program is not true. Essentially, an **assert** statement is a comment that is understood by the computer.

It is a good idea to change comments to **assert** statements when possible, because this allows the computer to help check that our programs are behaving as we wish. The disadvantage of assertions is that they slow down program execution a bit. This disadvantage is eliminated in well-tested production programs that must execute fast by instructing the compiler to ignore assertions.

Besides **assert** statements, there are specialized assertions called **invariants** that can be used in loops; invariants are also used in a language feature called the **module** that is introduced in a later chapter.

We have described assertions as if they are conditional failures; the program halts if the assertion is false. Given that the compiler is generating code to check assertions, this description is valid. But there is another way to look at assertions; in this other view, assertions are used to tell us what a program should accomplish. Ideally, a program contains enough assertions to specify the purpose of the program. And ideally, we should prove that whenever the program reaches an assertion, the assertion is necessarily true. If we are able to do this, we say we have proven that the program is **correct**, which means that it accomplishes its purposes as specified by its assertions. In this book we use assertions to specify only some of the requirements of certain programs, and we do not go into proofs of correctness.

COMPARISON OF STRINGS FOR RECOGNITION

We need to be able to compare one string with another for two purposes. One purpose is for the **recognition** of strings; in this we are concerned with whether two strings are the same or not. The other is to put string into an ordered sequence. String comparisons are made in logical conditions since their result is either true or false; the strings are the same or they are not. Here is an interactive program that reads and outputs words until it reaches the word *stop*:

```
% The "reading" program
% Read and print words up to "stop"
var word: string
var count: int := 0
put "Type some words, one to a line, ending with stop"
loop
    get word
    exit when word = "stop"
    count := count + 1
end loop
put skip, count, "words before stop"
```

This program requires the user to type a sequence of words:

Type some words, one to a line, ending with stop
soup
slow
sip
stop

3 words read before stop

The program's loop exits when *stop* is read.

SEQUENCING STRINGS

The other use of string comparisons is to sequence strings, to put them in order. Usually we speak of alphabetic order for alphabetic strings.

ABCDEFGHIJKLMNOPQRSTUVWXYZ

The alphabet and digits have the normal order among themselves: 0 comes before 9, A comes before Z, and a comes before z. Blanks have the lowest value. The operators $>$ and $<$ are used to compare the strings. The following comparisons are labelled as true or false:

	Comparison		Value	
"John"	>	"Jim"	true	
"John"	<	"Johnston"	true	
"McLeod"	>	"MacKay"	true	
"23"	>	"156"	true	(because 2 >1)

The following program reads in 10 names and outputs the one that is the last alphabetically.

```
% The "last" program
% Outputs name that is alphabetically last
var name: string
var final: string := "A "
put "Please type 10 last names"
for i: 1..10
    get name
    if name > final then
        final := name
    end if
end for
put "The alphabetically last is:", final
```

Here is an example of the use of this program:

Please type 10 last names
Clarke Lee Cordy Sevcik Fournier
Wortman Winslow Tsichritzis Gotlieb Jackson
The alphabetically last is: Wortman

COLLATING SEQUENCES

It is clear that the character "*A* " comes before "*C* " and that the string "*cat* " comes before "*dog* ". But the ordering is not so obvious for pairs such as (1) "*William* " and "*Williams* ", (2) "*Frank* " and "*Frank* " (with blanks at the end), and (3) "*ABC Electronics* " and "*A1 Taxi* ".

The Turing language has a rule that determines these orderings among strings. It is an extension of the idea of alphabetic ordering, as in a dictionary, but it must handle non-alphabetic characters as well as letters. The rule for strings is based on the ordering among individual characters. This character ordering is called the **collating sequence** and it tells us that

$$0 < 1 < 2 \ldots < 8 < 9$$
$$a < b < c \ldots < y < z$$
$$A < B < C \ldots < Y < Z$$

The collating sequence determines all character orderings, so it answers the following questions. Does a digit such as *1* come after a capital letter? Does a capital letter *A* come before small letter *a*? Does a blank or hyphen come before a letter?

There are two collating sequences that are in common use in computers. The ordering among characters as specified by each of these sequences is given here.

ASCII Collating Sequence:

> blank ! " # $ % & ' ( ) * + , — . /
> 0 to 9
> : ; < = > ? @
> A to Z
> [\ ] ^ _ `
> a to z
> { | } ~

EBCDIC Collating Sequence:

> blank ¢ . < (+ |& ! $ *) ; ¬ — / , % _ > ? : # @ ' = "
> a to z
> A to Z
> 0 to 9

ASCII stands for American Standard Code for Information Interchange and is pronounced as "askee". EBCDIC stands for Extended Binary Coded Decimal Interchange Code and is pronounced as "ebsidick" or sometimes as "ebkadick".

The EBCDIC sequence is used primarily on large IBM computers. Most newer computers such as the VAX and almost all microcomputers use the ASCII sequence. In most programs, the differences between the two sequences is not important, because they have the same ordering within capital letters, within small letters and within digits. However, there are some differences. With ASCII, "A12" comes before "ABC", and "ABC" comes before "Abc" but the opposite is true with EBCDIC. This means that certain Turing programs may not behave quite the same way on a microcomputer and on a large IBM computer, because comparison of characters is a bit different.

Whatever collating sequence is used, it determines the ordering of strings. The rule for sequencing strings is called **lexicographical ordering**. This rule defines ordering of any two strings *s* and *t* on a character by character basis as follows:

$s=t$ This is true when the strings are equal character by character and they have the same length.

$s<t$ To see if this is true, we compare s and t from left to right until either a character mismatches or until we run off the end of *s* or *t*. If a mismatched character is encountered at position P then $s(P)<t(P)$ means $s<t$. If the end of a string encountered without a mismatch, then $length(s)<length(t)$ means $s<t$.

Using this ordering, we can tell that

> *"John"* < *"Johnson"*   (because *"John"* is shorter)
> *"Frank"* < *"Frank"*   (because *"Frank"* is shorter)
> *"S Cook"* < *"Steve Cook"*   (because blank comes before *"t"*).

You should be warned that some programming languages, such as PL/1, use a slightly different rule, which handles strings of different lengths as follows: Before comparing strings of different lengths, the shorter string is extended on the right with blanks and then the comparison is done. This extending is called **blank padding**. In a language, such as PL/1, with blank padding *"Frank"* is considered to be equal to *"Frank"*, even though $length("Frank") < length("Frank")$. Since Turing does not use blank padding, we know that if $s = t$ then s and t have the same length.

THE INDEX FUNCTION

There is a method of checking to see if one string is a substring of another. The *index* function is used, as is shown here:

> **var** *i:* **int**
>
> ...
>
> *i := index("elephant", "h")*   *% i becomes 5*

This sets *i* to *5*, which is the position or *index* of the substring *h* in the string *elephant*. If the substring occurs more than once in the string, the first occurrence is reported, so *i* is set to *1* and not *3* here:

> *i := index("elephant", "e")*   *% i becomes 1*

If the substring does not occur in the string, then zero is returned:

> *i := index("elephant", "f")*   *% i becomes 0*

The substring can be more than one character:

> *i := index("Dear Mrs Brown", "Mrs")*   *% i becomes 6*

This sets *i* to be *6*.

As an example of the use of the *index* function, here is a program that reads a line and replaces an occurrence of *Mrs* by *Ms*.

```
% The "lib" program
%   Replace "Mrs" by "Ms" in a line
var line: string
get line: *
const pos := index(line, "Mrs")
if pos not = 0 then  % Found "Mrs"?
    line := line(1..pos - 1) + "Ms" +
        line(pos + 3..*)   % Mrs becomes Ms
end if
put line
```

The index function can be used to check if a character is one of a set of characters. For example:

> **if** *index("AEIOU", c)* **not** = *0* **then**

If *c* is a single character, this tests to see if *c* is a capital letter vowel.

CHAPTER 8 SUMMARY

In this chapter we have given methods of manipulating strings of characters. We introduced character string variables and we explained how to put strings together, to take them apart, and to find their lengths. Using these basic string operations, we can write programs which can modify strings in various ways, including extending them on the left or right, or inserting or removing parts. The following important terms were presented:

Maximum length — each character string variable has a maximum length given in its declaration which determines the longest string which can be assigned to the variable. For example, if *s* is declared as **string** *(5)*, its maximum length is 5, and it can have the value *stick*, but not the value *sticky*. If the type of *s* is simply **string**, a default maximum length, typically 255, is used.

Null string — the string of length zero, that is, the string with no characters. In Turing programs, the null string is written as "".

Length of a string — the number of characters in a string. A character string variable can have any length from zero, for the null string, up to the maximum length of the variable.

length — a built-in function which can be used to determine the length of the string. For example, *length("HO")* has the value 2 and *length(s)* gives the current length of the character string variable *s*.

String overflow — this is an error that occurs when a string is too long. This can happen when a string value is assigned to or read into a string variable. It can also happen when a catenation of strings is longer than that allowed; this limit is typically 255.

Catenation (or concatenation) — means putting strings together, one after the other, to form another string. In Turing, the plus sign (+) indicates catenation. For example, "*pine* " + "*apple* " is equal to "*pineapple* ".

Substring — means a part of a string. For example, *sew* is a substring of *housewife* and *ale* is a substring of *salesman*. In Turing, the basic form of a substring of string *s* is

> *s(leftChar..rightChar)*

where *leftChar* and *rightChar* give the positions of the beginning and ending characters of the substring. There are two other forms of substrings:

> *s(leftChar..*)*
> *s(charPosition)*

The first of these is equivalent to *s(leftChar..length(s))*. The second selects a substring of length 1 and is equivalent to *s(charPosition..charPosition)*.

String comparisons — used to test character strings for equality and for ordering. Strings can be compared using the following operators:

<	comes before (less than)
>	comes after (greater than)
<=	comes before or is equal (less than or equal)
>=	comes after or is equal (greater than or equal)
=	equal
not =	not equal

Collating sequence — the order of individual characters, for example "*A* "<"*B* " and "*5* " <"*6* ".

Assertion — a statement of the form

> **assert** *condition*

placed in a program; acts like a comment that can actually be checked by the computer.

index — The *index* function returns the position of a substring inside a string. For example, *index("she ", "he ")* has a value *2* because *he* is a substring of *she* at position 2, but *index("he ", "she ")* is *0* because *she* is not a substring of *he*.

CHAPTER 8 EXERCISES

1. Which of the following comparisons of strings are true?

    (a)   "David Barnard" = "David T. Barnard "
    (b)   "E. Wong" = "Edmund Wong"
    (c)   "Mark Fox" = "Mark Fox"
    (d)   "Johnson" > "Johnson"
    (e)   "416 Elm St" >= "414 Elm Street"
    (f)   "Hume,Pat" >= "Holt,Ric"
    (g)   "Allen" = "Alan"

2. Suppose H and L have been declared to be **string** *(20)* and that these two statements have been executed:

    $H :=$ "house"
    $L :=$ "light"

    What do each of the following statements output?

    (a) **put** $L + H$
    (b) **put** $L + $ " " $+ H$
    (c) **put** $H + $ " " $+ L$
    (d) **put** $H(1..2)$
    (e) **put** $H(3..*)$
    (f) **put** $H(4) + L$
    (g) **put** $L(1) + H(2..*)$

3. Suppose that p has been declared as **string**, and that p has as its value a phrase, such as

    One swallow doesn't make a summer

    or

    An ounce of prevention is worth a pound of cure

    Write statements to accomplish each of the following.

    (a)   Find the first blank in p and set its location into the integer variable L.

    (b)   Set the fixed variable L to the location of the beginning of the last word in p.

    (c)   Change p by adding a period to its right end.

    (d)   Change p by replacing its first word by the character "*1*".

    (e)   Change p by extending it on the left by the phrase "*They say*".

    (f)   Set the fixed variable *count* to the number of words in p. You can assume that each word, except the last word, is followed by a single blank.

(g)   If *p* contains the word "pound" then replace it by the phrase 0.45 kilograms.

4.   Write a program that checks to see that the "*i* before *e* except after *c*" rule in spelling is followed. Your program should read a sequence of words until it finds the word *quit*. It should search for *i* and *e* appearing next to each other. If the combination is *ei* and is not immediately preceded by a *c*, then the string should be output together with an appropriate warning message. Similar action should be taken if *c* immediately precedes *ie*.

5.   Write a program that will accept names of persons entered in the form

     Louisa Logan Molyneux

and output

     Molyneux, L.L.

Make sure your program will work for any number of names before the surname and for names already abbreviated to initials. Arrange that the program will work for a number of entries on each run.

6.   Write a program which reads text and determines the percentage of words having three letters. For simplicity, use text without any punctuation.

Chapter 9

FILES OF DATA

The Turing programs that we have developed so far in this book have been interactive. They read input from the terminal keyboard and they output to the terminal screen. In this chapter we show how programs can handle files of data that are more permanent. This data can be saved from day to day or month to month. Most computer systems store files on magnetic disks or possibly on magnetic tapes. The way we use files is influenced by the basic software of the computer system we are using; in this chapter we will assume that we are using the Unix operating system.

READING FROM A FILE

The last chapter gave a program that reads and prints words until it reads the word *stop*. Here is a slightly modified version of that program:

```
% The "readstop" program
%     Read and print words up to "stop"
var word: string
var count: int := 0
loop
    get word
    exit when word = "stop"
    put word
    count := count + 1
end loop
put count, " words before stop"
```

If this program is stored in a Unix file called *readstop.t*, we compile it and run it this way:

$ *ttc readstop.t*	(Compile program)
$ *readstop.x*	(Execute program)
No time to stop and say hello	(Person types input data)
No	(Computer output)
time	
to	

3 words before stop

We have used our program interactively, meaning that we have typed data into it and it has responded to our typing.

We will show how this program can read data from a computer file instead of the terminal keyboard. We will assume that the file has been created by a Unix text editor such as the one called *ed.* The file is called *sampledata* and contains:

Here are words
such as stop and go

We can list this file as our terminal by the *cat* command:

$ *cat sampledata*
Here are words
such as stop and go

We can run our program and have it read this file using the symbol <.

$ *readstop.x* < *sampledata*
Here
are
words
such
as
5 words before stop

We write < *sampledata* to mean: receive input from the *sampledata* file. (In this context, < does not mean *less than.*)

INPUT-OUTPUT REDIRECTION

When we use the symbol < to specify that the input data comes from a file instead of from the terminal, this is called **input redirection**. We can also use **output redirection**, as is done here:

$ *readstop.x* > *temp*	(Create *temp* file)
Will this ever stop	(Person types input data)
$ *cat temp*	(Display *temp* file)
Will	
this	
ever	
3 words before stop	

In this example, the file called *temp* is created and holds the output of the program. The *cat* command prints this output.

We can redirect both input and output, as is done here:

$ *readstop.x* < *sampledata* > *temp*

This reads the *sampledata* file and places the output in the *temp* file.

STANDARD INPUT-OUTPUT STREAMS

There are two streams of data that our programs have read or witten. These are the **standard input** stream (the default input file) that is read by the **get** statement, and the **standard output** stream (the default output file) that is written by the **put** statement.

By default the standard input stream is connected to the terminal keyboard, but it can be redirected via < to be connected to a file. Similarly, the standard output is connected to the terminal screen unless it is redirected via > to a file.

A Turing program can read or write additional streams, besides standard input and output; before describing how this is done, we will see how a program detects if a stream contains more data.

DETECTING END-OF-FILE

The *readstop* program reads words until it finds the word *stop*. We can always put a word like *stop* in the data as a signal for a program to terminate, but this is inconvenient. In this section, we will show how a program can detect that there is no more data in a file, without the help of a special word like *stop*. This situation of having no more input data is called **end-of-file** or simply *eof*.

In Turing, a program is considered to be illegal (it gets an error message) if it tries to read a token when the file contains no more tokens. Fortunately, the Turing language provides these two constructs for determining if there are more words (tokens) in a file:

skip	This is used in a **get** statement; it skips characters until it finds the next token (word) or until it finds the end-of-file.
eof	This is a predefined function that is tested to see if the stream is at its end-of-file.

These two constructs are used in this program to read and count the words in a file:

```
% The "wordcount" program
%      Print the number of words (tokens) in the input
var word: string
var count: int := 0
loop
    get skip    % Skip to next token or to eof
    exit when eof
    get word
    count := count + 1
end loop
put "Number of words = ", count
```

If we use the file named *sampledata* containing the sentence

> Here are words
> such as stop and go

then we can have the *wordcount* program read this sentence:

> **$** *wordcount.x* < *sampledata*
> **Number of words = 8**

After the *wordcount* program reads the last word, *go*, it uses **skip** to skip to the end-of-file; the *eof* function becomes true, so the program displays the number of words and stops.

If there were no characters following the last word of the file then it would not be necessary to use **skip** because there would be nothing to skip. This situation rarely occurs in a system like Unix, because the last character of a line is usually a **new line** character, which specifies the ending of the line. Whenever we create a line in a file using a Unix editor, each line, including the last line, is terminated by a new line character. We use **skip** to get past these new line characters, as well as past other white space (blanks, tabs and form feed characters) to see whether end-of-file or another token comes next.

USING END-OF-FILE WITH NUMBERS

The *wordcount* program uses the pattern of **get skip** (to skip to the next token or to end-of-file) followed by exiting a loop when *eof* is true. We use **skip** first and check *eof* before reading the first token; this allows the program to work even if the file contains no tokens. This same pattern is used in the next program, which calculates the average and sum of the numbers in the data.

```
% The "averaging" program
%    Read numbers in the input stream.
```

```
%    Display their average, with count of numbers.
var number: real
var sum: real   := 0
var count: int   := 0
loop
    get skip    % Skip to next number or to eof
    exit when eof
    get number
    sum := sum + number
    count := count + 1
end loop
if count not = 0 then    % Avoid dividing by zero
    put "Average is ", sum/count
end if
put "Sum is ", sum
```

Programs such as this *averaging* program and the *wordcount* program generally read files as their input data. They can be used interactively, but there is a difficulty, and that is: How do we tell the program when we are finished typing. Under Unix, there is a convention for specifying that the end of a file is being typed; this is done by typing "*ctrl—d* ", as illustrated here.

```
$ averaging.x
4
8
12
ctrl—d     (Hold down control key and type d)
Average is 8
Sum is 24
```

After typing the three numbers, we type *ctrl-d* to specify the end of the data. (Beware that on some computer systems, end-of-file may be signaled by the interactive user in some other way.)

In the last two sections we have shown how to detect the end of the file when reading data a token at a time. In the next section we will show how end-of-file is detected when reading a line at a time.

READING A LINE AT A TIME

The method of input used so far in this book reads tokens. For example, this **get** statement reads a number, possibly preceded by white space:

```
var x: real
get x          % Read a token
```

This is called token-oriented input.

Sometimes we need to read a line at a time; this is done by **line-oriented** input, as illustrated here:

```
var input: string
get input:*      % Read line of data
```

The :* following *input* means that all the characters of the next line of data are to be read into the variable called *input.* If the next line being read is:

13 and 29 are numbers

then the **get** statement reads all these characters into *input*, changing *input* as if this statement has been executed:

input := "13 and 29 are numbers"

The string assigned to *input* includes any white space on the line. The new line character that ends the line is not part of the string assigned to *input*, the new line character is read but discarded. When using line-oriented input, the variable receiving the characters of the line must be able to hold the entire line being read. In this example, the *input* variable is declared as **string**, so its maximum length is 255; it can read a line containing at most 255 characters.

As a simple example of line-oriented input, here is a program that reads a file a line at a time to create a copy of the file.

```
% The "copy" program
%    Copy input stream to output stream
var line: string
loop
    exit when eof
    get line:*
    put line
end loop
```

This program does not use the **skip** construct, because line-oriented reading already skips to the next line (or to end-of-file). There are no extra characters to be skipped; so **skip** should not be used, because it would skip over white space in the file, preventing the *copy* program from faithfully copying all the file's characters.

Notice that the *eof* function is used in this program before reading from the file; this is allowed in Turing. Essentially, *eof* means: there are no more characters in the file. If the file is empty (contains no characters), *eof* will be true before the first read.

The *copy* program can be used under Unix to make a copy of *fileA* in *fileB*:

$ *copy.x* < *fileA* > *fileB*

If *fileB* did not exist, it is created; if it already exists, its previous contents are lost. When *copy* is used this way, it has the same result as the Unix *cp* command:

$ *cp fileA fileB*

However, *cp* is preferable for large files because it has been carefully tuned for efficiency.

We can use our *copy* program to list *fileA* on the terminal screen:

$ *copy.x* < *fileA*

when used this way, it has the same result as the Unix *cat* command:

$ *cat fileA*

Programs such as *cp* and *cat* that are used by many people for various purposes are called **utility** programs or simply **utilities**. Turing programs for manipulating files, such as the programs developed in this chapter, can be used as utility programs.

NUMBERING THE LINES OF A FILE

This section gives another example of reading a file a line at a time. This program is a utility that prints a file with line numbers in the left margin.

```
% The "numbering" program
%     Copy the input file, giving line numbers
%     on the left.
var lineNumber: int := 0
var line: string
loop
    exit when eof
    get line: *
    lineNumber := lineNumber + 1
    put lineNumber: 6, " " , line   % Output line number and line
end loop
```

Here is an example of using this program to number the lines of the file called *sampledata*:

$ *numbering.x* < *sampledata*

1 Here are words

2 such as stop and go

PROGRAMS AS DATA FILES

We can use a Unix editor or a Turing program to create a data file. Later we can use this file as input data for another Turing program. What is a bit surprising is the fact that a Turing program can be read by another Turing program. For example, we can use the *wordcount* program to count the number of tokens in the *numbering* program:

> $ *wordcount.x* < *numbering.t*
> **Number of words = 50**

(The exact number of tokens in the *numbering* program will vary according to the way the program is typed into the computer. For example, "**var** *line*: **string**" will be counted as only two tokens, one for **var** and one for "*line: string*", if there are no spaces surrounding the colon.)

We have run the executable version of *wordcount*, called *wordcount.x*, to count the tokens in the original source version of *numbering*, called *numbering.t*. Beware that *wordcount.t* cannot be directly executed, because it has not yet been translated to machine language. And *numbering.x* should not be used as input data to *wordcount.x*, because *numbering.x* consists of machine language rather than lines of readable text.

As an intriguing example of using a program as input data, here is the *numbering* program reading itself:

> $ *numbering.x* < *numbering.t*
> **1   % The "numbering" program**
> **2   %   Copy the input file, giving line numbers**
> **3   %   on the left**
> **4   var lineNumber: int := 0**
> **5   var line: string**
> **6   loop**
> **7   exit when eof**
> ... etc for rest of *numbering* program...

Other programs given in this chapter can read themselves. You may want to think about what each of these programs will do when reading itself.

FINDING A PATTERN IN A FILE

In this section we develop a program to locate certain strings of characters in a file. For example, suppose we want to locate *proceed* misspelled as *procede* in an essay. Our program to do this job will be called *find*, it is used this way:

> $ *find.x essay*
> *procede*

The command line means to execute *find.x* reading the file called *essay* and using *procede* as standard input data. (The Unix *grep* command, which is not explained in this book, is essentially a generalized version of the *find* program.)

The *find* program reads *procede* from the standard input stream using an ordinary **get** statement:

> **get** *pattern*

When the program reads from the *essay* file, it uses a new form of the **get** statement, as shown here:

> **var** *line:* **string**
>
> ...
>
> **get:** *1, line %Read from file number one*

In order to make the program more readable, we set *fileNo* to equal 1 and use it with our **get** statement and with *eof*:

> **const** *fileNo:=1*
> **var** *line:* **string**
>
> ...
>
> **get** *: fileNo, line:**   *% Read one line from file*
>
> ...
>
> **exit when** *eof(fileNo)*

We have defined *fileNo* to be 1; it represents the first (and only) file name, *essay*, on the command line. We have used a colon immediately following the keyword **get**; this specifies that *fileNo* is the number of a file and not a variable to be read. We use the form *eof(fileNo)* to check if there are more characters in the file.

If there are several files to be read or written by a program, their names are to be listed following the command name; in the program they correspond to files numbered 1, 2, 3, and so on. Here is the complete *find* program:

```
% The "find" program
%     Read a pattern string from the standard input.
%     Print lines (with their line numbers) from
%     the file containing this pattern.
const fileNo := 1   % Stream number of file.
var line: string
var lineNumber: int :=0
var pattern: string
get pattern
loop
    exit when eof(fileNo)
```

```
get : fileNo, line:*
lineNumber := lineNumber + 1
if index(line, pattern) not = 0 then   % Is pattern in line?
    put lineNumber: 6, " ", line
end if
```
end loop

This program uses the predefined function *index* whose value is zero if *pattern* is not present in *line* but, if present, the character position of the first occurrence of *pattern* in line. As an example of running this program, we can find the word *stop* in the file *sampledata*

$ *find.x sampledata*
stop

2 such as stop and go

The program has found that the word *stop* appears in line 2 of the file. If we have a file named *s* containing only the word *stop*, we could accomplish the same thing by running:

$ *find.x sampledata < s*
2 such as stop and go

As another example, we can locate all occurrences of the word *pattern* in the *find* program:

$ *find.x find.t*
pattern

> **2 %   Read a pattern string from standard input**
> **4 %   the file containing this pattern.**
> **8 var pattern: string**
> **9 get pattern**
> **14   if index (line,pattern) not =0 then % Is pattern in line?**

This is another example of a program reading itself.

Before developing more examples, we will review the ways **get** and **put** are used. Ordinarily, **get** reads from the keyboard, but it can be redirected to read from a file using <. Similarly, **put** outputs to the terminal screen, but can be redirected to a file using >. If we follow **get** or **put** by a colon and a file number, we can read from or write to other streams of data. The stream being used has a number that corresponds to the position of the file's name in the command line.

MERGING FILES

This section presents a program that reads two files and creates a third file. The two input files, which will be called A and B, are each assumed to be in alphabetic order. The third file will contain all items from files A and B, and will also be in alphabetic order. For example, if files A and B contain:

File A contents:

Abbott, Harold	421−1624
Mendell, Mark	882−1126
Perelgut, Steve	842−1882
Venus, Jan	242−1141

File B contents:

Bregman, Phyllis	211−8483
Galloway, David	817−2143

then we should be able to run our *merge* program as shown here:

$ *merge.x fileA fileB*

Abbott, Harold	**421−1624**
Bregman, Phyllis	**211−8483**
Galloway, David	**817−2143**
Mendell, Mark	**882−1126**
Perelgut, Steve	**842−1882**
Venus, Jan	**242−1141**

If we want to put the output into *fileC* instead of on the terminal screen, we write *merge.x fileA fileB > fileC.*

We have simplified the programming by assuming that each file contains at least one line. First the program reads one line from each file, then the program repeatedly writes the alphabetically first of the two lines, and reads another line from the file that provided the line just written. When there are no more lines from one file to be read, the rest of the lines from the remaining file are copied to the output stream and then the program stops. Here is the program.

```
% The "merge" program
%  ·   Read two input streams that are already
%      sorted into alphabetic order. Merge them into a
%      third alphabetic stream.
%      Assumption: each input file contains at least one line.
const fileA := 1   % First input stream
const fileB := 2   % Second input stream
assert not eof(fileA) and not eof(fileB)
```

```
    var lineA, lineB: string
    get: fileA, lineA:*   % Read line from fileA
    get: fileB, lineB:*   % Read line from fileB
    loop
        if lineA < lineB then   % Which line to write first?
            put lineA
            if eof(fileA) then
                loop   % eof on A, so copy rest of B
                    put lineB
                    exit when eof(fileB)
                    get : fileB, lineB:*
                end loop
                exit   % Program is finished
            else
                get: fileA, lineA:*
            end if
        else
            put lineB
            if eof(fileB) then
                loop   % eof on B, so copy rest of A
                    put lineA
                    exit when eof(fileA)
                    get : fileA, lineA:*
                end loop
                exit   % Program is finished
            else
                get: fileB, lineB:*
            end if
        end if
    end loop
```

Each file used by the *merge* program was either read from or written to, but not both. This pattern of reading a file but not also writing to it, or writing but not reading, is enforced by the Turing language. In other words, you are not allowed to read and write the same file.

In the *merge* program, as well as in all programs given in this chapter, each file has been read by starting at the beginning of the file and proceeding sequentially through the file. This method of reading or writing is called **sequential** input-output. There is a more general form of input-output that allows skipping around in a file, to read or write just parts of a file. This is called **random access** input-output. The Unix operating system supports random access to files, but this is not discussed in this chapter.

PROCESSING TEXT

We will now give a program that is a simple text editor; it uses character string variables in producing a personalized fairy tale. The program first reads in the name of a child and the name of a friend of the child from the default input stream. The program then outputs a story about the child and his or her friend. The basic text of the story is read from a file. The program simply reads the basic text and outputs the story. Whenever the program reads *CHILD* it substitutes the child's name and when it reads *FRIEND*, it substitutes the friend's name. In this example, the fairy tale has only been started. You can supply your own plot by providing more data.

```
%  The "story" program
%     Personalizes a story. Reads two names and uses
%     them to replace CHILD and FRIEND.
const storyFile := 1
var nameOfChild, nameOfFriend, word: string
var line: string := ""     % Start with empty line
const blank := " "
const maxLineLength := 50
put "Type names of two children"
get nameOfChild, nameOfFriend   % Names for CHILD, FRIEND
loop
    get: storyFile, skip   % Skip to next word or eof
    exit when eof(storyFile)
    get: storyFile, word
    if word = "CHILD" then
        word := nameOfChild
    elsif word = "FRIEND" then
        word := nameOfFriend
    end if
    if length(line) + 1 + length(word) <= maxLineLength then
        line := line + blank + word
    else     % Print line and start next line
        put line
        line := word
    end if
end loop
put line     % Print last line of story
```

The *storyFile* could contain:

> Once upon a time there lived a great
> fiery dragon. This fiery dragon had a
> friend named CHILD and CHILD has a friend
> FRIEND who lived nearby. Early one
> cold morning ...

As you can see in the program, words are added to the end of a line to a maximum line length of 50 characters. A blank is inserted between words.

Our program is a very simple computer **text editor**. A much fancier computer text editor operating under the Unix system was used in preparing the text you are now reading.

CHAPTER 9 SUMMARY

In previous chapters we used token-oriented input to read from the default (or standard) input stream, which is the keyboard. This chapter has introduced line-oriented input and has shown how to read and write files of data. There is a third form of input supported by Turing, called character-oriented input, that allows more precise control when reading. Since this last method of input is a bit complex, it is not covered in this chapter. The following important terms were discussed.

Input-output redirection — under the Unix operating system, the symbols
< and > can be used to cause reading from and writing to files.
For example, this Unix command

> **$** *copy.x < infile > outfile*

causes reading from the file called *infile* and writing to the file called *outfile*.

File numbers — a **get** or **put** statement can have a file (stream) number, as
in

> **const** *infile := 1*
> **var** *line:* **string**
>
> ...
>
> **get :** *infile, line:**   *% File number is 1*

This reads a line from file number 1, whose name is the first file given on the Unix command line; for example, in this command, file 1 is *essay.*

> **$** *find.x essay*

End-of-file detection — the *eof* predefined function is used to check if the input contains more characters. The *eof* function can accept an argument, as in *eof(2)*, to check if end-of-file exists on a file other than the default input stream. The **skip** construct used in a **get** statement skips characters up to the next token or to the end of file.

Line-oriented input — input can be read a line at a time:

> **var** *s:* **string**
>
> ...
>
> **get** *s :** % *Read to end of line*

This **get** statement reads the rest of the characters on the line into the string called *s*. If the line contains no characters (it was typed as just a return), then after the **get**, *length(s)=0.*

Programs as data — a program written in a language like Turing is typed into the computer the same way as ordinary character data. The program can be read by other programs (or by itself) as data, for example:

> **$** *wordcount.x < numbering.t*

Here the *wordcount* program is counting the number of words (tokens) in the *numbering* program.

Merging files — this means reading two files that are already in alphabetic order (or in some other increasing or decreasing order) and producing a third ordered file that contains the items from the input files.

Text processing or word processing — manipulation of files containing readable text, such as correspondence. The *story* program given in this chapter, which produces personalized fairy tales, is a simple text processing program.

CHAPTER 9 EXERCISES

1. For each of the programs given in this chapter, describe the results of having the program read itself as input data.

2. Write a program that looks up a person's phone number. For example:

> **$** *lookup.x phonebook*
> *Walsh*

This should print out all lines of the file that begin with the characters in *Walsh*. If the file called *phonebook* contains:

```
...
Vanderbok, Harold 2416 24th St          814−2165
Walsh, Albert       10 Kings College Rd  978−4044
```

| Walsh, HJ | 41 Madison Dr | 816—3612 |
| Williams, Alison | 123B Grandview | 816—3042 |

the program should output:

| **Walsh, Albert** | **10 Kings College Rd** | **978—4044** |
| **Walsh, HJ** | **41 Madison Dr** | **816—3622** |

3.   Write a program called *page* that outputs a file on the terminal a screen-full at a time. The user types a return to see the next full screen of data.

4.   What does this program do? Insert appropriate comments (%) documenting its purpose.

```
        % The "squash" program
        const maxWidth := 60
        var word: string
        get word
        put word
        var lineLength: int := length(word)
        loop
            get skip     % Skip to next word or to eof
            exit when eof
            get word
            if lineLength + length(word) < maxWidth then
                put " ", word ..
                lineLength := lineLength + length(word) + 1
            else
                put ""    % Start a new line
                lineLength := length(word)
                put word ..
            end if
        end loop
        put ""   % End last line
```

5.   Write a program which looks up Nancy Wong's telephone number and outputs it. You are given a set of data entries, each containing a name and a phone number. For example, the first entry might be

   "John Abel"   443—2162

6.   The *merge* program given in this chapter assumes that each input file contains at least one line. Re-write it so it works when either file or both are empty (contain no lines).

Chapter 10

ARRAYS

So far in our programming, each memory location for data had its own special name; each variable had a unique identifier. In this chapter we will introduce the idea that groups of data will share a common name and be differentiated from each other by numbering each one uniquely.

Suppose that we have a list of names of students. We could give the list the name *student* and identify the first name as *student(1)*, the second as *student(2)*, and so on. We call the number that is enclosed in parentheses the index of the **iist** or **array**. The reason why we should use this method of identifying variables may not be clear. We will have to do an example so that you can see the power of the new method. As an example, suppose you wanted to read in a list of names of 50 students and output them in reverse order, that is, last first. We would need to read in the entire list before we could begin the output. This means we must have a memory location for each name. We must be able to reserve this space by a declaration.

DECLARATION OF ARRAYS

For the list of names of students we would use a declaration

var *student:* **array** *1..50* **of** **string** *(20)*

Each name is a character string variable whose maximum length is allowed to be *20*. Each element of the array *student* is a string variable. In the declaration, after the keyword **array** we give the **range** of the index, namely from *1* to *50*.

Notice that the first element of the *student* array is *student(1)*. This element is a string of maximum length *20*. The 5th character of this sting is *strudent(1)(5)*; the first number in parentheses gives the element's array index, the second the character position of the desired character in the string.

HANDLING LISTS

We are now ready for the program that reverses the order of a list of names. Here the array index is the integer *i*.

```
% The "reverse" program
% Print list of names in reverse
var student: array 1..50 of string (20)
% Read list of names
for i: 1..50
    get student(i)
end for
% Output reversed list
for decreasing i: 50..1
    put student(i)
end for
```

Now, perhaps, you can see what a powerful programming tool the indexed variable can be. The index *i* that is counting the **for** loops can be used inside the loop to refer to the different members of the list. In the first **for** loop the names are read; the first name is stored in the variable *student(1)*, the second in *student(2)*, and so on. In contrast, the first iteration of the output loop outputs *student(50)*, the next *student(49)*, and so on.

Suppose, as a second example, we had a list of *50* integers and we wanted the sum of all the numbers. Here is the program:

```
% The "total" program.
% Read numbers and print their total.
var number: array 1..50 of int
% Read in numbers
for i: 1..50
    get number(i)
end for
% Find total
var sum: int := 0
for i: 1..50
    sum := sum + number(i)
end for
put "Sum = ", sum
```

In the last example, it is not necessary to read all the numbers and then add them up, but we did it that way just to show what is necessary for reading or summing a list. We could have written only one loop, combining the two operations.

```
% Read numbers and find total
var sum: int := 0
for i: 1..50
    get number(i)
    sum := sum + number(i)
end for
put "Sum = ", sum
```

In this example there is no need for an array since we could add each number to *sum* and not store the number at all. Commonly, there is more to be done that requires having the list still present. For instance we might want to divide each member of a list by the sum and multiply by 100. This would express each entry as a percentage of the group. To do this we would add these statements:

```
% Calculate percentage of total
for i: 1..50
    number(i) := round(number(i)* 100 / sum )
    put number(i)
end for
```

Inside the **for** loop the first statement results in each member of the list being operated on and changed to a percentage.

AN EXAMPLE PROGRAM

Arrays can be used in manipulating various kinds of lists. We will now give an example in which the list is the timetable for teachers in a high school. The timetable has been prepared as a list of data lines. Each line has a teacher's name, a period (1 to 6) and a room number.

The data lines look like the following:

(teacher)	(period)	(room)
"Ms. Weber"	1	216
"Mrs. Williams"	6	214
"Mrs. VanVeen"	1	103
"Ms. Weber"	4	200
"Mrs. Reid"	2	216
...		
"xxx"	0	0 (dummy entry)

A program is needed to output the timetable in order of periods. First, all teachers with their classrooms for the first period should be output; then all teachers with their classrooms for period 2 and so on up to period 6. The output from the program should begin this way:

PERIOD   **1**

Ms. Weber   **216**
Mrs. VanVeen   **103**

   ...

The following program produces this output:

```
1    % The "periods" program
2    %   Read timetable giving teachers, periods, and rooms,
3    %   then  print out in order of periods
4    var teacher: array 1..50 of string (20)
5    var period, room: array 1..50 of int
6    % Read the timetable
7    var i: int := 1
8    loop
9        get teacher(i), period(i), room(i)
10       exit when teacher(i) = "xxx"
11       i := i + 1
12   end loop
13   % Output the timetable by periods
14   for thisPeriod: 1..6
15       put skip, "PERIOD": 20, thisPeriod: 5, skip
16       for j: 1..i − 1
17           if period(j) = thisPeriod then
18               put teacher(j): 20, room(j): 5
19           end if
20       end for
21   end for
```

Our program is able to read in a timetable consisting of at most 50 data entries, including the dummy entry. If there are more than 50 entries in the timetable, then line 11 will eventually set i to 51; this value of i will be used in line 9 as an index for the *teacher, period*, and *room* arrays. This would be an error, because the declarations specify that 50 is the largest allowed array index. The problem is that the index is **out of bounds** in line 9 when i exceeds 50. When the program is executing, this would be detected and an error message would state that the array index is out of bounds. You should take care that array indexes in your programs stay within their declared bounds. In our example program, we can prevent bounds errors by changing line 10 to the following.

    exit when $i = 50$ **or** *teacher*$(i) =$ "*xxx*"

Our change guarantees that no more than 50 lines will be read. Unfortunately, the modified program fails to report the situation when there were too many data entries. We can remedy this problem by leaving line 10 as it was and following it by this:

> **if** *i = 50* **then**
> >   **put skip**, "***Error: Only 50 lines were read*"
> >   **exit**
> **end if**

The program now supplies a more appropriate error message than the system would provide, and continues on to give a period-by-period listing of the entries it has actually read.

When using arrays of strings, such as the *teacher* array, it is a good idea to give an explicit maximum length, which is 20 in this case:

> **var** *teacher:* **array** *1..50* **of string** *(20)*

The program would work if we omitted the 20 but it would require space for $50*255 = 12,750$ characters of teachers' names, because the default maximum length is 255. With this sort of declaration there is the danger that you will need more space than the computer can provide. By setting the maximum length to 20, the required space is only $50*20 = 1000$ characters.

TWO-DIMENSIONAL ARRAYS

It is possible to have arrays that correspond to entries in a **table** rather than just a single list. For instance, a table of distances between 4 cities might be

	1	2	3	4
1	0	20	30	36
2	20	0	12	20
3	30	12	0	15
4	36	20	15	0

We could call this array *distance* and *distance(1,4)* is 36 or *distance(3,4)* is 15. The first number in the parentheses refers to the row in the table, the second to the column. You can see that *distance(3,1)* has the same value as *distance(1,3)*; the table is symmetric in this case about the diagonal line running from top left to bottom right. All entries on this diagonal are zero; the distance from a city to itself is zero.

We must learn how to declare such a two-dimensional array. All that is necessary is to write

var *distance:* **array** *1..4, 1..4* **of int**

The first index is the number of rows, the second the number of columns. In mathematics, a two-dimensional array, such as *distance*, is called a **matrix**.

As an example, we will read in this table and store it in the memory. On each input data line we will enter one row of the data:

var *distance:* **array** *1..4, 1..4* **of int**
  for *i: 1..4*   *% For each row*
    for *j: 1..4*   *% For each item in a row*
      get *distance(i, j)*
    end for
  end for

In this program there is one **for** loop nested inside another. We have used two indexes, *i* to give the row number, *j* to give the column number. When *i = 1* the inner loop has *j* go from 1 to 4. This means the elements of the array on the first line are stored in these variables:

distance(1,1) *distance(1,2)* *distance(1,3)* *distance(1,4)*

These are the elements in row 1 of the table. Since our table is symmetric it does not matter if we interchange rows and columns, because we get exactly the same result. For most tables it *does* matter, and you must be careful.

ANOTHER EXAMPLE PROGRAM

We will illustrate the use of two-dimensional arrays in terms of a set of data collected by a consumers' group. This group has been alarmed about the recent rapid rise in price of processed wallalumps. They sampled grocery store prices of processed wallalumps on a monthly basis throughout 1982, 1983, and 1984 and observed that prices varied from 75 cents to 155 cents as the following table shows:

Month

	1	2	3	4	5	6	7	8	9	10	11	12
1982	87	89	89	89	85	85	85	75	90	100	100	100
1983	95	95	95	95	90	90	85	90	100	110	120	110
1984	110	110	115	115	115	100	100	110	120	140	145	155

These 36 prices were to be entered as data and a program was needed to analyze the price changes. We will read them into a table whose general element is *price (month,year)*. In this example the first index is the column number of the table, the second the row number. Although we usually do it the other way around it is more convenient in this example to do it this way. We will still read the table in a row at a time. This means that the inner **for** loop covers the first index range *1..12* of the *price* two-dimensional array.

The following program reads in the data and determines the average price for 1983:

```
% The "cost" program
%   Read in cost of wallalumps for 3 years, and print averages
var price: array 1..12, 1982..1984 of int
for year: 1982..1984    % For each year
    for month: 1..12    % For each month of the year
        get price(month,year)   % Read price of the month
    end for
end for
% Determine average price in 1983
var total: int := 0
for month: 1..12
    total := total + price(month,1983)
end for
put "Average 1983 price: ", total / 12
% ...add statements here to calculate other averages
```

In this program, the array *price* is declared so it can have a first index which can range from 1 to 12 and a second index which can range from *1982* to *1984*. Effectively, the *price* array is a table in which entries can be looked up by month and year. The first part of the program uses the input data to fill up the *price* array. The second part of the program sums the prices for each month during *1983* and calculates the average *1983* price.

We could as well calculate the average price for a particular month. For example, the following calculates the average price in February:

```
total := 0
for year: 1982..1984
    total := total + price(2, year)
end for
put "Average February price: ", total / 3
```

We could calculate the average price for the entire three-year period as follows.

```
total := 0
for year: 1982..1984
    for month: 1..12
        total := total + price(month,year)
```

      end for
    end for
    put *"Overal l average:"*, *total / 36*

This example has illustrated the use of two-dimensional arrays. It is possible to use arrays with three and more dimensions. For example, our consumers' group might want to record prices for five grades of processed wallalumps (that makes one dimension), each month (that makes two dimensions), for three years (that makes three dimensions). The array declaration

      var *price:* **array** *1..5, 1..12, 1982..1984* **of** **int**

would set up a table to hold all this data.

SUBRANGE TYPES

When we are programming, we often find that we are using a particular limited set of values. In the wallalump example, we are interested in the values *1982, 1983,* and *1984,* because they are the years of the survey. The **for** loop counter called *year* only holds the values *1982* to *1984.* We say *1982* to *1984* is a **subrange** of the integers and we write this subrange as *1982..1984.*

Turing provides a way to specify that a variable can be restricted to have values in a particular subrange. This is illustrated in a program that locates the first month of *1984* in which the price of processed wallulumps exceeds a dollar:

    ...declaration of *price* as before...
    ...read values of *price* array...
    var *month: 1..12 := 1*
    loop
        if *price(month,1984)* > *100* **then**
            put *"Price exceeded 1.00 in month number ", month*
            exit
        end if
        if *month* = *12* **then**
            put *"Price stayed below 1.00 all year "*
            exit
        end if
        month := month + 1
    end if

As you can see, *month* has been declared to have only values 1 to 12. In a similar way, we could declare *year* as a variable with the type *1982..1984.*

We could have declared month as **int** instead of 1..12 without changing the action of the program. It would still calculate and output the same thing. But the new declaration is better than the old because it tells someone reading the program a lot about the *month* variable. Without looking beyond the declaration we know the small set of values that will be given to the variable. This means it is easier to read and understand the program; when programs start getting long and complex, it is important to keep them as understandable as possible. Besides helping the reader, the new declaration may help the compiler to do a better job in translating the program; since it knows more about *month*, it may be able to produce a faster or smaller machine language program from the program. And when we use ranges the computer can help us locate errors; for example, if *month* has a range of *1..12* but is accidently assigned the value 93482, the computer can warn us of the problem.

We would not declare *total* to be a subrange because we do not know much about its values. The prices are read from the data and do not fit neatly into subranges, as the twelve months of the year do.

NAMED TYPES

When a particular data type is used several times in a program, it is convenient to give the type a name instead of writing out the type repeatedly. For example, if the subrange *1..12* appears several times in our wallalump program, we can name it this way:

> **type** *monthType: 1..12*

We say *monthType* is a **named type**. Then we can use it in successive declarations such as:

> **var** *month: monthType*
> **var** *price:* **array** *1982..1984, monthType* **of** int

In general any type can be given a name and this type name can be used in following declarations. For example, we could give a name to the type **array** *1982..1984,monthType* **of int** and then declare *price* using this type name.

We can give our declarations in any order, as long as the declaration of each item appears before it is used. For example, here are our declarations again, this time with names given to the beginning and ending years.

> **const** *firstYear := 1982*
> **const** *lastYear := 1984*
> **type** *monthType: 1..12*
> **type** *yearSpan: firstYear..lastYear*

var *month: monthType*
var *year:* **array** *yearSpan, monthType* **of int**

Suppose we modify our program so that it uses *firstYear* where it uses *1982*, *lastYear* where it uses *1984*, *lastYear* − *firstYear* + *1* where it uses 3 and 12*(*lastYear* − *firstYear* + *1*) where it uses 36. Our program still works as before. But now it can be easily changed to handle another year's data, by simply changing the definition of *lastYear* to

const *lastYear* := *1985*

This sort of flexibility is important because it makes it easier to keep programs up to date.

ARRAYS OF ARRAYS

We can have arrays of any type including **int** and **real**. Since any array itself is a type, we can have an array whose parts are another array. This sounds confusing but an example should make it clear. If we have a year's data, say month by month prices, then we can place these in an array:

type *yearsData:* **array** *1..12* **of int**
var *thisYear: yearsData*

The twelve prices for one year can be recorded in the *thisYear* array. But if we are interested in three years, we can use

type *yearsData:* **array** *1..12* **of int**
var *period:* **array** *1982..1984* **of** *yearsData*

Period contains all the data for the three years and *period(1983)* contains the data just for *1983*. The data for February *1983* is held in *period(1983)(2)*. This is equivalent to our old variable called *price* where the same data was in *price(1983,2)*. In the case of *period(1983)(2)* we use the first index *(1983)* to pick a year's array of data and the second (2) to pick a month within the year. With *price(1983,2)* we choose the year and month at the same time with the index pair *(1983,2)*.

The only advantage of using the *period* array instead of *price* is that with *period* we can deal with an entire year at a time. We can assign arrays to arrays, so if we want to set the prices in *1984* to be the same as those in *1983*, we can change all 12 month values by writing the assignment

period(1984):=period(1983)

With *price* we would have to write a loop to copy the 12 values one at a time. Although arrays can be assigned, they cannot be compared, so we are *not* allowed to write *period(1982) = period(1983)* in a condition to test if the *1982* prices are the same, month by month, as the *1983* prices.

INITIALIZATION OF ARRAYS

When a variable is declared, it is often convenient to give it an initial value, as in

var *total:* **real** := 0.0

When a **const** is declared, an initial value is always required, as in

const *size* := 10

We call these numbers (*0.0 and 10*) **initial values**.

If the declared item is an array, there is a special notation for the initial value, for example

const *child:* **array** *1..2* **of string** (5) := **init** ("*Adam*", "*Sarah*")

This sets up the *child* array so that *child(1)*="*Adam*" and *child(2)*="*Sarah*". If the *child* array is going to change, we declare it as **var** instead of **const**.

To initialize an array in a declaration, we have to give the type, for example, **array** *1..10* **of string** (5), and inside the **init** construct we must give as many items as there are elements of the array. If the array has two dimensions, we give its values row by row, as in

var *a:* **array** *1983..1984, 1..2* **of string** (11) :=
    init ("*outstanding*", "*worldclass*", "*good*", *exceptional*")

For example, this sets *a(1983,2)* to "*worldclass*". The values in **init** are given in the order such that the left indexes increase more slowly than the right indexes, as in *a(1983,1), a(1983,2), a(1984,1), a(1984,2)*.

For arrays of arrays we use nested **init** constructs, as in

type *hemisphere:* **array** *1..2* **of string** (10)
var *b:* **array** *1983..1984* **of** *hemisphere* :=
    init (**init** ("*outstanding*", "*worldclass*"),
        init ("*good*", "*exceptional*"))

The first nested **init** sets *b(1983)(1)* to "*outstanding*" and *b(1983)(2)* to "*worldclass*".

The following program illustrates the use of initialized arrays. It reads a year, such as *1984*, and a day in the year, such as *33*, and prints a date, such as *Feb 2, 1983*. The **const** array *monthName* holds the names of the months, namely, *Jan, Feb, March* and so on. The *monthLength* array is initialized to hold the number of days in each month. It is a variable instead of a constant because its February entry is adjusted to 28 or 29 depending on whether the year is a leap year.

A leap year is detected by seeing if the year is evenly divisible by 4. This test is written as

> if *year* mod *4 = 0* then

The **mod** (modulus) operator gives the remainder of the year divided by 4. If this remainder is zero, we have a leap year.

```
% The "dating" program
% Read a year and a day number in the year; print month and date
const monthName: array 1..12 of string (5) :=
        init ("Jan", "Feb", "March", "April", "May", "June",
             "July", "Aug", "Sept", "Oct", "Nov", "Dec")
var monthLength: array 1..12 of 28..31 :=
        init (31, 28, 31, 30, 31, 30,
             31, 31, 30, 31, 30, 31)
            % 30 days hath September, April, June, and November
var year: int
var dayInYear: int
loop   % Infinite loop to read then print dates
        loop   % Keep asking till reasonable numbers are given
            put "Give year and number of day in year"
            get year, dayInYear
            if 1900 <= year and year <= 3000 and dayInYear >= 1 then
                if year mod 4 = 0 then   % Year divides evenly by 4 (leap yr)?
                    monthLength(2) := 29   % Adjust length of February
                    exit when dayInYear <= 366
                else
                    monthLength(2) := 28
                    exit when dayInYear <= 365
                end if
            end if
        end loop

        var precedingDays: int := 0
        var month: int := 1
        loop   % invariant: precedingDays = sum for i =1 to month − 1 of
            %            monthLength (i)
            exit when dayInYear <= precedingDays + monthLength (month)
            precedingDays := precedingDays + monthLength (month)
            month := month + 1
        end loop
        % Print date, e.g., The date is Oct 31, 1983
        put "The date is ", monthName (month), " ",
                dayInYear - precedingDays, ", ", year
end loop
```

DYNAMIC ARRAYS

In the examples of arrays we have given so far, we could tell the size of each array before running the program. These arrays have **compile-time bounds** meaning the computer determines the array's size before running the program.

Turing allows us to use **dynamic** arrays, whose upper bounds are noi known until run time. This program contains a dynamic array named *list*.

```
% The "percent" program
%    Read n and then a list of n numbers.
%    Print each number and the percentage
%    it is of the total of the numbers

    var n: int    % How many numbers to be read
    put "Type an integer n and then n numbers"
    put "For each number, its percent of total is printed"
    get n
    var list: array 1..n of real   % Dynamic array of n numbers
    var sum: real := 0
    for i: 1..n   % Read the n numbers
        get list(i)
        sum := sum + list(i)
    end for
    put skip, "Number": 12, "Percentage"
    for i: 1..n   % Compute percentages; print results
        put list(i): 5, (list(i)/sum)*100: 15
    end for
```

Here is an example of the use of this program:

Type an integer n and then n numbers
For each number, its percent of total is printed
3
10   40   '0

Number	Percentage
10	12.5
40	50
30	37.5

In this program, we have used the dynamic array, called *list*, the size of *list* is read from the input data.

ARRAYS AS DATA STRUCTURES

We have spoken of structured programming and shown how control flow is structured in a program. Now we can speak of the structure of data. Giving variables identifiers that are meaningful has been the only way we could systematize data so far. But with arrays we find that data can be structured or organized into one-dimensional forms called lists, or two-dimensional forms called tables. We can use higher-dimensional arrays when we need them.

When we approach a problem and want to solve it by creating a computer program we must decide on the data structures we will use. We must decide in particular whether or not we need to establish arrays for any of the data, or whether single variables will serve us well enough.

Arrays will be useful whenever we must store groups of similar pieces of information. They are not necessary when small amounts of information come in, are processed, and then go out.

OTHER DATA STRUCTURES

Just so that you do not think that single variables and arrays are the only kind of data structures we can have, we will mention a few others.

One common structure is the **tree** structure. The easiest way to think of a tree is to imagine a family tree. At the risk of being called chauvinists we will show only the male members in the tree and talk of fathers and sons. This keeps it simple.

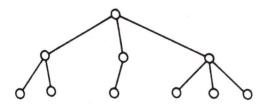

TREE STRUCTURE

The diagram is showing a man with three sons. The first son has two sons, the second one son, the third three. The grandfather is the **root** of the tree. The tree is of course growing upside down. The lines joining the relatives are called **branches**; the people themselves are **nodes**.

The data we might store could be the names of the people, and the tree structure would have to be stored also. The way it is done is to have **pointers** stored with the data to give the structure. Each father entry requires a pointer for each of his sons.

A list can also be arranged with elements and pointers instead of in an array. This means that some of the information stored is used to describe the data structure and some to give the data. With arrays, the structure is given by the fact that one element follows right next to the preceding element. It does not need a pointer.

Later we will be investigating other data structures in detail. Often we will use the array structures to implement structures like trees or lists with pointers from one element to another.

CHAPTER 10 SUMMARY

This chapter has introduced array variables, which are used for manipulating quantities of similar data. An array is made up of a number of elements, each of which acts as a simple, non-array variable. The following terms are used in describing arrays and their uses.

Array declaration — sets aside memory space for an array. For example, the declaration

> **var** *cost:* **array** *1..4* **of real**

sets aside space for the array elements *cost(1)*, *cost(2)*, *cost(3)* and *cost(4)*. Each of these elements can be used like a simple, non-array **real** variable.

Array index (sometimes called array subscript) — used to designate a particular element of array. For example, in *cost(i)*, the variable *i* is an array index. An array index can be any arithmetic expression, and can even include array elements.

Array bounds — the range over which array indexes may vary. For example, given the declaration

> **var** *price:* **array** *1..12, 1982..1984* **of int**

an array element of *price* can be specified by *price(m,y)*, where *m* can range from 1 to 12 and *y* can range from *1982* to *1984*.

Out-of-bounds index — an array index which is outside the bounds specified in the array's declaration. This is an error.

Subrange type — a type such as *1982..1984* that specifies a subrange of another type. *1982..1984* is a subrange of the type **int**.

Named type — any type, for example, *1..12*, can be given a name and then used in declarations.

Multiply-dimensioned arrays — arrays requiring more than one index, such as the *price* array given above.

Arrays of arrays — these are similar to multidimensioned arrays. Each index is written in its own parentheses, for example *period(1982)(2)* rather than *price(1982,2)*.

Initialized arrays — an array can be initialized in its declaration, for example

var *rating:* **array** *1..3* **of real** *:=* **init** *(— 0.5, 0.0, 0.5)*

Dynamic arrays — arrays whose size is not known until run time. Turing allows the upper bound(s) of arrays to be determined at run time, for example

> **var** *n:* **int**
> **get** *n*
> **var** *a:* **array** *1..n* **of real**   % *Dynamic array*

CHAPTER 10 EXERCISES

1. What does the following program output?

    ```
    % The "flowers" program
    var poem: array 1..2 of string (6)
    poem(1) := "A rose "
    poem(2) := "Is "
    for sayItAgain: 1..3
        for part: 1..2
            put poem(part)
        end for
    end for
    put poem(1)
    ```

2. What does the following program output?

    ```
    % The "rumors" program
    var he, she: array 1..4 of string (10)
    put "Here they are "
    for who: 1..4
        get he(who), she(who)
    end for
    put skip, skip, he(1), " says ", she(2), " loves ", he(2)
    ```

```
put "However ", skip
for who: 2..3
    put she(who), " says ", he(who+1), " says "
end for
put she(2), " is just shopping around "
```

The input data is:

John Ann Fred Judy Ed Alice Bill Jane

3. What does this program output?

```
% The "polish " program
var name: array 1..50 of string (10)
var price: array 1..50 of int
var n, p: int
get n
for i: 1..n
    get name(i), price(i)
end for
get p
for i: 1..n
    if price(i) > p then
        put name(i)
    end if
end for
```

The input data is:

```
3
"Johnson's"          518
"Lemon Oil"          211
"Domino"             341
300
```

4. Write a program which reads yesterday's and today's stock-market selling prices and outputs lists of rapidly rising and rapidly falling stocks. A typical data entry will look like this:

"General Electric" 93.50 81.00

The entry gives you the company's name followed by yesterday's price, followed by today's price. Your program should output a list of companies whose stock declined by more than 10 per cent, and then a list of companies whose stock rose by more than 10 per cent.

5.   What will the following program output? What error would occur if *germ* were inserted into the data just before "*all done*"?

Explain how this error can be avoided by changing one declaration. Add statements so that if more than six objects are read in, the program will output "Thank you, you have been a wonderful audience", and quit.

```
% The "singout" program
var object: array 1..8 of string
var verse: int := 1
put "Song of the Green Grass", skip
loop
    get object(verse)
    exit when object(verse) = "all done"
    if verse = 1 then
        put "There was a tree"
    else
        put "And on that", object(verse − 1)
        put "there was a ", object(verse)
        put "The prettiest", object(verse)
        put "That you ever did see"
        for decreasing v: verse..2
            put "And the ", object(v),
                " was on the ", object(v − 1)
        end for
    end if
    put "And the tree was in the ground"
    % Belt out the chorus
    put skip, "And the green grass grew all around, all around"
    put "And the green grass grew all around", skip
    verse := verse + 1
end loop
```

The input data is:

tree branch nest bird wing feather flea "all done"

6.   Do you know the song about the old lady who swallowed a fly? If so, write a program to output its words. Otherwise, if you know the song "Alouette", write a program to output its words. Otherwise, if you know the song "The Twelve Days of Christmas", write a program to output its words. Otherwise learn one of these three songs and repeat this exercise. (Note the **if**...**elsif**...**elsif**...**else** form of this question.)

7. You work for the Police Department and you are to write a program to try to determine criminals' identities based on victims' descriptions of the criminals. The police have data describing known criminals. These data entries have the form

    name   height   weight   address

    Here is an example:

    "Joey MacLunk" 67   125   "24 Main St."

    There is another set of data giving descriptions of criminals participating in unsolved crimes. Here is such a set:

    | "14 Dec: Shop Lifting" | 72 | 190 |
    | "9 Nov: Purse Snatching" | 66 | 130 |
    | "6 Nov: Bicycle Thievery" | 67 | 135 |

    The two numbers give the criminal's estimated height and weight. Write a program which first reads in the file of data entries describing the unsolved crimes. Then it reads the file entry giving the known criminals' names, descriptions, and addresses. Each known criminal's height and weight should be compared with the corresponding measurements for each unsolved crime. If the height is within 2 inches and the weight is within 10 pounds, your program should output a message saying the criminal is a possible suspect for the crime. (Note: Joey MacLunk is not a real person!)

Chapter 11

DESIGN OF PROGRAMS

STEP-BY-STEP REFINEMENT

Most of the examples of programming so far have been short. Nevertheless we have emphasized some of the aspects of good programming. These were:

1. Choosing meaningful words as identifiers.

2. Placing comments in the program to increase the understandability.

3. Paragraphing loops and selection statements to reveal the structure of control flow.

4. Choosing appropriate data structures.

5. Reading programs and tracing execution by hand, to strive for correctness before machine testing.

All of these are important even in small programs, but it is only when we attempt larger programs that our good habits will really start to pay off.

And when we work on larger programs we will find that we must develop their design in stages. Programs are devised to solve problems mechanically; we must move from a **specification** of what the problem to be solved is, to a solution, which is a well-structured program for a computer. The solution to the problem will be done by designing the program.

The original specification of a problem will be in English, with perhaps some mathematical notation. The solution will be in Turing. What we will look at in this chapter is the way we move from one of these to the other. We will be discussing a method whereby we go step by step from one to the other. This systematic method we will refer to as **step-by-step refinement**. Sometimes we say that we are starting at the top, the English-language specification of the problem, and moving down in steps to the bottom level, which is the Turing program for the solution. We call this the **top-down approach** to program development.

TREE STRUCTURE TO PROGRAM DEVELOPMENT

To illustrate the technique of structuring the design of programs by the step-by-step refinement, or the top-down approach, we need a problem as an example. We need a problem that is large or difficult enough to show the technique, but not so large as to be too long to follow. If a program is too long and involved, we will use another technique that divides the job into subprograms and does one subprogram at a time. This is called **modular programming**. It is another form of structured programming. But it must wait until we have learned about subprograms and modules.

The example we choose is sorting a list of names alphabetically. We will now start the solution by trying to form a tree which represents the structure of our attack. The root of the tree is the specification of the problem. In the first move we show how this is divided into three branches:

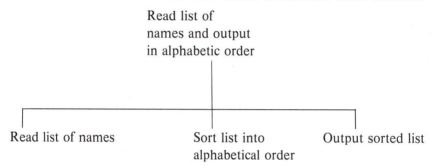

At each of the three nodes that descend from the root we have an English statement. These statements are still "what-to-do" statements, not "how-to-do-it."

We will be moving down each branch of the solution tree replacing a statement of what to do by an algorithm for doing it. As we develop the final program the algorithms will not necessarily be in the Turing language. We will use a mixture of English and Turing at each node until in the nodes farthest from the tree root we have a Turing program.

CHOOSING DATA STRUCTURES

Before we try to add more branches to the solution tree, we should decide on some data structures for the problem of sorting the list of names. We need not make all the decisions at this stage, but we can make a start.

We will use an array of character strings called *name* to hold the list of names to be sorted. The length of this list we will call *n* and we will allow names up to 30 characters in length. What we are deciding on is really the declarations for the Turing program, and for now we have decided that we need

> **const** *maxList := 100*
> **type** *nameType:* **string** *(30)*
> **var** *n: 0..maxList*
>
> ...
>
> **var** *name:* **array** *1..n* **of** *nameType*

In these declarations we are allowing a maximum size for the list of 100 names. The actual list will have *n* names, and we must read this number in as part of the input before the declaration of *name*. We will input and output one name on each line. We will assume for the moment that we will keep the sorted list in the same locations as the original list. The names will have to be rearranged, and this means some swapping will be needed.

GROWING THE SOLUTION TREE

Having decided on these data structures, we are prepared to continue the process of structuring the solution tree. We can see how to develop the left and right branches now, even as far as transforming them into Turing program segments. We will still have to refine the middle branch. Here is the tree now:

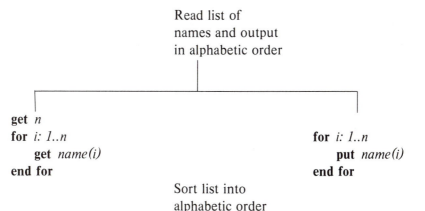

At this stage we must face up to designing an algorithm for producing a sorted list. We will do it by interchanging elements of the list two at a time. We will be swapping elements.

DEVELOPING AN ALGORITHM

We want the names to be in the sorted list so that each name has a larger value than the name ahead of it in the list. In the sorted list

> *Holt*
> *Horning*
> *Hull*
> *Hume*

we see that each name is alphabetically greater than the one preceding it.

In our solution tree one branch must be developed further; this is, "Sort list into alphabetic order." We have seen from the example that a sorted list has the largest value in the last position. This is also true of the list if an element is removed from the end. The new last element is the largest one of the smaller list. So our next refinement in the solution is to arrange the list in this way. We write:

> **for decreasing** *last* from *n* to second,
>> swap elements so largest of list up to *last* is in *name(last)*
>
> **end for**

In the list of four names, *last* begins with a value of 4, and the names are swapped so *Hume* is in position 4. Then *last* is set to 3 and the names are swapped so *Hull* is in position 3. Then *last* is set to 2 and *Horning* is placed in position 2. The only remaining name, *Holt*, is left in position 1, and the list is alphabetized. This is why the **for** has second as the limit. The first part of this can be written in Turing as

> **for decreasing** *last: n..2*

But we must still refine the part,

> swap elements so largest of list up to *last* is in *name(last)*

We will now refine this part; it becomes

> **for** *i: 1..last* − *1*
>> **if** *name(i)* > *name(i* + *1)* **then**
>>> swap elements number *i* and *i* + *1*
>>
>> **end if**
>
> **end for**

We must now refine the statement "swap elements number *i* and *i* + *1* ". This swapping is done by temporarily placing *name(i)* in *temp*.

> **const** *temp := name(i)*
> *name(i) := name(i* + *1)*
> *name(i* + *1) := temp*

Now we can assemble the complete program.

```
% The "sort" program
% Sort list of n names alphabetically
type nameType: string (30)
var n: int
% Read name list
put "list length = "..
get n
var name: array 1..n of nameType
put "Enter names one to a line"
for i: 1..n
    get name(i)
end for
% Sort list into alphabetic order
for decreasing last: n..2
    % Swap elements so largest of list
    %   up to last is in name(last)
    for i: 1..last- 1
        if name(i) > name(i + 1) then
            % Swap elements i and i + 1
            const temp := name(i)
            name(i) := name(i + 1)
            name(i + 1) := temp
        end if
    end for
end for
put "Here is sorted list"
% Output sorted name list
for i: 1..n
    put name(i)
end for
```

Here is a sample display:

list length = *5*
Enter names one to a line
Andrews
Cameron
Allen
Baker
Dawson
Here is sorted list
Allen

Andrews
Baker
Cameron
Dawson

Notice that the English parts of the solution tree remain as comments in the final program. Comments are not added after a program is written, so that it can be understood at a later date, but are an integral part of the program construction process.

ASSESSING EFFICIENCY

In this approach to problem solution we have moved step by step to refine the statement of the problem in English into a program in a language that is acceptable to a computer, namely Turing. In the process, as we constructed the solution tree, we gradually replaced statements of what is to be done by statements of how it is to be done; we devised an algorithm for performing the process. The algorithm was expressed in English, or a mixture of English and Turing. Then finally we had a Turing program.

Nowhere during this process have we spoken about the efficiency of the method that we have chosen, that is, the efficiency of our algorithm. This is because the issue of efficiency complicates the solution. Since in structured programming we are trying to control complexity, we have in this first attempt eliminated efficiency from our considerations.

This means that to find a more efficient algorithm we may need to back up to an earlier point in the solution tree and redo certain portions. In practice afterthoughts must be allowed to improve a method of solution. The only reason to reject afterthoughts is that the work in incorporating them may not be justified, considering the gain that would result.

In our particular example you can see that it is possible, at a certain stage, that the list might be sorted and that there is no need to keep on to the bitter end. What we should incorporate is a way of recognizing that the list is sorted so that the mechanical sorting process can stop.

A BETTER ALGORITHM

What we will do is to back up in the solution tree to the point where the middle branch stated, "Sort list into alphabetic order". We have translated this essentially by the statement, "Swap elements of *name* in such a way that at the end of the swapping process the list is sure to be sorted."

We are going to change now to the statement, "Swap elements of *name* in such a way that at the end of the swapping process the list would be sorted, and stop either when the list **is** sorted or when the normal end of the swapping process is reached." You can see that we are going to have a counted loop with a conditional exit. What we must add to the counted loop is the exit

> **exit when** *sorted*

But how do we know when the list is sorted? We must devise a method to test whether or not the list is sorted. You will notice that if the inner loop does not swap any names, the list **must** be sorted. We should have a **boolean** flag called *sorted* that can be set to **true** to indicate that the list is sorted or **false** to indicate that the list is not sorted.

We would have to initialize this loop by setting *sorted* to **true** in its declaration inside the outer loop. We want *sorted* to be changed to **false** if swapping takes place in the inner **for** loop. This can be accomplished if we set it to **true** just before we enter the inner loop and set it to **false** if any swapping does take place. The altered part of the program is as follows.

```
    % Sort list into alphabetic order
    for decreasing last: n..2   % Exit if sorted
        var sorted: boolean := true   % Assume list is sorted;
        %   if swapping is done, list is not sorted
        % Swap elements so largest of list
        %   up to last is in name(last);
        %   if there is swapping, set "sorted" to be false
        for i: 1..last − 1
            if  name(i) > name(i + 1) then
                sorted := false
                const temp := name(i)
                name(i) := name(i + 1)
                name(i + 1) := temp
            end if
        end for
        exit when sorted
    end for
```

BETTER ALGORITHMS

In our example we could see that an improvement in the efficiency of the sorting algorithm could be achieved, and we backed up the solution tree and redid a portion to incorporate the improvement. This was an easier job than trying to think about efficiency in the first place. This is why in the step-by-step refinement method we do not consider efficiency at first. In a way we were lucky that our algorithm could be modified so readily. We might have done the swapping in an entirely different way, in which we would not be able to detect a sorted list by the absence of swapping on any iteration of the process.

To see how this might be, suppose that to sort this list each element were compared with the last element. If it were larger, the two would be swapped. With the largest in the last position the list would be shortened by one and the process repeated. The difficulty here is that the fact that no swapping occurs in any round only means that the largest is already in the last position, not that the list is sorted. We have no way of seeing that the list is sorted unless we compare each list member with its next-door neighbor. And this is what we did in our sorting method.

So our method is more suited to this particular improvement than a method that involves swapping by comparison of each element with one particular element. If we had started this way we would have had to revise completely. To say that efficiency considerations are left until after a first algorithm is programmed produces disadvantages. For many standard processes like sorting, various algorithms have been explored, their efficiencies evaluated, and the best algorithms determined. The method we have developed is good for short lists, up to about 20 items, but is too slow for long lists.

The method we have described is called the **bubble sort**. A modification of this was devised by Donald Shell and is known as the **Shell sort**. If the list is reasonably long this is a much more efficient method. Perhaps you can see that it is really a series of bubble sorts, starting with a large space between elements being compared and swapped if necessary, and going down to the comparison of next-door neighbors. The altered part of the sort program which uses the Shell sort method is this:

```
% Sort list into alphabetic order
var space: int := n
loop
     space := floor(space/2)
     exit when space < = 0
     for i: space + 1..n
          var j: int := i − space
          loop
               exit when j < = 0
               if name(j) > name(j + space) then
                    const temp := name(j)
                    name(j) := name(j + space)
```

```
            name(j + space) := temp
            j := j– space
         else
            j := 0
         end if
      end loop
   end for
end loop
```

The best, or optimal, algorithm often depends on the problem itself. For instance, one algorithm may be best for short lists, another for longer lists. Establishing the best method is very difficult and depends on circumstances. Always try to pick a good algorithm if you are programming a standard process. At least avoid bad algorithms. Very often, programs are already written using good algorithms and you can use them directly in your own program. We can create programs from subprograms that are already made for us. Then one of the branches of your solution tree is filled by a **prefabricated subprogram**. We need only learn how to hook it up to our own program. We can also create subprograms of our own. This technique is called **modular programming** and it is an additional way to conquer problem solving, by dividing the problem into parts.

CHAPTER 11 SUMMARY

In previous chapters we concentrated primarily on learning a programming language; we have covered variables, loops, character strings, arrays and so on. In this chapter, the focus has been on designing programs.

The method of program development which we described is based on the idea of dividing the problem into parts: the divide-and-conquer strategy. Each of these parts in turn is divided into smaller parts. This continues until eventually the solution to the problem has been broken into small parts which can be written in a programming language like Turing. We will review this method of program design using the following terms:

Top-down approach to programming. When using a computer to solve a problem, you should start by understanding the problem thoroughly. You start at the "top" by figuring out what your program is supposed to do. Next you split your prospective program into parts, for example, into a reading phase, a computation phase, and a outputting phase. These phases represent the next level in the design of your program. You may continue by defining the data which these phases use for passing information among themselves, and then by writing Turing statements for each of the phases. The

Turing statements are the bottom level of your design; they make up a program which should solve your problem. In larger programs, there may be many intermediate levels between the top - understanding the problem completely - and the bottom - a program which solves the problem. (Beware: top-down program design does **not** mean writing your program from the top of the page to the bottom! The top level in top-down design means gaining an understanding of the problem to be solved, rather than writing the first line of Turing.)

Step-by-step refinement. When you are writing a program, you should start with an overall understanding of the program's purpose. You should proceed step by step toward the writing of this program. These steps should each refine the proposed program into a more detailed method of solving the problem. The last step refines the method to the level where the computer can carry out the required operations. This means that the final refinement results in a program which can be executed by the computer. As you can see, the idea behind top-down programming is step-by-step refinement leading from the problem statement to the final program.

Tree structures to program design. In this chapter we have illustrated top-down programming by drawing pictures of trees. The root, or base, of the tree is labelled by the statement of the problem. Once the problem has been refined into subproblems, we have our tree grow a branch for each subproblem. In turn, each subproblem can be divided, resulting in sub-branches, and so on. When you are actually solving problems, you will probably not actually draw such a tree. However, you may well use the idea behind drawing this tree, namely, step-by-step refinement leading from problem statement to final program.

Use of comments. One of the purposes of comments, in a program is to remind us of the structure of the program. Comments are used to tell us that a particular sequence of Turing statements has been written to solve one particular part of the problem.

CHAPTER 11 EXERCISES

1. You have been given the job of writing a program to read a list of names and output the names in reverse order. In your top-down approach to writing your program, you first decided your program should have the overall form:

(a) Read in all of the names;

(b) Output the names in reverse order;

Next, you decided that the names will be passed from part (a) to part (b) via an array declared by

>   **var** *name:* **array** *1..50* **of** *nameType*

The index of the last valid name read into this array will be passed to part (b) in a **int** variable called *howMany*. Making no changes to this overall form, you must now complete the program. Include comments at the appropriate places to record the purpose of the two parts of your program. Answer the following questions about your completed program.

-   Can you think of another way to write part (a) of your program without changing part (b)? How?

-   Can you think of another way to write part (b) of your program without changing part (a)? How?

2. The school office wants a list of all *A* students and a list of all *B* students. The input line should be of the form:

>   *"David Tilbrook"* *A—*

Each grade is *A,B,C,D* or *F*, which may be followed by + or −. The school's programmer has designed the following two possible structures for a program to read the input and output the two required lists.

First program structure: (a) Read names and grades and save all of them in arrays; (b) Output names having *A* grades; (c) Output names having *B* grades;

Second program structure: (a) Read names and grades and save only those with *A* 's or *B* 's in arrays; (b) Output names having *A* grades; (c) Output names having *B* grades;

Suppose the final program will have room in arrays to save at most 100 students' names. What advantage does the second program structure have over the first one? You do not need to write a program to answer these questions.

3. A company wants to know the percentage of its sales due to each salesman. For each salesman there is an identification number and the dollar value of his sales. The top-down design of a program to output the desired percentages has resulted in this program structure:

(a)   Read in salesmen's numbers and sales and add up total sales;

(b)   Calculate each salesman's percentage of the total sales;

(c)   Display the salesmens' numbers and percentages.

Parts (a) and (c) have been written in Turing. You are to write part (b) in Turing, add declarations and complete the program. Here is part (a):

```
% Read in salesmen and sales, total sales
totalSales := 0
i := 1
loop
    get salesman(i), sales(i)
    exit when salesman(i) = "noone"
    totalSales := totalSales + sales(i)
    i := i + 1
end loop
n := i
```

Here is part (c) written in Turing:

```
% Display salesmen and percentages
put "    salesman","    percent"
for i :1..n
    put salesman(i): 10, percent(i): 10
end for
```

You are to complete the program without changing parts (a) and (c).

Chapter 12

SUBPROGRAMS

Up to now you have seen how a program is used to direct a computer to solve a particular problem. In this chapter you will see how parts of a program can be separated out into subprograms and how subprograms can be used to solve problems a piece at a time.

Once programs reach a certain size, perhaps 100 lines, they start to be difficult to understand and update. One reason we use subprograms is to make it easier to write and modify programs. Another reason is that we can use parts of old programs (the parts are subprograms) in new programs. Subprograms are building blocks that are used in constructing software.

PREDEFINED SUBPROGRAMS

Some subprograms are so useful that they are made available along with the programming language. These subprograms are said to be **predefined** (or **built-in** or **predeclared**). For example, the *sin* subprogram is predefined and we can use it in any Turing program. Here *x* is set to the sine of *2.81* radians.

    var *x:* **real** *:= sin(2.81)*

Radians are one way of measuring angles; if the angle is in degrees instead of radians, we use the predefined subprogram called *sind*.

We say *sin* is a **function**; it takes a value, such as *2.81*, and returns another value. A function is essentially the same as an operator such as +, which accepts certain values and returns another. Here are three examples of uses of predefined functions with their values:

Use of function   Value

length("London")   *6*
repeat("Ho", 3)   *"HoHoHo"*
intstr(67)   *"67"*

The *length* function determines the number of characters in a string. The *repeat* function catenates together a number of copies of a given string.

The *intstr* function takes an integer and produces the corresponding string, for example, *intstr(0)* = *"0"* and *intstr(216)* = *"216"*. There is a complete set of predefined **type transfer functions** in Turing that convert among the types **string**, **int** and **real**; these include the functions *intstr, strint, realstr* and *strreal.*

In Turing there are two kinds of subprograms: functions and procedures. The *randint* subprogram is an example of a procedure that is predefined. It takes an integer variable such as *i* and two integer values such as *1* and *5* and assigns to *i* an unpredictable value between *1* and *5* inclusive. For example, the following program prints strings of stars.

```
% The "randstr" program: prints patterns such as
%      **
%      *****
%      *
%      ***
%      (etc.)
var i: int
loop
    randint(i,1,5)        % Set i to 1, 2, 3, 4 or 5 randomly
    put repeat("*", i)    % Print i stars
end loop
```

The next section shows how to write procedures and a later section shows how to write functions.

PROCEDURES

A **procedure** is a subprogram that consists of a set of statements, that act together as a single large statement. Suppose you are writing a program that is to start out by printing this heading:

January Report of the Southeastern
North Dakota Music Lovers Club
J.S. Backhouse, President

We can write a subprogram named *printHeading* to carry out this task:

```
1    procedure printHeading
2        put repeat(" ",10), "January Report of the Southeastern"
3        put repeat(" ",14), "North Dakota Music Lovers Club"
4        put repeat(" ",16), "J.S. Backhouse, President"
5    end printHeading
         ...
6    printHeading
```

7   **put** *"The purpose of N.D.M.L.C. is to promote... "*

           ...

Lines 1 through 5 define or declare the procedure; as a result the name *printHeading* stands for lines 2 through 4, which are together called the **procedure body**. In these lines the predefined function *repeat* is used for printing sequences of blanks. Instead of using the *repeat* function, we can output a single blank in a field with a specified width; for example, the following two lines have the same affect.

>   **put** *repeat(" ",16), "J.S. Backhouse, President"*
>   **put** *" ":16, "J.S. Backhouse, President"*

Lines 2 through 4 are not executed until they are *called* or activated. The procedure is called by the statement *printHeading* on line 6. This line causes the computer to execute lines 2 through 4 and then to continue with line 7. When the procedure reaches its **end**, it **returns** to the **point of call**, that is, execution continues with line 7.

This example is small and specialized, so it hardly deserves to be a procedure. We will show how to make this procedure more useful by generalizing it to handle different months and different presidents.

PARAMETERS

We could get our *printHeading* procedure to print each month's report by changing line 2 to print *February* instead of *January*, then *March* instead of *February*, and so on. Similarly, we would eventually need to print the name of a new president. These changes are easy in this new version of the procedure:

1   **procedure** *printHeading(month:* **string**, *pres:* **string***)*
2   **put** *repeat(" ",10), month, " Report of the Southeastern "*
3   **put** *repeat(" ",14), "North Dakota Music Lovers Club "*
4   **put** *repeat(" ",16), pres, ", President "*
5   **end** *printHeading*

           ...

6   *printHeading(" January ", "J.S. Backhouse ")*
7   **put** *"The purpose of N.D.M.L.C. is to promote ..."*

This new version of our procedure has parameters named *month* and *pres*. Line 1, which is called the **procedure header**, can be written a shorter way:

>   **procedure** *printHeading(month, pres:* **string***)*

We have combined the declarations of the two parameters because they both use the **string** type.

A call to this new version of *printHeading* must supply particular strings for these parameters. This is done in line 6, which gives *month* the value *"January "* and *pres* the value *"J.S. Backhouse "*. *Month* and *pres* are called **formal** parameters; they correspond to the **actual** parameters *"January "* and *"J.S. Backhouse "*. We say an actual parameter is **passed** to its corresponding formal parameter, for example, *"January "* is passed to *month.* (Actual parameters are sometimes called **arguments** . Formal parameters are sometimes called **dummy arguments**. A formal parameter is sometimes called simply a **formal** and an actual parameter an **actual**.) For this activation of *printHeading*, it behaves as if it had been given these two **const** declarations:

> **const** *month:* **string** *:=* *"January "*
> **const** *pres:* **string** *:=* *"J.S. Backhouse "*

If later in the program we used the statement

> *printHeading("February ", "J. Lennon ")*

the computer would print the heading with *February* instead of *January* and *J. Lennon* instead of *J.S. Backhouse.*

We now switch to a new example: the problem of converting from an integer such as *216* to a string such as *"$2.16 "*. We will give a procedure and then a function that does this conversion.

The following part of a program makes the conversion from a non-negative integer to an equivalent dollar string.

```
1        assert i >= 0
2        % Convert integer i to dollars, so if i = 10, s become $0.10
3        var t: string := intstr(i,0)  % Convert i to a string, e.g., 10 becomes " 10 "
4        if length(t) = 1 then
5            t := "00" + t
6        elsif length(t) = 2 then
7            t := "0" + t
8        end if
9        s := "$" + t(1..length(t)- 2) + "." + t(length(t)- 1..*)
```

Line 1 documents the requirement that the dollar amount must not be negative. Line 3 uses the predefined function *intstr* to convert *i* to a string of digits.

Before inserting the decimal point, we must extend the string so it contains at least three digits. This is done by lines 4 through 8 which add one or two leading zeroes as required to make the length of *t* at least 3. Finally, line 9 adds the leading *"$"* and inserts the decimal point; for example, if *t = "216 "* then line 9 is equivalent to:

$$s := "\$" + "2" + "." + "16"$$

We will now package this part of a program to make it into a subprogram.

VARIABLE AND CONSTANT PARAMETERS

It would be handy to have a statement called *makeDollar* that converts an integer to a dollar string. For example, we could use this new statement to set string *u* to "*$2.16*" in the following:

> **var** *u:* **string**
> *makeDollars(216,u)*   % Sets u to: $2.16

What is required is a procedure named *makeDollar*, which can be defined by

> **procedure** *makeDollar(i:* **int, var** *s:* **string** *)*
>
> ... copy lines 1 through 9 from previous section ...
> **end** *makeDollar*
>
> ...
>
> **var** *k:* **int**
> ...compute value of *k*...
> **var** *u:* **string**
> *makeDollar(k,u)*
> **put** "*You owe me*", *u*

We have sandwiched lines 1 through 9 between the procedure header and its **end**. Now we can use *makeDollar* throughout our program whenever we want to make a conversion from an integer to dollars. Besides that, we can save the *makeDollar* procedure and use it in future programs.

The declaration of *s* is preceded by the keyword **var**, so we say *s* is a **variable parameter** in the *makeDollar* procedure. A parameter is declared to be **var** when the parameter is modified by the procedure body. In this example, the pocedure assigns to formal parameter *s*, and this changes actual parameter *u*. Parameters declared without **var**, such as *i*, are **constant parameters**; the procedure body is not allowed to modify constant parameters.

LOCAL DECLARATIONS

Inside the *makeDollar* procedure we have a declaration for the variable *t*. This variable *t* is private to or **local** to this procedure, which means that *t* can be accessed inside the procedure but not outside of it. We say *t*'s **scope** is the body of the procedure. Each time the procedure is called, *t* is created or re-created.

Similarly, formal parameters *i* and *s* are local to the procedure. This is analogous to counter *c* in this **for** loop:

    for *c: 1..100*
        ...body of **for** loop...   (*c*'s scope is this body)
    end for

As has been explained before, counter *c* can be accessed inside the loop but not outside it, so we say *c* is local to the loop.

GLOBAL DECLARATIONS

A subprogram can use declarations that appear outside and before the subprogram. For example, the *readName* procedure given here assigns to the variable *name*.

    var *name:* **string**

    ...

    procedure *readName*
        put *"Please give your name, then type return "*
        get *name:**   % Read entire line*
    end *readName*

    ...

    readName   *% Call to the procedure*

We say *readName* uses a **global declaration**, because *name* is declared outside of the *readName* procedure. Note that for *name* to be accessed by *readName*, *name's* declaration must appear ahead of the procedure.

We have two ways of giving information to a subprogram: we can use parameters to explicitly pass the information at each call, or we can have the subprogram access global declarations.

If the subprogram is to be given different items at each call, for example, *makeDollar* is given different integer values and different variables, then parameters should be used. If the subprogram is intended for a specialized purpose, such as reading a string into a particular variable, then it is not necessary to use a parameter; the variable's global declaration can be accessed in the subprogram body.

If a program contains many subprograms that access global variables, things can get confusing because it is difficult to keep track of the flow of information. A Turing language construct, the **module**, is introduced later in this book to help solve this problem. A module controls flow of information by collecting a set of subprograms together with the variables accessed by these subprograms.

FUNCTIONS

We have developed example subprograms called *printHeading*, *makeDollar*, and *readName*. These three were procedures, and they are activated by a **procedure call statement**, such as

> *printHeading("January", "J.S. Backhouse")*

The other kind of a subprogram is the function and is called when we need to compute a value, for example, the predefined function *intstr* is called when we need the **string** value corresponding to an **int**.

We will now give a function, called *intDollar*, that converts integers to dollars.

> **function intDollar**(*i:* **int**): **string**
> **var** *s:* **string**
> ...copy lines 1 to 9 to convert integer *i* to string *s*...
> **result** *s*
> **end** *intDollar*

Note that this uses the same lines (1 to 9) that were used in *makeDollar*. The first line (the **header**) of this function, ends with a colon and the keyword **string**, This specifies that the type of the value of the function will be a **string**. The value of the function is given in the **result** statement, which returns string *s*. We use *intDollar* to produce values in the same way we use predefined functions, for example:

> **put** *intDollar(216)*   *% Prints: $2.16*

Notice that, in this function, *s* is a local variable, rather than being a **var** parameter as was the case in the *makeDollar* procedure.

The only purpose of *s* in the function is to hold the dollar string until it is used in the **result** statement. We can shorten the function by eliminating *s* as is done here.

> **function** *intDollar(i:* **int**): **string**
> **assert** *i* >= *0*
> *% Convert integer i to dollars, so intDollar(10) = "$0.10"*
> **var** *t:* **string** := *intstr(i,0)*
> **if** *length(t)* = *1* **then**
>   *t* := *"00"* + *t*
> **elsif** *length(t)* = *2* **then**
>   *t* := *"0"* + *t*
> **end if**
> **result** *"$"* + *t(1..length(t)−2)* + *"."* + *t(length(t)−1..*)*
> **end** *intDollar*

This version of *intDollar* does not need *s* because its value is computed as a part of the **result** statement.

In the language of mathematics, *intDollar* does a *mapping* from non-negative integer values to string values. This means that for each non-negative integer, this function produces a string. For any mathematical mapping or function *F* with argument (actual parameter) *x*, we get the value *F(x)*. Some mappings require more than one argument. For example, the integer addition operator $+$ is a mapping that takes two arguments to produce its result; it maps arguments 2 and 7 to the result 9. One of the properties of mathematical functions is that they never modify their arguments. So if $x = 4$ and we determine $y = F(x)$ then *x* is still 4.

The purpose of the **function** construct in the Turing language is to allow us to define mappings. Since a mapping never changes its arguments, parameters of a Turing function are not allowed to be declared **var**. For example, the following would not be allowed.

> **function** *intDollar*(**var** *i:* **int**)**: string**   % *Illegal!*

because this would allow *i* to be changed. In a similar vein, a function is not allowed to modify global variables (either directly by assigning a value to the global variable or by calling procedures that cause modifications to global variables).

If a function has any effect other than producing its result, we say it has **side effects**. The Turing language constrains its functions so they never have side effects. The **put** statement is considered to have side effects, because it changes the output stream. The **get** statement also has side effects because it changes the position where reading is being done in the input stream. Since functions in Turing must not have side effects, they are not allowed to contain **put** or **get** statements.

Sometimes when a function is being tested, it is convenient to output intermediate results to see if they are reasonable. To allow for this possibility, when a **put** or **get** is detected in a function, a Turing compiler gives an error message stating that the **put** or **get** statement should not appear in the function, but still allows the program to run.

Procedures (as opposed to functions) do not contain **result** statements. Instead, a procedure accomplishes its purposes by making changes to **var** parameters and to global variables and by using **get** and **put** statements.

THE RETURN STATEMENT

In a function the **result** statement gives the function's value, and it cuases immediate return from the function to the point of call. A **result** statement cannot appear in a procedure, but there is another statement that causes immediate return from a procedure. This is the **return** statement, written simply as:

> **return**

We do not use this statement in examples in this chapter, because most procedures are clearer if they return implicitly when the procedure's **end** is encountered. The **return** statement is generally only used in exceptional situations. For example, a **return** might be used within a loop in the first part of a procedure if it is determined that the remainder of the procedure should not be executed.

PROCEDURES VERSUS FUNCTIONS

The *makeDollar* procedure and the *intDollar* function have the same purpose: to convert an integer to dollars. You may ask: (1) which provides a better way of doing the conversion, and (2) why does a language like Turing need to support two kinds of subprograms: procedures and functions.

The answer to the first question is that *intDollar* is simpler to use because it produces a value directly, as in

> **put** *" You owe me "*, *intDollar(j)*

By contrast to do the same thing with *makeDollar* requires the use of a variable:

> **var** *j:* **int**
> ...
> **var** *u:* **string**
> *makeDollar (j, u)*
> **put** *" You owe me "*, *u*

Generally when it is possible to use a function, this is better than using a procedure. However, functions cannot always be used.

One situation where procedures are used is to compute several values. A function can return only one value, via its **result** statement, but a procedure can return a separate result in each of its **var** parameters. (Later when the **record** type is introduced, you will see that it can be used to allow a function to return a set of values. This makes functions more widely useful.)

Procedures are also needed when global variables or parameters are to be updated, or when **get** and **put** statements are to be used.

PRE CONDITIONS AND POST CONDITIONS

We use **assert** statements to specify conditions that must be true for a program to be correct. Subprograms are essentially small programs within a larger program, and they have special forms of assertions called **pre conditions** and **post conditions**. For example, the *intDollar* function can be written as

> **function** *intDollar(i:* **int** *)s:* **string**
>   **pre** *i* > = *0*
>   **post** *s(1)* = "*$* " **and** *s(length(s)− 2)* = ". "
>   ...same body as before, but without the **assert** statement...
> **end** *intDollar*

The **pre** condition specifies that the function is to be called only with a non-negative parameter. The **post** condition specifies that the returned string starts with a dollar sign and contains a decimal point at the appropriate place.

The header line of the function contains the declaration of identifier *s*, which represents the value of the function. The only place where this identifier can be used is in the **post** condition. This is because *s* only has a value after the execution of the **result** statement. As soon as the **result** statement is executed, the **post** condition is checked to make sure that it is true. Procedures can have **pre** and **post** conditions just like those of functions.

The **post** condition given in this example documents some easily specified requirements for a correct answer, but it does not document all the requirements. As it is given, it allows certain unacceptable values of *s* such as "*$.+5* " for *i* = 5. To be complete, the **post** condition must also specify (1) that all characters of *s* except the "*$* " and the "." should be digits, (2) that at least one digit should appear to the left of the decimal point, and (3) that the value of the string *s*'s digits considered as an integer should equal *i*. Since these extra requirements are clumsy to write, we have countented ourselves with a **post** condition that gives some but not all of the requirements. In the language of mathematics, we say this is a **necessary** but not a **sufficient post** condition for the correctness of the function.

Suppose we have a subprogram that has complete (necessary and sufficient) **pre** and **post** conditions. We say the subprogram is **formally**

correct if we can prove that the true **pre** condition followed by the execution of subprogram's statements results in a true **post** condition. This idea of proofs of correctness is very helpful in getting our programs to do what we need them to do. We will not explore the idea further now, but instead will consider more aspects of subprograms.

AN EXAMPLE FUNCTION

We will give an example of a function that is used in mathematics. Given a triangle, with sides *a* and *b* forming a right angle, the third side *c* is called the hypotenuse. Pythagoras' theorem from geometry states that:

> The sum of the squares of the two sides *a* and *b* is equal to the square of the hypotenuse *c*.

This means that given *a* and *b*, we can compute *c* as the square root of the sum of *a* squared and *b* squared. This calculation is done here:

> % *The* "*hypot*" *program*
> % *Read sides of right triangle and output the hypotenuse*
> **function** *hypotenuse(a, b:* **real** *):* **real**
>   **result** *sqrt(a** 2 + b** 2)*
> **end** *hypotenuse*
> **put** "*Give lengths of two sides* "
> **var** *x, y:* **real**
> **get** *x, y*
> **put** "*Hypotenuse is* ", *hypotenuse(x, y)*

The **result** statement computes *a* squared as $a^{**}2$ and *b* squared as $b^{**}2$. It sums these and uses the *sqrt* predefined function to calculate the square root, which is the hypotenuse.

The function *hypotenuse* has **real** formal parameters, but its actual parameters can be of type **int** as in:

> **put** "*For sides 3 and 4, hypotenuse is* ", *hypotenuse(3,4)*

Just as in assignment statements, these integer values are automatically converted to **real**. But **real** values cannot be passed to **int** parameters, so if *z* is **real** we cannot pass *z* to *intDollar:*

> **var** *z:* **real** *:= 8.74381*
> **put** "*You owe me* ", *intDollar(z)* % *Illegal!*

As in assignment statements, **real** values must be explicitly converted to **int**; the **put** statement can be legally written as:

> **put** "*You owe me* ", *intDollar(round(z))*

Notice that a function, such as *intDollar*, can have as its actual parameter the value of another function, such as *round(z)*.

DYNAMIC ARRAY PARAMETERS

Sometimes we need a subprogram that can handle arrays of various sizes. For example, the function named *sum* shown in this example, adds up the elements of an array of any size.

```
% Sum elements of array
function sum(a: array 1..* of real): real
    var total: real := 0
    for i: 1..upper(a)   % Size of a is upper(a)
        total := total + a(i)
    end for
    result total
end sum

...
var b: array 1..250 of real
... compute elements of b...
put "Sum of elements of b:", sum(b)
```

The upper bound of a formal parameter array can be given as *, as is done for the array named *a* in this example. This means that *a* has the same upper bound as the array which is passed to it as an actual parameter. In this example, *b* is the actual parameter, so the upper bound of *a* is 250. The **for** statement in this example uses the notation *upper(a)*; this gives the upper bound of *a*. Note that if another array besides *b* is passed to *a*, then *upper(a)* will not necessarily be 250. An array such as *a* whose size is not known until run time is called a **dynamic array**.

We call *upper* an **attribute** and it is essentially a predefined function. For arrays of more than one dimension, *upper* requires a second parameter to specify the dimension. For example, given the declaration:

var *x:* **array** *1..5, 2..20, 1..18* **of real**

we have *upper(x, 1) = 5, upper(x, 2) = 20* and *upper(x, 3) = 18*. There is also the *lower* attribute, for example, *lower(x, 2) = 2*.

DYNAMIC STRING PARAMETERS

We can give the upper bound of a **var string** formal parameter as *. This means the formal parameter receives the maximum length from its actual parameter. We say the formal parameter is a **dynamic string**. For example, here is a procedure that inserts a string called *word* into another string called *target*.

> **procedure** *insert*(**var** *target:* **string** *(*)*, *word:* **string**, *place:* **int** *)*
>   **pre** *0 < = place* **and** *place < = length(target)*
>   **and** *upper(target) > = length(target) + length(word)*
>   *target := target(1..place) + word + target(place + 1..*)*
> **end** *insert*
>
> ...
>
> **var** *s:* **string** *(25) := "Alexander Bell"*
>
> ...
>
> *insert(s, "Graham", 10)   % Note blank at end of Graham*

In this example, *s* is passed to *target*, so *target*'s maximum length is 25. Inside the *insert* procedure, *upper(target)* gives the maximum length of the actual parameter passed to *target*.

You may have noticed that the second parameter, *word*, is declared as **string** without the star. Why, you might ask, is one parameter declared with the star and the other without. The answer is that the first parameter is declared as **var**, and this means that *target* becomes a new name for *s*. Since target and *s* are really the same variable, they must have the same maximum lengths.

By contast, *word* is a constant parameter that is initialized to the value "*Graham*". Since *word* cannot be assigned to, its maximum length is of no great importance. We could declare *word* as **string**(*), but since *word* is a constant parameter, this would be equivalent to simply **string** without the star. It would not have been reasonable to declare *target* to be of type **string** without the star, because then *s*, whose maximum length is 25, could not be passed to *target*, the only variables that could be passed to *target* would be those declared as **string** with no explicit maximum length.

The only place where * can be used as an array upper bound or a string maximum length is in a formal parameter. Note that it is **not** allowed to use a star to specify a function's type.

> **function** *intDollar(i:* **int** *):* **string** *(*)   % Not legal!!*

The reason this is illegal is because the result of a function does not have a corresponding actual parameter.

MATCHING TYPES OF ACTUAL AND FORMAL PARAMETERS

The Turing language does not allow types of values to be freely inter-mixed. For example, it does not allow integers to be compared to strings, so the comparison *"elephant'* $>$ *27* is not legal. Because of restrictions like these, we say Turing is a **strongly typed** language.

Similar restrictions apply when passing parameters to subprograms. There is the obvious restriction that the number of actual parameters must be the same as the number of formal parameters. There are separate rules for matching parameters of **var** and non-**var** parameters:

*Rule for constant (non-**var**) parameters.* An actual parameter passed to a constant formal parameter must be **assignable** to the formal parameter's type. For example, we can pass 924 to a constant formal parameter whose type is **int**, but we could not pass *"elephant "* to this formal parameter.

*Rule for variable (**var**) parameters.* Since a **var** parameter can be assigned to in the procedure body, the actual parameter must be a variable and not just a value; so we cannot pass *"rabbit "* or *x+2* to a **var** parameter. The types of the actual and formal parameters must be **equivalent**. So, variable *x* whose type is the subrange *1..10* can only be passed to a formal parameter with an integer subrange with equal limits (1 and 10). Similarly, variable array *a* with type **array** *1..12, 1..7* **of real** can only be passed to a **var** formal parameter with equal bounds and with **real** as its element type.

We will give some examples using these rules with **var** parameter *v* and non-**var** parameter *c*.

```
procedure sqr(var v: 1..100, c: 1..10)
    v := c** 2
end sqr
var a: 1..100 := 6
var b: 1..10 := 4
... call to sqr occurs here ...
```

Here are some calls to *sqr* that could occur immediately following *b*'s declaration.

1. *sqr(a, b)*   % Fine, sets *a* to 16

2. *sqr(b, a)*   % Illegal because *b*'s type is not equivalent to *v*'s type

3. *sqr(a, 5)*   % Fine sets *a* to 25

4. *sqr(5, b)*   % Illegal, 5 is not a variable

5. *sqr(a, a)*   % Fine, sets *a* to 36. Note that the
           % actual parameter *a* given after the comma
           % initializes run-time constant *c* to 6.

When it is allowed to pass an actual parameter to a formal parameter, we say they are **compatible**. In Turing there are two kinds of compatibility: (1) type equivalence is required for **var** parameters and (2) assignability is required for non-**var** parameters.

There is a restriction on actual parameters that are arrays. If the size of an actual parameter array is not known at compile time, then it is a dynamic array and its corresponding formal parameter must have its upper bound(s) declared as star. For example, if array *A* has an upper bound that is not known until run time then *A* can only be passed to a formal parameter with * as upper bound. A similar restriction applies to strings; namely, a string with a run-time maximum length can only be passed to **var** formal parameters having * as maximum length.

AN EXAMPLE: HANDLING MATRICES

We will develop some procedures that handle matrices. (Due to its Latin origin, the plural of matrix is usually written matrices, although matrixes is acceptable.) In mathematics, a matrix is a two-dimensional array, such as

> **var** *A:* **array** *1..2, 1..3* **of real**

This is called a 2 by 3 matrix because it has 2 rows and 3 columns. In Turing an element of *A* is written *A(i,j)*, but in mathematics we write A_{ij}.

Sometimes we need to read and print matrices. Here are procedures that do the reading and printing.

```
        procedure getMatrix(var M: array 1..*, 1..* of real)
            for i: 1..upper(M,1)  % Each row of M
                for j: 1..upper(M,2)  % Each column of M
                    get M(i, j)
                end for
            end for
        end getMatrix

        procedure putMatrix(M: array 1..*, 1..* of real)
            for i: 1..upper(M,1)  % Each row of M
                for j: 1..upper(M,2)  % Each column of M
                    put M(i, j): 15 ..  % Next element of row on same line (..)
                end for
```

```
            put " "   % Start new line after printing row
        end for
    end putMatrix
```

These two procedures can be used in many different programs. We will use them in a program that does a calculation called **matrix multiplication**, that combines two matrices to form a third matrix.

Our program will read and print two matrices X and Y, and then will compute and print their product matrix Z. To carry out this computation, it is required that the number of columns of X is the same as the number of rows of Y.

We will use a procedure named *multMatrix* that will calculate Z using X and Y. We will give *multMatrix* procedure later, but first here is the program.

```
procedure getMatrix(var M: array 1..*, 1..* of real)
    ...as already given...
procedure putMatrix(M: array 1..*, 1..* of real)
    ...as already given...
procedure multMatrix(var C: array 1..*, 1..* of real,
    A,B: array 1..*, 1..* of real)
    ...to be given...

% Read sizes of matrices and declare matrixes
var rowsX, colsX, colsY: int
get rowsX, colsX, colsY
const rowsY := colsX   % Y is to have as many rows as X has columns
var X: array 1..rowsX, 1..colsX of real
var Y: array 1..rowsY, 1..colsY of real
var Z: array 1..rowsX, 1..colsY of real

% Read and print matrix X
getMatrix(X)
put "Matrix X:"
putMatrix(X)

% Read and print matrix Y
getMatrix(Y)
put skip, "Matrix Y:"
putMatrix(Y)

% Calculate and print matrix Z
multMatrix(Z, X, Y)
```

put skip, *"Product matrix Z:"*
putMatrix(Z)

This program uses *getMatrix* two times, to read X and Y, and uses *putMatrix* three times, to print X, Y, and Z. The program could read this input data:

2	3	4		(sizes of matrices)

3	5	7		(2 by 3 matrix X)
1	6	2		

3	3	2	7		
5	2	1	10	(3 by 4 matrix Y)
9	4	5	4		

After printing matrices X and Y, the program calculates and prints their product, which is:

97	47	46	99
51	23	18	75

Notice that the result has 2 rows (corresponding to X's 2 rows) and 4 columns (corresponding to Y's 4 columns).

For this data, each element of the 2 by 4 product matrix Z is calculated as

$$Z(i,j) = X(i,1) * Y(1,j) + X(i,2) * Y(2,j) + X(i,3) * Y(3,j)$$

For example:

$$
\begin{aligned}
Z(2,3) &= X(2,1) * Y(1,3) + X(2,2) * Y(2,3) + X(2,3) * Y(3,3) \\
&= (1*2) + (6*1) + (2*5) \\
&= 2 + 6 + 10 \\
&= 18
\end{aligned}
$$

Notice that $Z(2,3)$ is calculated by using each element in row 2 of X and each element in column 3 of Y.

The general mathematical formula for computing elements of product matrix Z is

$$Z_{ij} = \sum_{k=1}^{p} X_{ik} \, Y_{kj} \qquad (\sum_{k=1}^{p} \text{ means to sum terms 1 to } p)$$

where p is the number of columns of X (and also the number of rows of Y). This formula is calculated by the Turing statements

$Z(i,j) := 0$
for $k: 1..p$
     $Z(i,j) := Z(i,j) + X(i,k) * Y(k,j)$

end for

These statements appear in the *multMatrix* procedure, with X, Y, and Z replaced by A, B, and C and p replaced by *upper (A,2)*.

The *multMatrix* procedure uses * for upper bounds of the arrays, so that various sizes of matrixes can be multiplied. The first **for** loop executes *upper(A,1)* times; this is once for each row of C. For each of these rows, the next **for** loop executes *upper(B,2)* times; this is once for each element of C in the row. For each such element $C(i,j)$, the innermost loop executes *upper(A,2)* times (which is the same as *upper(B,1)* times), to compute the value of $C(i,j)$.

```
% Matrix multiplication C := A*B
procedure multMatrix(var C: array 1..*, 1..* of real,
                         A,B: array 1..*, 1..* of real)
   pre upper(A,2) = upper(B,1)  % cols of A = rows of B
   for i: 1..upper(A,1)  % Each row of C
      for j: 1..upper(B,2)  % Each col of C
         C(i,j) := 0
         for k : 1..upper(A,2)  % Each col of A (and each row of B)
            C(i,j) := C(i,j) + A(i,k) * B(k,j)
         end for
      end for
   end for
end multMatrix
```

A whole set of procedures could be written for performing other matrix manipulations, such as matrix addition, subtraction, finding the *determinant*, and so on.

CHAPTER 12 SUMMARY

This chapter has introduced subprograms. Subprograms are used as building blocks for constructing programs. The reasons for using subprograms in programs include:

1. Dividing the program into parts that can be written by different people.

2. Dividing a program into parts that can be written over a period of time.

3. Making a large program easier to understand by building it up out of conceptually simpler parts.

4. Factoring out common parts of a program so they need not be written more than once within a program. As a result the program will take up less space in the computer's memory.

5. Factoring out commonly used parts of programs so they can be used in a number of different programs.

6. Separating a program into parts that can be individually tested.

There are two kinds of subprograms in Turing: procedures and functions. Essentially, each procedure provides a new kind of statement and each function provides a new kind of operation. The following important terms were discussed.

Predefined subprograms — these include mathematical functions such as *sqrt* (square root) and *sin* (the sine function). There is also the *randint* predefined procedure for generating random numbers. See the appendix for more details.

Subprogram declaration — gives a name to a procedure or function. A subprogram declaration in a Turing program must appear textually before it is called. A procedure can be declared using this form:

> **procedure** *procedureName*(...formal parameters...)
>   ...declarations and statements...
> **end** *procedureName*

A function can be declared using this form:

> **function** *functionName*(...formal parameters...): *returnType*
>   ...declarations and statements...
>   **result** ...returned value...
> **end** *functionName*

If a subprogram has no parameters, the parameters and their enclosing parentheses are omitted from the declaration.

Calling a subprogram (invoking a subprogram) — causing a subprogram to be executed. A procedure is called by a statement of the form:

> *procedureName* (...actual parameters...)

If the procedure has no parameters, then the list of actual parameters and the parentheses are omitted. A function is called by using its name, followed by a parenthesized list of actual parameters if required, in an expression.

Formal and actual parameters — the formal parameters are declared in the subprogram header and the actual parameters appear in the call to the subprogram. In the following, the formal parameter is *i* and the actual parameter (or argument) is *x*.

```
function sqr(i: real ): real
    result i**2
end sqr
var x: real
get x
put "X squared is: ", sqr(x)
```

Variable and constant parameters — a formal parameter declared using **var** is called a variable parameter and can be changed in the subprogram. The variable parameter gives a new name to the actual parameter; any change to the formal parameter changes the actual parameter. A formal parameter declared without **var** is called a constant parameter and cannot be changed.

Local declarations — declarations made inside a subprogram are said to be local to the subprogram. Identifiers declared in a subprogram can only be accessed in the subprogram. A variable declared in a subprogram is created each time the subprogram is called and deleted when the subprogram returns to the point of call.

Global declarations — declarations outside and preceding a subprogram can be accessed in the body of the subprogram. These declarations are global to the subprogram.

pre and **post** conditions — the **pre** condition is an assertion that must be true when the subprogram is called. The **post** condition is an assertion that must be true when the subprogram returns to the point of call.

Dynamic formal parameters — a formal array parameter can be declared with its upper bound(s) specified as * and a formal string parameter can be declared with its maximum length specified as *. These are called dynamic formal parameters and take their upper bounds and sizes from their corresponding actual parameters.

```
procedure readNames(var name: array 1..* of string(*))
    for i : 1..upper(name)  % Read each string in array
        get name(i)
    end for
end readNames
```

Here *name* is a dynamic array of dynamic strings. The *upper* attribute is used to find the upper bound of *name.*

Compatibility of parameters — an actual parameter passed to a **var** formal parameter must have a type that is equivalent to the type of the formal parameter. If the formal parameter is not **var**, the actual parameter must be assignable to the formal parameter's type.

CHAPTER 12 EXERCISES

1.   What does the following program output? List the formal parameters and actual parameters.

```
% The "numbers" program
procedure absolute(m: int, var n: int)
    if m >= 0 then
        n := m
    else
        n := -m
    end if
end absolute
var output: int
for i: -2..2
    absolute(i, output)
    put output
end for
```

2.   What does the following program output? List the actual parameters and formal parameters in the program.

```
% The "weather" program
var temperature, rain: array 1..31 of real
var time: int
procedure average(list: array 1..* of real, howMany: int)
    var total: real := 0
    for i: 1..howMany
        total := total + list(i)
    end for
    put total / howMany
end average
get time
for day: 1..time
    get temperature(day), rain(day)
end for
put "Average temperature: "..
average(temperature, time)
put "Average rainfall: "..
average(rain, time)
```

Assume the program reads this data:

5 45.0 0 47.2 0 48.0 .3 47.5 2.1 48.0 0

3. Write a procedure that sorts an array of names into alphabetic order. For example, your procedure could be used in the following:

```
% The "order" program
var workers: array 1..100 of string (20)
procedure sort(var names: array 1..* of string (*), size: int)
    ...you write this part...
end sort

for i: 1..100
    get workers(i)
end for
sort(workers, 100)
for i: 1..100
    put workers(i)
end for
```

4. What does this program output?

```
% The "ditty" program
procedure MacDonald
    put "Old MacDonald had a farm"
    put "E I E I O"
end MacDonald

var animal, noise: string
loop
    get animal, noise
    exit when animal = "stop"
    MacDonald
    put "And on that farm he had a ", animal
    put "E I E I O"
    put "With a ", noise, "— ", noise, " here, a ",
        noise, "— ", noise, " there"
    put "Here a ", noise, " there a ", noise,
        " everywhere a ", noise, "— " ,noise
    MacDonald
    put ""    % Skip line
end loop
```

Assume the data being read is:

duck quack cow moo stop silence

5. What does the following program output? How could you change this program so each output line ends with a period.

```
% The "encore" program
procedure singLine(left,middle,right: string ,repeats: int)
    var line: string := left
    for i: 1..repeats
        line := line + middle + " "
    end for
    put line, right
end singLine


procedure MacDonald
    singLine("Old MacDonald","had ", "a farm ", 1)
    singLine("", "E I ", "O ",2)
end MacDonald


var animal, noise: string

loop
    get animal, noise
    exit when animal = "stop"
    MacDonald
    singLine("And on that ","farm he had a ",animal, 1)
    singLine("", "E I ", "O ", 2)
    singLine("With a ",noise, " here ", 2)
    singLine("A ", noise, " there ", 2)
    singLine("Here a ", noise, "", 1)
    singLine("There a ", noise, "", 1)
    singLine("Everywhere a ", noise, "", 2)
    MacDonald
    put ""   % Skip line
end loop
```

Assume the data being read is:

duck quack cow moo stop silence

6. What does the following procedure do? Write a small program that uses this procedure.

```
procedure metric(var width: real)
    width := 2.54 * width
end metric
```

7. What does the following function do? Write a small program that uses this function.

> **function** *convert(inches:* **real** *):* **real**
>> **result** *2.54 * inches*
> **end** *convert*

8. Write a function that replaces each sequence of blanks in a string with a single blank. For example, your function could be used in this program.

> *% The "squash" program*
> **function** *deblank(s:* **string** *):* **string**
>> ...you write this part...
> **end** *deblank*
> **const** *testPattern :=* "*Here   is a test   sentence*"
> **put** *testPattern*
> **put** *deblank(testPattern)*

Chapter 13

SEARCHING AND SORTING

When a large amount of information is stored in a computer, it must be organized so that you are able to get at the information to make use of it. This problem of **data retrieval** is at the heart of all business operations. Records are kept of employees, customers, suppliers, inventory, in-process goods, and so on. These records are usually grouped in some way into what are called **files**. We might have, for example, a file of employee records, a file of customer records, an inventory file, and so on. Each file must be kept up to date.

A file that we all have access to is printed in the telephone book. It consists of a series of **records** of names, addresses, and telephone numbers. We say that there are three **fields** in each of these records: the name field, the address field, and the phone-number field. The file is in the alphabetic order of one of the three fields, the name field. We say that the name field is the **key** to the ordering of the file. The file is in alphabetic order on this field because that is how it can be most useful to us for data retrieval. We know someone's name and we want the phone number. We might also want the address and that too is available. The telephone company also has the same set of records, ordered using the phone-number field as the key.

In this chapter we will be investigating how a computer can search for information in a file and how records can be sorted. In later chapters we will look at record structures and the storage of files in secondary memory.

LINEAR SEARCH

One way to look for data in a file is to start at the beginning and examine each record until you find the one you are looking for. This is the method people use who do not have large files. But for more than about 12 records it is not a good filing system. It will serve as an example to introduce us to the idea of searching mechanically and give us a bad method to compare our better methods to. We will create a file which consists of names and telephone numbers but the file will not be ordered by either name or number.

We will keep the file in two one-dimensional arrays, one called *name* and one called *number*. The element *number(i)* will be the correct telephone number for *name(i)*. We will read this file, then read a list of names of people whose phone numbers are wanted. Here is the program to do this job. We are assuming that our file of names and phone numbers is entered so that the name has no blanks in it.

```
% Look up pho ne numbers in directory
%    The "phones" program
const direcSize := 50
const dummy := "*"
type nameType: string (20)
type numberType: string (8)
var name: array 1..direcSize of nameType
var number: array 1..direcSize of numberType
var friend: nameType
var place, fileSize: 1..direcSize
% Read in file of names and numbers
put "Enter phone directory"
put "name": 18, "phone"
fileSize := 0
for i: 1..direcSize
    get name(i), number(i)
    exit when name(i) = dummy
    fileSize := fileSize + 1
end for
put "End with dummy name *"
loop
    put "Enter friend's name"
    get friend
    exit when friend = dummy
    % Look up friend's number
    place := 1
    loop
        exit when place > fileSize or friend = name(place)
        place := place + 1
    end loop
    if friend = name(place) then
        put number(place)
    else
```

```
        put "unlisted"
      end if
   end loop
```

Here is a sample display:

Enter phone directory

name	phone
Perrault,R.	*483—4865*
Borodin,A.	*782—8928*
Cook,S.A.	*763—3900*
Enright,W.H.	*266—1234*
*	*999—9999*

End with dummy name *
Enter friend's name
Borodin,A.
782—8928
Enter friend's name
Davies,R.
unlisted
Enter friend's name
*

We have stored the phone number as a character string because of the dash between the first three and the last four digits. The names must be typed without any blanks or else enclosed in quotes.

TIME TAKEN FOR SEARCH

In the last section we developed a program for a linear search. The searching process consists of comparing the friend's name, *friend*, with each name in the file of names *name(1), name(2), name(3)*, and so on until either the name is found or the end of the file is reached. For a small file, a linear search like this one may be fast enough, but it can be time-consuming if the file is lengthy.

If there are *n* records in the file and the name is actually in the file, then on the average there will be *n*/2 comparisons. The largest number of comparisons would be *n* if the name were last in the file, the least number would be 1 if the name were first. A file of 1000 names would require 500 comparisons on the average. This gets to look rather formidable. It is for this reason that we do something to cut down on the effort. What we do is to sort the file into alphabetic order and then use a method of searching called **binary searching**. We will look at sorting later, but first we will see how much faster binary searching can be.

BINARY SEARCH

The telephone book is sorted alphabetically and the technique most of us use for looking up numbers is similar to the technique known as binary searching. We start by opening the book near where we think we will find the name we are looking for. We look at the page that is open and compare any name on it with the name being sought. If the listed name is alphabetically greater we know we must look only between the page we are at and the beginning of the book. We have eliminated the second part of the book from the search. This process is repeated in the part that might contain the name until we narrow the search down to one page.

In binary searching, instead of looking where we think we might find the name, we begin by looking at the name in the middle of the file and discard the half in which it cannot lie. This process cuts the possible number of names to be searched in half at each comparison.

A file of 16 names would require a maximum of 4 comparisons: one to cut the list to 8, another to 4, another to 2, and another to 1. Of course, we might find it earlier, but this is the **most** work we have to do. It is the maximum number of comparisons. With a linear search of 16 records we might have to make 16 comparisons, although 8 is the average. If we have a file of 1024 records, the binary search takes a maximum of 10 comparisons. This can be calculated by seeing how many times you must divide by 2 to get down to 1 record. Put mathematically, 1024 is equal to

$$2*2*2*2*2*2*2*2*2*2$$

Just one more comparison, making 11 altogether, will let you search a list of 2048 entries. Then 4096 can be done with 12 comparisons. You can see how much more efficient binary searching can be when the file is a long one.

A PROCEDURE FOR BINARY SEARCH

We will now design a program for doing a binary search and write it so that it can be called as a procedure. When we write

   search(basicFile, key, size, location)

we are asking for the value of *location* for which *basicFile(location)=key*, where *basicFile* is an array of *size* items declared as of type *nameType*. If the *key* is not in the file, *location* will be set to zero.

We will develop the algorithm for the binary search in two stages as an illustration of step-by-step refinement. We will write out our proposed solution in a form that is a mixture of English and Turing.

```
loop
    Find middle of file
    if middle > = key then
        Discard last half of file (after middle)
    else
        Discard first half of file (including middle)
    end if
    exit when only one element is left
end loop
if remaining element = key then
    location := index of remaining element
else
    location := 0
end if
```

It will be important to know the *first* and *last* of the remainder of the file at any time in order to establish the *middle* and to discard the appropriate half. We initially set *first* to *1* and *last* to *size*. Then to find the middle we use

$$middle := (last + first) \textbf{ div } 2$$

It will not matter that this division is truncated as the process of finding the middle is approximate when the number of entries in the file is an even number. Refining the expression, "Discard last half of file (after *middle*)" becomes

$$last := middle$$

and, "Discard first half of file (including *middle*)" becomes

$$first := middle + 1$$

The procedure can now be written:

```
% Locate key using binary search
procedure search(basicFile: array 1..* of nameType, key: nameType,
    size: int, var location: int )
        var first,last,middle: int
        % Initialize the search loop
        first := 1
        last := size
        % Search until file is exhausted
        loop
            % Find middle of file
            middle := (first + last) div 2
            if basicFile(middle)> = key then
                % Discard last half of file (after middle)
```

```
                last := middle
            else
                % Discard first half of file (including middle)
                first := middle + 1
            end if
            % Exit when only one element is left
            exit when first = last
        end loop
        if basicFile(first) = key then
            location := first
        else
            location := 0
        end if
    end search
```

A program that uses this procedure can now be written. We will use it to look up telephone numbers. We will replace the following serial search in the *phones* program:

```
        place := 1
        loop
            exit when place > fileSize or friend = name(place)
            place := place + 1
        end loop
        if friend = name(place) then ..
```

this becomes:

```
        search(name, friend, fileSize, place)
        if place not = 0 then ...
```

We are assuming that the file of names is sorted alphabetically. The procedure *search* should be included in the main program before it is called.

You will notice that the binary search program has more instructions than the linear search that it is replacing. Each step is more complicated, but the process is much faster for a large file because fewer steps are executed.

SEARCHING BY ADDRESS CALCULATION

We have seen that the efficiency of the searching process is very much improved by having a file sorted. The next method of searching uses data organized in a way so there is "a place for everything, and everything in its place".

Suppose you had a file of *n* records numbered from *1* to *n.* If you knew the number of the record, you would immediately know the location. The number would be the index of the array that holds the file entries. Each entry would have a location where it belonged. The trouble usually is to find the location of a record when what you know is some other piece of information such as a person's name.

Files are sometimes arranged so that they are organized on serial numbers that can be calculated from some other information in the record. For example, we could take a person's name and, by transforming it in a certain definite way, change it into a serial number. This transformation often seems bizarre and meaningless, and we say the name is **hash-coded** into a number. When the number has been determined, the location is then definite and you can go to it without any problem.

Usually with hash coding it happens that several records have the same hash code. This means that, instead of the code providing the address of the exact record you want, what you get is the address of a location capable of containing several different records. We call such a location a **bucket** or **bin**. We then must look at the records in the bin to find the exact one we are interested in. Since the number is small they need not be sorted. A linear search is reasonable when the number of items is small.

If fixed-size bins are used to store the file, it is important to get a hash coding algorithm that will divide the original file so that roughly the same number of records is in each bin.

As an example of a hash-coding algorithm, suppose that we had 1000 bins and wanted to divide a file of 10,000 records into the bins. The file might already have associated with each record an identifying number. For example, it might be a Social Insurance number or a student number. These numbers might range from 1 to 1,000,000. One way to divide the records into bins would be to choose the last three digits of the identifying number as the hash code. Another hash code might be formed by choosing the third, fifth, and seventh digit. The purpose is to try to get a technique that gives about the same number of records in each bin. More complicated hashing algorithms may be necessary.

SORTING

We have already developed a sorting program as an example of step-by-step refinement in a previous chapter. The method we used is called a **bubble sort**. Each pair of neighboring elements in a file is compared and exchanged, to put the element with the larger key in the array location with the higher index. On each exchange pass, the element with the largest key gets moved into the last position. The next pass can then exclude the last position because it is already in order. We also showed a better method for longer lists called the **Shell sort**.

We have shown that the binary search technique is much more efficient for a large file than a linear search. In the same way, although a bubble sort is a reasonable method for a small file, it is not efficient for a large file. What we usually do to sort a large file is to divide it into a number of smaller files. Each small file is sorted by a technique such as the bubble sort, then the sorted smaller files are merged together into larger files. We will look at an example in which two sorted files are merged into a single larger sorted file.

MERGING OF SORTED FILES

We will develop a procedure called *merge* to merge *file1*, which has *size1* records ordered on the field *keyFile1*, with *file2*, which has *size2* records ordered on the field *keyFile2*, and store it in *file3*. We will invoke this procedure with the statement

$$merge(keyFile1, size1, keyFile2, size2, keyFile3)$$

Here is the *merge* procedure:

```
% Merge two sorted files
procedure merge(keyFile1: fileType, size1: int,
        keyFile2: fileType, size2: int, var keyFile3: fileType)
    var i1,i2,i3: int := 1
    % Merge until all of one file is used
    loop
        exit when i1 > size1 or i2 > size2
        if keyFile1(i1) < keyFile2(i2) then
            keyFile3(i3) := keyFile1(i1)
            i1 := i1 + 1
        else
            keyFile3(i3) := keyFile2(i2)
            i2 := i2 + 1
        end if
        i3 := i3 + 1
    end loop
    % Add remaining items to end of new file
    loop
        exit when i1 > size1
        keyFile3(i3) := keyFile1(i1)
        i1 := i1 + 1
```

```
            i3 := i3 + 1
        end loop
        loop
            exit when i2 > size2
            keyFile3(i3) := keyFile2(i2)
            i2 := i2 + 1
            i3 := i3 + 1
        end loop
end merge
```

EFFICIENCY OF SORTING METHODS

The number of comparisons required to merge the two previously sorted files in our example is *size1* + *size2*. To sort a file of length *n* by the bubble sort we can count the maximum number of comparisons that are needed. It is

$$(n - 1) + (n - 2) + (n - 3) + ... + 1$$

This series can be summed and the result is

$n(n - 1)/2$ which is
$n^2/2 - n/2$

When *n* is large, the number of comparisons is about $n^2/2$, since this is very large compared to $n/2$. We say the execution time of the algorithm varies as n^2; sorting 100 items takes 100 times the number of comparisons that sorting 10 items does. We will now make calculations to see why merging is useful for sorting long files. To sort a file of *n* items, by first using a bubble sort on two files $n/2$ in length then merging, requires $n^2/4 - n/2$ for the bubble sort and *n* for the merge. This makes a combined total of

$n^2/4 + n/2$ comparisons.

Using a bubble sort on the whole file gives a result of

$n^2/2 - n/2$ comparisons.

When *n* is 100, the bubble sort merge method requires 2,550 comparisons, the straight bubble sort requires 4,950 comparisons. We can keep dividing files and subfiles, sorting them by merging, with further improvements. In the limit we have a **successive merge sort** that is efficient enough to be used for large files.

CHAPTER 13 SUMMARY

This chapter has introduced the idea of the structure of files in main memory and presented methods of searching and sorting that are used to handle files. These methods manipulate files of records. Each record consists of one or more fields.

A search is based on a key, such as a person's name, that appears as one field in a record of a file. A linear search locates the desired record by starting at the first record and inspecting one record after another until the given key is found. A linear search is slow and should not be used for large files; a faster search method, such as binary search, should be used for large files.

A binary search requires that the file be ordered according to the key field of the records. An unordered file can be ordered using one of the sorting methods discussed in this chapter. The binary search inspects the middle record to determine which half of the file contains the desired record. Then the middle record of the correct half is inspected, to determine which quarter of the file contains the desired record, and so on, until the record is located.

If the key is a number that is identical to the index of the desired record then no searching is required, because the key gives the location of the record. Sometimes the key can be manipulated to create a hash code that locates a small set of records, called a bucket, that includes the desired record.

A file of records can be ordered using the bubble sort. This method repeatedly passes through the file, interchanging adjacent out-of-order records until all records are in order. The bubble sort is slow and should not be used for large files; the Shell sort is faster for somewhat longer files but a still faster sorting method, such as sorting by merging, should be used for large files.

A file can be sorted by merging in the following manner. First the file is divided into two sub-files and each of the sub-files is sorted by some method, such as the Shell sort. Then, starting with the first records of the two sub-files, the ordered file is created by passing through the sub-files and successively picking the appropriate (smaller key or alphabetically first key) record. If the sub-files are large, they should be sorted by a fast method, such as a merge, instead of by a Shell sort.

CHAPTER 13 EXERCISES

1. Prepare a file of names and addresses, enter the file and order it alphabetically. Now try looking up the address of a friend in your file.

2. Write a program that maintains a lost and found service. First the program reads entries giving found objects and the finders' names and phone numbers. For example, this entry

    "Siamese cat" "Miss Mabel Davis" 714—3261

    means Miss Mabel Davis, having phone number *714—3261*, found a Siamese cat. These entries are to be read and ordered alphabetically and then a similar set of entries for losers of objects is to be processed. If a lost object matches a found object, then the program should display the name of the object as well as the finder, the loser and their telephone numbers. Assume the loser entries are not alphabetized. Process each loser entry as it is read, using a binary search.

Chapter 14

IMPROVING PROGRAM RELIABILITY

Throughout this book, we have emphasized structured programming techniques; these include step-by-step refinement, programming without the **goto** statement, choosing good variable names and so on. These techniques make it easier to write correct programs. We have also given techniques for testing and debugging programs. In this chapter we will collect and expand upon these techniques for making sure a program works.

PROGRAM SPECIFICATION

The **specifications** for a program tell what the program must do to solve a problem. Before starting to write a program, the programmer needs the detailed specifications for the program. Suppose the problem is to prepare pay checks for the employees of a company; there is an entry giving each employee's name and amount of payment. The programmer needs to know the format of the data entry as well as the format for the pay checks. These formats are part of the specifications for the program to prepare pay checks.

Sometimes the program specifications are not completely agreed upon and written down. If an employee's entry indicates an amount of *$0.00*, this may mean that the employee is on leave and is to receive no pay check. If the programmer does not know the special significance of *$0.00* — because the specifications are not complete — he may write a program that prepares hundreds of worthless pay checks. Often programs fail to handle special situations such as *$0.00* correctly. If the programmer is in doubt, he should check the specifications and make sure they are complete.

ERROR PREVENTION

Errors are sometimes made in the preparation of data for a program. Amounts may be entered incorrectly; more data may be supplied than anticipated. The method of handling data errors may be given in the program specifications, or it may be left to the discretion of the programmer. Sometimes a programmer can write his program so that it detects and reports bad data. This is called **defensive programming**. Some programs are written to accept absolutely any data; after reporting a bad data item, the program ignores the item or attempts to give it a reasonable interpretation. If a program is written assuming no data errors, bad data items may prevent the program from doing its job. It is the programmer's responsibility to make the program sufficiently defensive to solve the problem at hand.

The quality of a computer program is determined largely by the attitudes and work habits of the programmer. Some programmers underestimate the programming task. They write programs too quickly, they do not test their programs sufficiently, and they are too willing to believe that their programs are correct.

Most programs, when first written, contain some errors. This is not surprising when you consider the vast number of possible programming errors and the fallibility of every programmer. The programmer should take the attitude that a program is not correct until it is shown to be correct.

One good method of preparing computer programs is to write them using a soft lead pencil. This allows easy corrections and improvements by erasing and replacing lines. The program should be entered into the computer only when the programmer feels confident that no more changes are required. This method of program preparation can save the programmer a lot of time. The savings come because it is easy to change a program when it is still on paper and fresh in the programmer's mind. Each later change requires the programmer to relearn the program before he can confidently make modifications. A few minutes of desk-checking a program can save hours of debugging time. The programmer who tries to do it right the first time comes out ahead, saving time and writing programs with fewer errors.

PROGRAM CORRECTNESS

The most effective way to make sure a program works correctly is to study the program thoroughly. It should be read again and again until the programmer is thoroughly convinced that it is right.

It helps if a second programmer reads and approves the program.

Ideally, the second programmer should read the program after its author feels that it is correct, but before it is submitted to the computer. The second reader provides a new point of view and may be able to find typical errors such as incorrect loop initialization.

This process of studying programs to make sure they are correct can be called "proving program correctness". Sometimes programs are proven correct using a mathematical approach; proving that a program is correct is then similar to proving that a theorem in geometry is true. More often, programs are proven correct by a non-mathematical, common-sense approach. The program is considered to have errors until proven correct.

In Turing the use of assertions in the form of preconditions and post conditions in a program lets the computer detect the existence of run-time circumstances which would produce an incorrect result. These do not insure that the program is correct. For one thing: not all required pre and post conditions might be included; the assertions may be incomplete or, for that matter, incorrect themselves. Most certainly, if the execution is interrupted by the failure, the program was not correct. A truly correct program would not need assertions except as comments to increase understandability.

PROGRAMMING STYLE

A program should be easy to read and understand; otherwise the job of studying it to verify its correctness will be hopeless. The programmer should strive for a good **programming style**, remembering that other readers will be in a hurry and will be critical of sloppiness or unnecessary confusion in the program. It commonly happens that as a programmer makes a program clearer and easier to understand, ways to improve or correct the program are discovered.

It takes work to write programs that are easy to read — just as it takes work to write clear English. Good writing requires care and practice. One way of making programs readable and understandable is to give them a simple organization — so the reader can easily learn the relationship among program parts. We have previously presented step-by-step refinement and division into subprograms, often called modular programming, as techniques for designing programs. As well as aiding in the writing of programs, these techniques help make programs easier to read.

USE OF COMMENTS AND IDENTIFIERS

One of the rules of good programming style is this: comments and identifiers should be chosen to help make a program understandable. Comments should record the programmer's intentions for the parts of the program. It is a good idea to write comments as the program is being written.

Better programs require fewer comments, because the program closely reflects the intentions of the programmer. Programs become more difficult to read if they are cluttered with obvious comments such as

> *% Increase n by 1*
> *n := n + 1*

Comments are usually needed to record:

- **Overall purpose of a program**. What problem the program is to solve. As well, comments may be used to record the program's author and its date of writing.

- **Purpose of each major program component**: function, procedure or module, similar to the comments for an overall program.

- **Purpose of a collection of statements**. Such a comment might give the purpose of a loop.

- **Assumptions and restrictions**. At certain points in a program, assumptions and restrictions may apply to variables and the data. For example, one program part may assume that another program part has set *numberOfAccounts* to a positive number less than 20 to indicate the number of customer accounts. Usually an assertion, if used, is self-explanatory.

- **Obscure or unusual statements**. As a rule, such statements should be avoided. If they are required they should be explained.

Well-chosen identifiers make a program easier to read. Each identifier should record the function of the named object. For example, an array used to save account numbers should be named *accountNumber* and not *list*. A procedure used to read accounts should be named *readAccounts* and not *p1* or *Margaret*.

If a variable has a very simple purpose, such as indexing through an array, a one-letter name such as *i, j,* or *n* may be appropriate. This is because these letters are commonly used for indexing in mathematics. But if the index variable has some additional meaning, such as counting input data entries, a longer name may help the reader.

Avoid abbreviations, such as *tbntr* for table entry. Avoid acronyms, such as *sax* for sales tax. Unless abbreviations or acronyms are well known to the reader before seeing the program, they impose an extra memorization task that interferes with understanding the program.

Avoid meaningless identifiers such as *a, b, c, d*, and *temp1*. A single-letter identifier such as *d* is sometimes appropriate for a simply-used variable when the name *d* is relevant, for example, when it stands for diameter. Adding a digit such as 1 or 2 to the end of an identifier, as in *temp1*, can be confusing unless it explains the purpose of the named object.

TESTING

After the program has been written and studied to verify its correctness, it should be tested. The purpose of testing is to run the program to demonstrate that it is working properly.

The tests must be chosen with care because only a limited number of them can be run. Consider a program designed to sort any list of 100 names into alphabetic order. Certainly we could not test it exhaustively by trying every possible list of 100 names. We would be testing for years! Rather than exhaustive testing we need to design tests which try every type of situation the program is to handle.

Well-designed tests should point out any errors in the program. Ultimately, testing demonstrates errors better than it demonstrates program correctness. When testing reveals an error, that is, a **bug**, in the program, the programmer is faced with a **debugging** task. We shall present debugging techniques later. Right now, we will give techniques for testing.

The programmer will need to study the program in order to design good tests. The tests should make each statement execute at least once — but this is not enough. Suppose the statement

   average := total/count

is tested and computes the desired average. This does not demonstrate that all is well; it may be that in some situations *count* can become zero. If this statement is executed with *count* set to zero, the statement does not make sense. So, not only should every statement be executed, but it should be executed for the type of situation it is expected to handle. Care should be taken to:

   — **Test end conditions**. See that each loop is executed correctly the first time and last time through. See that indexes to arrays reach their smallest and largest possible values. Pay particular attention to indexes and counters which may take on the value zero.

— **Test special conditions**. See that data which rarely occurs is handled properly. If the program displays error messages, see that each situation requiring such a message is tested.

Designing tests to exercise all end conditions and special conditions is not easy - but it is worthwhile in terms of program reliability.

The programmer should be able to tell from test results if the program is executing correctly. Sometimes this is easy because the program outputs intermediate results as it progresses. Sometimes the programmer will need to add special output statements to verify that the program is running correctly. These statements can:

Display messages to record the statement being executed. For example, a message might say: *Reading accounts procedure entered.*

Output values of variables. This allows the programmer to verify by hand that the values are correct. The best time to output variables is when subprograms start and when they finish, so the programmer can verify that variables were modified correctly.

Display warnings of violated assumptions. Suppose a procedure is used to set *where* to the index of the smallest number in a list of 12 numbers. The assumption that *where* receives a value from *1* to *12* can be tested by

> **if** *where* $<$ *1* **or** *where* $>$ *12* **then**
> **put** "*error: where* $=$ ", *where*

Care must be taken to design appropriate output statements for testing. Too much output will not be read by the programmer; too little will not give the programmer sufficient information about the execution of the program.

Ideally, tests should be designed before the program is submitted to the computer. With the program still fresh in mind, the programmer can more easily invent tests that try out every statement. Sometimes a programmer discovers that parts of a program are difficult to test; a slight change in the program may overcome this difficulty. It is best to make these changes when the program is still on paper, before time has been invested in entering the program into the computer. Designing tests requires the programmer to read the program with a new point of view. It sometimes happens that this point of view uncovers errors in the program. The best time to fix these errors is when the program is still on paper.

As programs become larger, it becomes increasingly difficult to test them thoroughly. Large programs can be tested by first testing the modules individually. Then the modules are combined into larger modules and these are tested and so on. The process is called **bottom-up testing**. This method of testing uses specially-written test programs that call the modules with various values of parameters, shared variables, and input data.

Whenever a program is modified, it should be retested. All the changed parts should be tested. In addition, it is a good idea to test the entire module containing changes, or even the entire program. The reason is that modifications often require a precise understanding of the surrounding program, and this understanding is sometimes not attained. Very commonly, program modifications introduce errors.

DEBUGGING

A program has bugs (errors) when it fails to solve the problem it is supposed to solve. When a program misbehaves we are faced with the problem of debugging — correcting the error. The program's misbehavior is a symptom of a disease and we must find a cure. Sometimes the symptom is far removed from the source of the problem; erroneous statements in one part of a program may set variables' values incorrectly and trigger a series of unpredicted actions by the program. When the symptoms appear via incorrect program output, the program may be executing in a different part. The programmer is left with a few clues: the incorrect output. It is necessary to solve the mystery and cure the disease. Solving these debugging mysteries can take more time than writing the program.

When a program contains a bug, this means that the programmer made at least one mistake. We can categorize programmer errors as follows:

Errors in entering the program; *procedure* might be mistyped as *procdeure*. These are typing errors.

Errors in using the programming language. The programmer did not understand a language construct. For example, the **return** statement cannot be used in functions; it can be used only in procedures.

Errors in writing program parts. Although a particular program part was properly designed, it was not correctly written in Turing. For example, a loop designed to read in account records might always execute zero times because of writing the loop's terminating condition incorrectly.

Errors in program design. The program parts and their interactions might be improperly designed. The program designer might forget to provide for the initialization of variables used by some procedures. He might overlook the fact that one procedure, say, *displayAccounts*, should be called only after calling another procedure, say, *readAccounts*.

Solving the wrong problem. The programmer did not understand the nature of the problem to be solved. He may have misunderstood the program specifications. Perhaps the specifications were not correct or complete.

This list of possible errors has proceeded from the least serious to the most disastrous. The first kind of errors, such as typing errors, can be corrected easily once detected. The last kind of error, misunderstanding the purpose of the program, may require scrapping the entire program and starting over again.

Some programmers are overly optimistic and immediately conclude that any bugs in their programs are not very serious. Such a programmer is quick to make little changes in his program to try to make the symptoms of the problem disappear. The wise programmer knows that program misbehavior is an indication of sloppiness and that sloppiness leads easily to disastrous errors. Program misbehavior is taken as a sign that the program is sick — it should have a checkup by studying it.

The overly optimistic programmer is forever saying, "I just found the last bug." When the wise programmer finds a bug, it is assumed that there are more.

Many of the least serious errors, such as misspelled keywords, are automatically pointed out by error messages, because the error results in an illegal Turing program. These errors are usually easy to fix. Some errors are particularly treacherous; they seem to defy attempts to correct them. Here is some advice — some of it repeated from earlier parts of this book — to help you track down treacherous bugs.

Read all error messages. In their hurry to read their program's output, some programmers fail to notice error messages. These messages may pinpoint a bug.

The first error messages may help more than later ones. This is because the first messages are closer to the source of the problem. Later messages may simply indicate that a previous error is still causing trouble.

Beware of confusion between l and 1. Some people can consistently read $x := x + l$ to mean increase x by one. Errors like this can be found by reading the program character by character — as a computer does! In general, the human tendency to read what we expect to be there, rather what is actually there makes debugging difficult.

Beware of misspellings. Some words are easily misspelled. A person who is concentrating on understanding a program may overlook *receipt* occasionally spelled as *reciept.*

If everything else fails in the debugging effort, the programmer is forced to rerun the program to gain more information about the errors. The programmer may add statements to output variables or to trace the program's execution. These statements are designed using the same techniques used in testing to show programs work properly. If the original tests had been carefully enough designed, there is a good chance they would have pinpointed the error and eliminated later time-consuming debugging.

CHAPTER 14 SUMMARY

In this chapter we have listed techniques for making sure a program works. There are a vast number of ways a program can be wrong, so the programmer should learn to be careful at all the stages of program preparation. When a programmer is too hasty to submit a program to the computer, the result is persistent bugs and excessive time spent in debugging. The following important techniques and terminology were presented.

Program specifications — explanation of what a program is to do. This should include the forms of the input and output data and the type of calculation or data manipulation to be performed. Essentially, program specifications explain how the computer is to be used to solve a particular problem.

Programming habits — the way a programmer goes about his work. Ideally, he should take the slow but sure approach, completing a program in pencil and thoroughly studying it before submitting it to the computer.

Program correctness — a program should be studied to verify that it satisfies its specifications. Formal proof of correctness is difficult.

Programming style — if the style is good, then the program can be easily read and understood.

Use of comments and identifiers — good programming style requires that comments and identifiers be chosen to make a program understandable. Comments should record the programmer's intentions; identifiers should record the function or use of the named object.

Testing — running a program to demonstrate that it meets its specifications. Tests should be designed to try every type of situation the program is to handle. Ultimately, testing is better at demonstrating bugs than demonstrating program correctness.

Debugging — correcting errors in a program. Debugging can be the most difficult and time-consuming part of trying to make a program work. These difficulties can be minimized by using the techniques listed in this chapter.

CHAPTER 14 EXERCISES

1. In this exercise you are to use defensive programming. Modify the program given in the chapter on arrays so that it will handle errors in the data gracefully. The program reads a list of names and outputs the list in reverse order.

2. Try to write a program that is completely correct before you submit it to the computer. Have a friend help you by studying your program for errors after you are convinced that it is free of errors. Record the time you spend preparing the program and record any programming errors you make. Your program should perform one of the following tasks:

    (a) The program should read a series of integers followed by the dummy value 9999. Output the sum of the positive integers and the number of negative integers.

    (b) The program should read and output a list of alphabetically ordered names. If a name is repeated in the data, it should be output only once.

Chapter 15

THE RECORD
DATA TYPE

We have seen that the **array** data type is used for storing a sequence of values. In an array, all the values are necessarily of the same type, for example, we can have an **array** of integers, but not an **array** that consists partly of strings and partly of integers. The chapter introduces a new data type, called the **record**, whose components can have different types.

RECORDS AND FIELDS

It is often convenient to store information as a set of entries or records. Each record consists of a number of fields, for example, in a checkbook, each record consists of four fields; these fields contain the check number, the date, the name of the party receiving the check, and the amount of the check. A record in a telephone book consists of a name field, an address field, and a telephone number field.

A collection of records, such as a checkbook, is called a file of records. In many cases the file is ordered by a particular field, which is called the key; for example, telephone books are in alphabetic order by name.

A Turing **record** is a collection of several fields and is particularly suitable for records in a file. As a simple example, suppose that we want to describe each entry in the telephone book as a record. We would identify the entire record by the identifier *customer* and the three fields as

> *customer.name*
> *customer.address*
> *customer.phoneNumber*

Here is a diagram showing the fields in the *customer* record:

| *name* | *address* | *phoneNumber* |

The field identifiers are a composite of their own identifiers, *name, addresss* and *phoneNumber* and the whole record's identifier, *customer*. The composite is constructed by putting a dot, or period, between the record name and the field name.

The record structure would be declared this way.

```
var  customer:
      record
            name: string (18)
            address: string (23)
            phoneNumber: string (8)
      end record
```

This record data type consists of two levels of naming. At the first level we have the identifier of the record declared, namely *customer*. The next level has three fields declared. Each of these has its own type. So it is possible to have each field with a different type. Here, all the fields are of type **string**, but each has a different maximum length.

MOVING RECORDS

One of the reasons for having records is that they make it simple to program the movement of a whole record from one place to another. When a move is to take place, the location that will receive the record must be declared using the same record data type. Here we create *custType*, which is a pattern for creating record variables, each having the same structure.

```
type  custType:
      record
            name: string (18)
            address: string (23)
            phoneNumber: string (8)
      end record
var customer, workSpace: custType
```

The record *workSpace* will have all the same fields as *customer. name, address*, and *phoneNumber*. But its fields will be referred to as *workSpace.name, workSpace.address*, and so on. We say that the record variables *customer* and *workSpace* have the same record type.

To move the record *customer* into the record *workSpace* we need only write

```
workSpace := customer
```

This is equivalent to the group of assignment statements

>*workSpace.name := customer.name*
>*workSpace.address := customer.address*
>*workSpace.phoneNumber := customer.phoneNumber*

ARRAYS OF RECORDS

Just as other types such an **int** may form arrays, records may form arrays. Each member of the array of records has the same type. For the telephone-book records, an array of *100* such records could be declared by

>**var** *telephoneBook:* **array** *1..100* **of** *custType*

An array of records can be used for grouping records for sorting purposes. A procedure for sorting a group of *customer* records will be given. The records are to be sorted using simple bubble sort method on the key *phoneNumber*. The **type** *custType* and the array of records called *customer* will be global to the procedure. The only parameter that the procedure has is *numberOfRecords*. A *workSpace* record is declared as a local constant with the type *custType*.

>**procedure** *sortRecords(numberOfRecords:* **int** *)*
> *% Sort records by phone number*
> **for** *i: 1..numberOfRecords − 1*
>   **for** *j: 1..numberOfRecords − i*
>   **if** *customer(j).phoneNumber >*
>   *customer(j + 1).phoneNumber* **then**
>   *% Swap customer(j) and customer(j + 1)*
>   **const** *workSpace: custType := customer(j)*
>   *customer(j) := customer(j + 1)*
>   *customer(j + 1) := workSpace*
>   **end if**
>   **end for**
> **end for**
>**end** *sortRecords*

In this example we have an array that contains records. The records in this example contain fields that are all strings. In general a record can contain any type, including other records.

INPUT AND OUTPUT OF RECORDS

The record is a convenient form for moving groups of fields around in the main memory of the computer. But we have not yet said how such structures may be read into or written out from the main memory. The input-output statements that we have had so far, the **get** and **put**, can be used to read or output individual fields of a record in exactly the same way as the values of individual variables are read or output.

Here is a program that reads a file of at most *25* customer records, sorts them and outputs them:

```
% The "recsort" program
%    Read, sort by number, and output customer records
const inFile := 1
const outFile := 2
type custType:
    record
        name: string (18)
        address: string (23)
        phoneNumber: string (8)
    end record
const maxRecords := 25
var customer: array 1..maxRecords of custType
var numberOfRecords: int

procedure readRecords(var numberOfRecords: int)
    % Read records into array
    var i: int := 0
    loop
        get : inFile, skip      % Skip to next name or to eof
        if eof(inFile) then
            numberOfRecords := i
            exit
        end if
        if i = maxRecords then     % Must stop reading
            numberOfRecords := i
            put "Error: Too many records for 'recsort'"
            exit
        end if
        i := i + 1
        get : inFile, customer(i).name, customer(i).address,
            customer(i).phoneNumber
    end loop
```

end *readRecords*

...copy *sortRecords* procedure here...

procedure *writeRecords(numberOfRecords:* **int** *)*
    for *i: 1..numberOfRecords*
        put *: outFile, customer(i).phoneNumber: 10,*
            customer(i).name: 20, customer(i).address
    end for
end *writeRecords*

% Read, sort and write records
readRecords(numberOfRecords)
sortRecords(numberOfRecords)
writeRecords(numberOfRecords)

This program uses two files, called *inFile* and *outFile*. To run this program under Unix, we could use the command:

    $recsort.x phoneBook sortedBook

The *phoneBook* file could contain:

Johnston,R.L.	"53 Jonston Cres."	491−6405
Keast,P.	"77 Kredle Haven Dr."	439−7216
Lipson,J.D.	"15 Weedwood Road"	787−8515
Mathon,R.A.	"666 Regina Ave."	962−8885
Crawford,C.R.	"39 Treatherson Ave."	922−7999

The resulting *sortedBook* file would be produced as:

439−7216	Keast,P.	77 Kredle Haven Dr.
491−6405	Johnston,R.L.	53 Jonston Cres.
787−8515	Lipson,J.D.	15 Weedwood Road
922−7999	Crawford,C.R.	39 Treatherson Ave.
962−8885	Mathon,R.A.	666 Regina Ave.

In the *recsort* program, the identifier *numberOfRecords* is used both as the name of a global variable, declared before the three procedures, and as the name of the formal parameter of each procedure. We could eliminate these parameters, and just have the procedures directly access *numberOfRecords* as a global variable. Instead, we have chosen to explicitly pass a parameter to each procedure to emphasize that the action of the procedures is determined by the number of records. Notice that the *numberOfRecords* parameter for *readRecords* is declared **var** because this is the procedure that counts the records and assigns the count to *numberOfRecords*.

CHARACTER-ORIENTED INPUT

The *recsort* program reads the fields of each record using token-oriented input. In the input file, each address was surrounded by quotation marks, so that the whole address (and not just the number part) would be read into *customer(i).address*.

There is a more flexible form of input that can be used to read fields containing blanks that are not surrounded by quotation marks. To illustrate, suppose that each field in the *phoneBook* file has a particular width: the *name* field is 18 wide, *address* is 23 wide and *phoneNumber* is 8 wide. Here is an example line:

Lipson,J.D.   15 Weedwood Road   787— 8515

We can input this line by replacing the **get** statement in *readRecords* by:

```
get : inFile, customer(i).name: 18,
     customer(i).address: 23, customer(i).phoneNumber: 8
```

The number following each field being read gives the number of characters to read. This method of input is useful when fields in a file occupy a fixed number of columns.

Sometimes fields in a file are separated by a special character such as a colon or a tab character. We handle this situation using character-oriented input to read exactly one character at a time. The basic construct we use is:

```
get ch: 1    % Read one character into ch
```

For example, if the *name* field is terminated by a colon, it can be input this way:

```
var ch: string (1)    % Variable to hold input characters
customer(i).name := ""    % Start as null
loop    % Read name a character at a time
    get ch: 1    % Read one character
    exit when ch = ":"    % Reached end of name?
    customer(i).name := customer(i).name + ch
end loop
```

Reading the *address* field is similar. Since the *phoneNumber* field contains no blanks and ends at the end of a line, it can be read using token-oriented input.

BINDING TO RECORDS

When using the **record** data type, it is common to keep referencing a particular record. For example, the **get** statement in the *readRecords* procedure references the *customer(i)* record three times, once for each field. We can avoid re-writing the name of a record such as *customer(i)* by using the **bind** construct:

> **bind var** *c* **to** *customer(i)*
> **get** *: inFile, c.name, c.address, c.phoneNumber*

The **bind** construct declares *c* as a new name for *customer(i)*. The keyword **var** means *c* can be changed, as happens in the **get** statement here. Since *c* is just a re-naming of *customer(i)*, any change to *c* is also a change to *customer(i)*. (Note: a change to *i* during the scope of *c* does not affect which record it is bound to.)

We can bind to more than one thing at a time; for example:

> **bind var** *a* **to** *customer(j)*, **var** *b* **to** *customer(j + 1)*
> **if** *a.name* > *b.name* **then**
>   % *Swap a and b*
>   **const** *workSpace: custType* := *a*
>   *a* := *b*
>   *b* := *workSpace*
> **end if**

The scope of *a* and *b* lasts from the **bind** down to the end of whatever construct contains the **bind**; for example, if the **bind** occurs inside a **for** statement, then *a* and *b* can be used until **end for**. Throughout the scope of a **bind**, the variable being bound to (*customer* in this case) cannot be accessed. At the end of the scope, *customer* can again be accessed.

The **bind** construct can make programs more efficient as well as easier to read. Efficiency is gained when the item being bound to contains an index. The index requires a calculation which is performed once, at the **bind**, rather than being repeatedly re-calculated.

Although we have described **bind** only in terms of binding to records, in the general case, any variable can be bound to.

FILE MAINTENANCE

As an example of reading and writing files we will program a simple file maintenance operation. We will assume that there exists on the disk a file of *customer* rcords called *oldFile* and we want to update this file by adding new customers. The information about the new customers is in a file called *actionFile*. Each line in this file corresponds to a **transaction** that must be **posted** in the file to produce an up-to-date customer file, which we will call *newFile*. This is an example of **file maintenance**. The file *oldFile* is ordered alphabetically by *customer.name* and the transactions must also be arranged alphabetically. This program will be very similar to the merge program of a previous chapter, except that the two files being merged now contain records.

```
% The "update" program
%    Read old and action files that are both ordered
%    Merge these to produce the new ordered file
type custType:
    record
        name: string (18)
        address: string (23)
        phoneNumber: string (8)
    end record
var customer, transaction: custType
const oldFile := 1
const actionFile := 2
const newFile := 3
const dummy := "zzzzzzzzz"


procedure readRecord(fileNo: int, var c: custType)
    if eof(fileNo) then
        c.name := dummy
    else    % Read record and skip end-of-line character
        get : fileNo, c.name: 18, c.address: 23, c.phoneNumber: 8, skip
    end if
end readRecord


procedure writeRecord(fileNo: int, c: custType)
    put : fileNo, c.name: 18, c.address: 23, c.phoneNumber: 8
end writeRecord


% Do first reads to initialize customer and transaction records
readRecord(oldFile, customer)
readRecord(actionFile, transaction)


loop
    exit when customer.name = dummy and
            transaction.name = dummy
    if customer.name < transaction.name then
        writeRecord(newFile, customer)
```

> *readRecord(oldFile, customer)*
> **else**
> > *writeRecord(newFile, transaction)*
> > *readRecord(actionFile, transaction)*
> **end if**
> **end loop**

This program uses the *dummy* name, which is set to all *z*'s, as a way to signify the end of either the old file or the action file. This *dummy* is never read or written, but instead is used as the value of the *name* field when the corresponding file has reached its end of file. Since this *dummy* come alphabetically after any real name, *dummy* forces remaining records in either the old or action file to be written to the new file.

This program has used *custType* as the type of formal parameters. This allowed all fields of a record to be passed to a procedure by just passing the record.

CHAPTER 15 SUMMARY

In this chapter we introduced programming language constructs for manipulating records. The following important terms were discussed:

Record — a collection of fields of information. For example, a record might be composed of a name field, an address field, and a telephone number field.

record type — the Turing construct for records. For example, this declaration establishes a record type called *direcEntry* with name, address, and telephone number fields.

> **type** *direcEntry:*
> > **record**
> > > *name:* **string** *(18)*
> > > *address:* **string** *(23)*
> > > *phoneNumber:* **string** *(8)*
> > **end record**
> > **var** *client: direcEntry*

client is a variable whose type is a record.

Array of records — to declare an array of records of the record type *direcEntry* we use the declaration:

> **var** *phoneBook:* **array** *1..50* **of** *direcEntry*

This creates an array of 50 records where each record has the same fields as *client*. We write *phoneBook(5).name* to refer to the name field of the fifth record in the array.

Assigning records — if two record variables are of the same type as each other, one can be assigned to the other by a single assignment statement. For example, we can write

$$phoneBook(5) := client$$

to assign the three fields of *client* to the corresponding three fields of *phoneBook(5)*.

Dataset — a file of information residing on secondary storage, typically on a disk or tape.

bind — a variable or a part of a variable can be renamed using a **bind**, for example:

$$\textbf{bind var } c \textbf{ to } customer(i)$$

This makes *c* stand for the *customer(i)*. The keyword **var** specifies that *c* can be changed.

Character-oriented input — this is a method of input in which the number of characters to be read is given explicitly, for example

$$\textbf{get } c: 14$$

This reads *14* characters into variable *c*.

CHAPTER 15 EXERCISES

The exercises for this chapter are based on a data processing system to be used by Apex Plumbing Supplies. For each of its customers, Apex has a record with the fields:

Name	(20 char)
Address	(20 char)
Balance	(integer)
Credit limit	(integer)

These records are entered from the keyboard. However, they are to be transferred to a disk file. A sample of the data is shown:

Abbot Plumbing	94 N.Elm	3116	50000
Durable Fixit	247 Forest Hill	0	10000
Erico Plumbing	54 Gormley	9614	5000
...			

The exercises for this chapter require you to write programs for various parts of the data processing system for Apex.

1. Enter data and create a master file for Apex Plumbing Supplies. You may use the Unix editing method for this.

2. Write a program to read an old version of the master file for Apex, sort the file, creating a new master file that is guaranteed to be in alphabetic order according to the name field.

3. Write a program that takes an existing master file for Apex and creates a new master file by deleting or adding new customer records. For example, the transaction data entries for your program might be

Davis Repair	4361 Main	2511	10000
Erico Plumbing	delete	0	0

   You can assume that the transactions are in alphabetic order. If the address field of the transaction specifies *delete*, the account is to be deleted from the file; otherwise it is an addition.

4. Write a program that reads the Apex master file and outputs the list of customers whose balances exceed their credit limits.

5. Write a program that reads the Apex master file and outputs a bill for each customer whose balance is greater than zero. For example, for the file record

Davis Repair	4361 Main	2511	10000

   your program should output

   to: Davis Repair
       4361 Main

   Dear Sir or Madam:
       Please remit $25.11 for plumbing supplies.
           Thank you,

       John Apex, Pres.
       Apex Plumbing Supplies
       416 College St.

6. Write a program that updates the master file using billing and payment transactions. A billing transaction is an entry of the form

name	(columns 1−20)
amount	(columns 41−50)

   For each billing transaction, the balance of the account is to be increased by the specified amount. A payment transaction is an entry of the form

name (columns 1—20)
amount (columns 41—50)
CR (columns 51—52)

For each payment transaction, the balance of the account is to be decreased by the specified amount. The billing and payment entries are in order.

Chapter 16

DATA STRUCTURES

In the last chapter we introduced the idea of records. By using these data structures we could move a group of items of data around in the computer as a unit. Also, we can have arrays of records.

Arrays of single variables, records, and arrays of records are examples of what we generally call **data structures**. Just as we systematize our programs by attempting to write well-structured programs, we systematize the way in which data is stored. We structure data.

In this chapter we will describe other structural forms for data and give examples of how these structures are useful to us. We will describe data structures called **linked lists** and **tree structures**. There are many kinds of lists, for example, **stacks, queues, doubly linked lists**, and so on. Tree structures can be limited to **binary trees**, or may be more general.

Turing contains a feature called **pointers** that can be used to implement linked lists but it is possible to implement all of these data structures without pointers using arrays instead. We will do this first, and then in the next chapter we will show how Turing pointers can be used.

LINKED LISTS

Suppose that we had a file of records stored in an array called *data*. The records are arranged in sequence on some key. For simplicity, we will consider that each record consists only of a single field which is the key to the ordering. We know that if the order is ascending and no two keys are identical, then

$$data(i + 1) > data(i)$$

The difficulty with this kind of data structure for a file comes when a new item is to be added to the file; it must be inserted between two items. This means we would have to move all the items with a key higher than the one to be inserted, one location on in the array. For example, you can see what happens when we insert the word *dog* in this list:

	before	after inserting *dog*
data(1)	cat	cat
data(2)	duck	dog
data(3)	fox	duck
data(4)	goose	fox
data(5)	pig	goose
data(6)	—	pig

Any list that is changing with time will have additions and deletions made to it. A deletion will create a hole unless entries are moved to fill the hole.

When the list changes with time we can use the data structure called the **linked list**. In the linked list each item has two components, the data component and the linking component or **link**. We associate with each entry in the *data* array an entry in a second array of integers called *link*. The number stored in *link(i)* is the index of the next entry in the sequence of the *data* array. This means that the actual or **physical sequence** in the *data* array is different from the **logical sequence** in the list. Here is an example showing our previous list as a linked list. The start of the list is stored in the integer variable *first*.

		first	3		
data(1)	pig	*link(1)*	0
data(2)	fox	*link(2)*	4
data(3)	cat	*link(3)*	5
data(4)	goose	*link(4)*	1
data(5)	duck	*link(5)*	2
data(6)	—	*link(6)*	—

Here is a diagram of this:

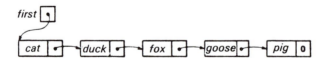

You can follow the list by beginning with the value of *first*, which is 3. The first entry will be in *data(3)*; it is *cat*. By looking then at *link(3)* you find a 5 which is the index of the next list item, *data(5)*, which is *duck*. You follow the list down until you reach a *link* whose value is 0; this is the signal that you have reached the end of the list. Other signals can be used, such as having a negative number.

INSERTING INTO A LINKED LIST

To see the merit of a linked list we must see how to insert new entries. We will add *dog* in its proper list position. We will do this first by hand; afterwards we will have to program it for the computer. We will place *dog* in *data(6)* since it is an available or free location. We must now change the values of certain of the links so that the new entry will be inserted. We must put a value into *link(6)* and change the value of the *link* of the entry before *dog*, which is *cat*, to point to *data(6)*. This means that *link(3)* must be changed to 6 and *link(6)* must be set to 5 so that the entry after *dog* is *duck*, which is *data(5)*. The linked list then becomes:

	first		3
data(1)	*pig*	*link(1)*	0
data(2)	*fox*	*link(2)*	4
data(3)	*cat*	*link(3)*	6
data(4)	*goose*	*link(4)*	1
data(5)	*duck*	*link(5)*	2
data(6)	*dog*	*link(6)*	5

Here is a diagram:

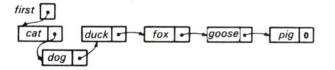

To add *dog*, one *link* must be changed and one set. No movement of the existing items in *data* is necessary. This is surely an improvement over moving half the list, on the average, to insert a new entry. The cost of this improved efficiency of operation comes in having to reserve memory space for the *link* array. This array gives the structure of the list and is stored explicitly for a linked list. In an array, the sequence or structure is implicit; each entry follows its neighbor. We will use other kinds of structures that require us to store the structure information explicitly.

MEMORY MANAGEMENT WITH LISTS

With linked lists, some of the memory is used for structure information and some for data. For any list, as the list grows, we use more memory; as it shrinks, we use less. This means we must reserve enough memory to hold the longest list that we ever expect to have. But we should not waste memory. As we stop using certain elements of the array by deleting entries, we must keep track of where they are, so when additions occur we can reuse these same elements. To keep track of the available array elements we keep them together in a second linked list. The list of available array elements does not have any useful information in the *data* part, but it is structured as a list using values in the *link* part. We must keep track of the beginning of this list so we keep the index of its beginning in a integer variable *available*.

Here is an array of 10 elements that stores our previous data items in a different set of locations and has the available space linked up:

	first	10		*available*	7
data(1)	goose		link(1)		9
data(2)	fox		link(2)		1
data(3)	—		link(3)		6
data(4)	duck		link(4)		2
data(5)	—		link(5)		0
data(6)	—		link(6)		5
data(7)	—		link(7)		3
data(8)	dog		link(8)		4
data(9)	pig		link(9)		0
data(10)	cat		link(10)		8

In these arrays there are two linked lists, one containing the actual data, the other containing elements available for use. Each list has a pointer to its start; each has a last element with a link of 0. Every element of the array is in one list or the other.

The next problem is to write a procedure for adding a new item to the list. We will develop the algorithm for this using step-by-step refinement.

PROCEDURE FOR INSERTING INTO A LINKED LIST

The first step is to construct a solution tree. We will presume the value to be added is in the variable *entryData*:

	Insert *entryData* into linked list	
Obtain storage element with index *entry* from available list	Place *entryData* in storage element *entry*	Insert storage element with index *entry* into the linked list

The expansion of the left branch of the solution tree requires us to find the index *entry* of the first element of the list of available elements and remove the element from the list. Here is the program segment that does this:

> *entry := available*
> *available := link(available)*

The middle branch is also simple. It is

> *data(entry) := entryData*

We must expand the right branch still further:

Insert storage
element with
index *entry* into
the linked list

if *entryData* goes first in list **then**
  place element at beginning of list
else find place to insert *entryData*
  and adjust links to make insertion
end if

entryData will go first in the list if either the list is empty or *entryData* is less than the first element of the list. So we can write, "if *entryData* goes first in list," in this way:

> **if** *first = null* **or** *entryData < data(first)* **then**

We have assumed that *null* is a named constant whose value is zero. We can write, "Place element at beginning of list," in this way:

> *link(entry) := first*
> *first := entry*

For the part of the program after the **else** we need to examine the entries in the list and compare them with *entryData*. The index of the element being compared we will call *next*. The index of the previously compared element we will call *previous*. We need to keep track of this previous element, because if

> *entryData < data(next)*

we must insert our element with index *entry* between *previous* and *next.*
Here is the program segment for this:

> *% Find place to insert new data*
> *previous* := *first*
> *next* := *link(first);*
> **loop**
> > **exit when** *next* = *null* **or** *entryData* < *data(next)*
> > *previous* := *next*
> > *next* := *link(next)*
>
> **end loop**
> *% Adjust links to make insertion*
> *link(previous)* := *entry*
> *link(entry)* := *next*

The whole procedure can now be written out. We are presuming that *data,*
link, first, and *available* are global to this procedure. The type of the entries
in the list is *entryType,* which could be **string** *(5)* for our example, but the
procedure would also be correct for other types such as **int**.

% Insert new data into linked list
procedure *insertData(entryData: entryType)*
> *% Obtain storage element for new data*
> **var** *entry:* **int** := *available*
> *available* := *link(available)*
> *% Place entryData in storage element*
> *data(entry)* := *entryData*
> *% See if new data goes first in list*
> **if** *first* = *null* **or** *entryData* < *data(first)* **then**
> > *link(entry)* := *first*
> > *first* := *entry*
>
> **else**
> > *% Find place to insert new data*
> > **var** *previous:* **int** := *first*
> > **var** *next:* **int** := *link(first)*
> > **loop**
> > > **exit when** *next* = *null* **or** *entryData* < *data(next)*
> > > *previous* := *next*
> > > *next* := *link(next)*
> >
> > **end loop**
> > *% Adjust links to make insertion*
> > *link(previous)* := *entry*
> > *link(entry)* := *next*
>
> **end if**

end *insertData*

So far we have ignored a potential problem in our *insertData* procedure. The conditions for both the **if** statement and the **exit when** use an element of the *data* array which may have the index *null(0)*. It seems we are in danger of having an out-of-bounds subscript. It turns out that this is not a problem because in Turing if the left part of a condition test (such as *first = null*) determines the result, then the right part (such as *entryData< data (first)*) is not evaluated.

DELETING FROM A LINKED LIST

The process of deletion is very similar. We will just record the complete procedure.

```
% Delete specified data from linked list
procedure deleteData (oldData: entry Type)
        % Find the item to be deleted
        var old: int := first
        var previous: int
        loop
            exit when data (old) = oldData
            previous := old
            old := link (old)
        end loop
        % Remove item from list
        if  first = old then
            first := link (old)
        else
            link (previous) := link (old)
        end if
        % Add storage element to free list
        link (old) := available
        available := old
end deleteData
```

Before using these two procedures we must set *first* to *null*, set *available* to *1*, and *link(i)* to *i + 1*, and so on, with the exception of the last element which should have a *null* link.

RECORDS AND NODES

We have used links that are in separate arrays from the arrays that hold the actual data values. Sometimes we collect the data and the link to form a record. For example, we could use these declarations

> **type** *nodeType:*
> > **record**
> > > *data: entryType*
> > > *link:* **int**
> > **end record**
> > **var** *list:* **array** *1..maxList* **of** *node*

Each item in the list is called a **node**. With these declarations, we refer to the data in node *i* as *list(i).data* and the link as *list(i).link*. The next chapter, which introduces the **pointer** type, gives examples of list processing using records as nodes.

STACKS

In the preceding sections we showed how to insert and delete items for a linked list. The insertions and deletions could be anywhere in the list. In each case, as the list of data items was changed, a second linked list of available storage elements was maintained. A deletion from the list of data items resulted in an addition to the list of available elements; an addition in the data list produced a deletion in the available list. The actions involving the available storage list were much simpler. This is because the additions and deletions for it always were to the beginning of that list. A list that is restricted to having entries to or removals from the beginning only is called a **stack**. The situation is similar to a stack of trays in a cafeteria. When you want a tray you take it off the top of the stack; when you are through with a tray you put it back on the top. When a list is used as a stack, we often call the pointer to the beginning of the list *top*. When an entry is removed from the top we say we have **popped** an entry off. The value of *top* must then be adjusted to point at the next entry. When we add an entry we say we have **pushed** it onto the stack.

Because a stack change only occurs at one end, it is convenient to implement a stack without using a linked list; an ordinary array will do. In our examples, a linked list is necessary for our stack of available storage elements because they are scattered all over. Stacks have other uses so we will show how a stack can be implemented using an array. We will call the array *stack*. The bottom of the stack will be in *stack(1)*, the next entry in *stack(2)*, and so on. Sorry if our stack seems to be upside down! Here is a stack of symbols:

top	*4*
stack(1)	$+$
stack(2)	$-$
stack(3)	$+$
stack(4)	$/$

This sort of stack is often used in compilers for translating arithmetic expressions into machine language.

Before using the stack we initialize it to be empty by setting *top* to zero:

$$top := 0$$

To add an item to the stack we can call the procedure *push*:

procedure *push(symbol: entryType)*
    top := top + 1
    stack(top) := symbol
end *push*

To remove the top item from the stack we can call the procedure *pop*:

procedure *pop(***var** *symbol: entryType)*
    symbol := stack(top)
    top := top − 1
end *pop*

The variable *top* and the array *stack* must be global to the *push* and *pop* procedures. Stacks may be implemented in other ways than shown here.

RECURSIVE PROCEDURES

If we want to read a list of integers and output it in reverse order then we can program it this way using a stack.

    % Output numbers in reverse order
    loop
        exit when there are no more numbers to read
        Read number *n*
        Push number *n* onto the stack
    end loop
    loop
        exit when stack is empty
        Pop number *n* from the stack
        Write number *n*
    end loop

Another way of programming this is by using a recursive procedure, which is a procedure that calls itself. In the execution of a recursive procedure there is an implicit stack.

```
% The "reverse" program
procedure outputInReverse
    var n: int
    get n
    if n not = − 1 then
        outputInReverse   % Output any other numbers
        put n
    end if
end outputInReverse
outputInReverse
```

Here is a sample display:

```
    5
    10
    − 1
    10
    5
```

The main program calls *outputInReverse*. This causes local variable *n* to be created and *5* is read into it. Next, *outputInReverse* calls itself, which creates a new local variable called *n*, which has *10* read into it. These two local variables are quite separate from each other even though they have the same name. Next, *outputInReverse* calls itself again, but finding that *− 1* has been read it returns. This return is to the activation of *outputInReverse* where *n* is *10*. After *10* is output, the return goes back to the activation in which *n* is *5* and *5* is output. Then a return is made to the main program and execution is complete.

Each new recursive call to *outputInReverse* creates a new copy of local variable *n*. These variables are stacked in a LIFO manner (last in first out), so that each return finds the previous value of *n*. Because of this implicit creation of a stack of variables, we do not have to implement one.

QUEUES

Another specialized type of list is a **queue**. For it, entries are made at the end of the list, deletions are made from the beginning. Rather than search for the end of the list each time an entry is made, it is usual to have a pointer indicating the last entry. Queues involve using things in a manner referred to as, **First in first out** (FIFO) or, **First come first served**

(FCFS). This is the usual way for a queue waiting for tickets at a box office to operate.

A queue is not as easy as a stack to implement using an array. It is always growing at one end and shrinking at the other. If an array is used, when the growth reaches the maximum limit of the array, we start it at the beginning again. Here is a queue of people waiting for a bus. We have a maximum of 8 elements. Five people are in the queue. The first person to board the bus is named *Green.*

first 6		*last 2*
queue(1)		*Whalon*
queue(2)		*Johnston*
queue(3)		—
queue(4)		—
queue(5)		—
queue(6)		*Green*
queue(7)		*Linnemann*
queue(8)		*Jacobs*

Here are procedures used to *enter* or *leave* this queue. We will use a constant named *maxQueue* whose value is *8* so we can easily change the maximum size of the queue. Before using these procedures the queue can be initialized to be empty by setting *first* to *1* and *last* to *maxQueue.*

```
const maxQueue := 8
procedure enter(name: entryType)
    last := last + 1
    if last > maxQueue then
        last := 1
    end if
    queue(last) := name
end enter

procedure leave(var  name: entryType)
    name := queue(first)
    first := first + 1
    if first > maxQueue then
        first := 1
    end if
end leave
```

We have used wrap around or modulo arithmetic in that we wanted *first* and *last* to keep increasing until they reach *maxQueue* and then to wrap back to *1.* The **if** statements in the *enter* and *leave* procedures make sure that wrap around occurs. There is a **mod** operator that accomplishes wrap around by returning the remainder of dividing one number by another. We can write

first := (first **mod** *maxQueue) + 1*

This means to set *first* to one more than the remainder of *first* divided by *maxQueue.* As long as *first* has a value of *1, 2* up to one less than *queueSize*, then this just adds one to *first.* But if *first* equals *maxQueue* then **mod** returns a value of zero which added to one causes *first* to be assigned the value one. So we can shorten the *enter* and *leave* procedures by using **mod**.

Queues can be implemented by linked lists as well as by simple arrays. Queues are used in **operating systems** such as Unix that operate multi-user computer systems. Different jobs requiring service are placed in different queues, depending on the demands they are making on the system's resources and the priority that they possess to be given service. Also, in programs that simulate other systems such as factories, queues are maintained to determine the length of time jobs are required to wait to be served when other jobs are competing for the same production facilities.

TREES

A linked list is an efficient way of storing a list that is changing with time, but it introduces an inefficiency in retrieval of information from the list. In an earlier chapter we saw that a binary search for an item in a list is much more efficient for long lists than a linear search. Unfortunately, there is no possibility of doing a binary search in a linked list; we must start at the beginning and trace our way through. There is no direct access to the middle of a linked list. It is for this reason that a more complicated data structure called a **tree** is used. We can get the efficiency of a binary search by having the elements linked into a **binary tree structure**.

To show how a binary tree is formed, we will look at the example of our list of names of animals:

```
        3   → cat
     2       → dog
             duck
  1          → fox
             goose
             pig
             snake
```

To do a binary search we should begin in the middle. (We have added *snake* to the list so the list has a middle entry.) If we are looking for the name *cat* we find that *cat* < *fox*, so we then discard the middle entry and the last half of the list. The next comparison is with the middle entry of the remaining list, namely with *dog*. Since *cat* < *dog* we eliminate the last half of the smaller list. By this time, we are down to one entry, which is the one we are looking for. It took three comparisons to get there. A linear search for *cat* would, as it happens, have taken only 1 comparison. On the **average**, the binary search takes fewer comparisons than a linear search. A short list is not a good example for showing off the efficiency of binary searching, but it is much easier to write out all the possibilities.

We will now look at the binary tree that would be used to give the same searching technique. Here it is:

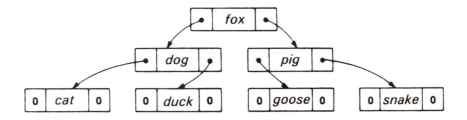

Each data element in the tree structure consists of three parts, the *data* itself and two links that we designate as *leftLink* and *rightLink*. The word *fox* is in a special position in the tree, called the **root**. From *fox* we have **branches** going to the left to *dog* and to the right to *pig*. In a sense, *dog* is in the root position of a smaller tree, what we call the **left subtree** of the main tree. *pig* is at the root of the **right subtree**. The words *cat, duck, goose,* and *snake* are at the end of branches and are called **leaves** of the tree. All the data elements are in **nodes** of the tree; *fox* is the **root node** and *cat* is a **leaf node**. To search for an entry in a binary tree, we compare the element in the root node with the one we are seeking. If the root is the same, we have found it. If the root is larger we follow the *leftLink* to the next entry; if smaller, we follow the *rightLink*. We are then at the root of a smaller tree, a tree with half as many entries as the original. The process is then repeated until the looked-for data is found.

Here is our tree structure as it might be stored in three arrays called *data, leftLink,* and *rightLink*. The variable *root* holds the link to the root element. We have jumbled up the sequence to show that the actual order in the *data* array makes no difference. A zero link is used to indicate the end of a branch.

		root	4

	data	*leftLink*	*rightLink*
(1)	goose	*0*	*0*
(2)	snake	*0*	*0*
(3)	dog	*6*	*7*
(4)	fox	*3*	*5*
(5)	pig	*1*	*2*
(6)	cat	*0*	*0*
(7)	duck	*0*	*0*

Starting at *root*, we find the root is in *data(4)*. *leftLink(4)* leads us to *data(3)* which is *dog*. *rightLink(3)* leads us to *data(7)* which is *duck*. You can see how it works.

A tree structure is a **hierarchical structure** for data; each comparison takes us one **level** down in the tree. The file system of Unix has a tree structure. It has a root directory named "/" and contains internal nodes that are file directories. The leaves of the tree are data files.

ADDING TO A TREE

To add a data item to a tree structure we simply look for the element in the tree in the usual manner, starting at the root. If the element is not already in the tree, we will come in the search to a link that is null (zero). This is where the element belongs. In our example, if we want to add *cow*, we would start at *fox*, then go to *dog*, then to *cat.* At this point we would want to follow the right link of *cat*, but we find a zero. If we stored the new entry in *data(8)*, we would change *rightLink(6)* to *8* and set

data(8)	*leftLink(8)*	*rightLink(8)*
cow	*0*	*0*

As we add items to a tree, the tree becomes lopsided; it is not well balanced. Searching efficiency depends on trees being **well balanced**, so that in an information retrieval data bank using a tree structure, an effort should be made to keep the tree balanced. We started with a balanced tree and it became unbalanced by adding a new item. If a tree is grown from scratch using the method we have described for adding a new entry, it is unlikely to be well balanced.

DELETING FROM A TREE

Removing an entry from a tree is a more difficult operation than adding an entry. The same method is used to find the element to be deleted, but then the problem comes. It is not difficult if both links of the element to be deleted are zero, that is, if it is a leaf. We just chop it off and make the link pointing to it zero. If only one link is zero it is similar to an ordinary linked list and deletion is similar to that. We just bypass it.

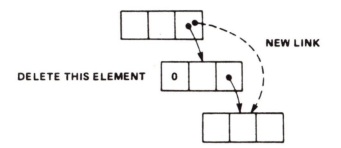

If neither link is zero in the element to be deleted, we must move another element into its position in the tree. In our original tree, if *fox* is to be deleted, it must be replaced by an element that is larger then all other elements in the left subtree or smaller than all the elements in the right subtree. This means that either *duck* or *goose* is the only possible choice. The one to be moved must be deleted in its present position before being placed in its new position.

Remember, in a linked structure, we never move a data item from its physical location in the data array; we only change the links to alter its logical position.

LISTING A TREE IN ORDER

Trees are used where searching and updating are the main activities. Sometimes we must list the contents of a tree. We must be systematic about it and be sure to list every node. We will show how to list it alphabetically.

An algorithm for listing a tree alphabetically can be written in this way:

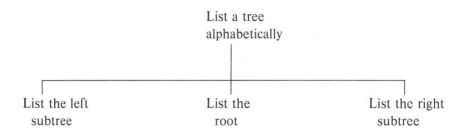

We see that we have described our algorithm in terms of three parts. The middle part, "List the root," is easy, but the other two require us to, "List a tree." This is exactly what our problem is, to "List a tree." We have defined the solution to a problem in terms of the original problem. This kind of definition is called a **recursive** definition of a solution. It seems rather pointless, as if we were just going in a circle, but it really is not. The reason it is not pointless is that the tree we are attempting to list when we say, "List the left subtree," is a smaller tree than the original tree when we said "List a tree." When we try to list the left subtree we get this solution:

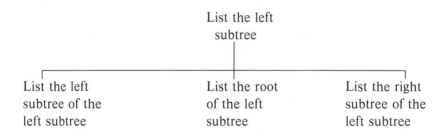

This time the left subtree of the left subtree has to be listed. It is smaller still. The algorithm is again repeated. Each application of the algorithm is on a smaller tree, until you reach a point where there is a zero link and there is **no** left subtree at all. Then the action of listing it is to do nothing: no tree, no listing. That is how recursive algorithms work. In programming terms, the algorithm calls itself over and over, each time to do a reduced task, until the task is easy to do.

In Turing a procedure may indeed call itself as we saw in the example of displaying a list of numbers in reverse order. Here is a Turing procedure for listing a tree in alphabetic order, given that its root is *root* and its data and links *data*, *leftLink* and *rightLink* are global variables.

```
procedure listTree(root: int)
    if root not = null then
        listTree(leftLink(root))
        put data(root)
        listTree(rightLink(root))
    end if
end listTree
```

Each time the procedure is entered for a new subtree, a different node is referred to by *root*. For this job, a recursive procedure is very easy to program. It is much more difficult to program this job non-recursively. In a recursive algorithm, each time a program calls itself, a record must be kept of the point in the program where the procedure was called, so that control can return properly. Each new activation of the procedure gets new parameters and local variables; in this example there are no local variables but each activation of *listTree* gets a different value of *root*. As the procedure recursively calls itself, a list is built of the points of return. Each point of return is added on top of the stack of other points of return. Finding the way back involves taking return points, one after the other, off this stack. This is all set up automatically by the compiler.

CHAPTER 16 SUMMARY

In previous chapters we have presented arrays and records, which are data structures provided by Turing. In this chapter we showed how to build up new data structures using arrays. Some of these new data structures use links to give the ordering of data items. The link (or links) for a given item gives the array index of the next item. The following important terms were discussed:

Linked list — a linked sequence of data items. The next item in the list is found by following a link from the present item. The physical order of a collection of items, as given by their positions in an array, is different from their logical order, as given by the links.

Inserting into a linked list — a new data item can be inserted by changing links, without actually moving data items.

Deleting from a linked list — a data item can be deleted by changing links, without moving data items.

Available list — the collection of data elements currently not in use.

Stack — a data structure that allows data items to be added, or pushed, onto one end and removed, or popped, from the same end. A stack does not require the use of links. A stack handles data items in a last-in-first-out (LIFO) manner.

Queue — a data structure that allows data items to be added at one end and removed from the other. A queue handles data items in a first-in-first-out (FIFO) manner.

Binary tree — a data structure in which each item or node has two links, a left link and a right link. The left link of a node locates another node and with it a subtree. Similarly, the right link locates a subtree. There is a unique beginning node called the root. If both links of a particular node are null, meaning they do not currently locate other nodes, then the node is called a leaf.

Recursive procedure — a procedure that calls itself. Each time the procedure is called, it is allocated new formal parameters and local variables.

CHAPTER 16 EXERCISES

1.   The Fly-By-Nite Airline company is computerizing its reservations system. There are four Fly-By-Nite flights with the following capacities:

flight #1	5 seats
flight #2	5 seats
flight #3	8 seats
flight #4	4 seats

The information for passenger reservations is to be stored in a linked list. At some point during the booking period, the following diagram might represent the current passenger bookings.

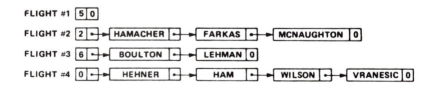

The above diagram shows the first element in each list holding the number of seats remaining. Each succeeding element holds the name of a passenger and either points to the next element or holds a 0 to indicate the end of the linked list.

In order to set up such a linked list system you will need two arrays. The first, called *flight*, will contain the four *first* elements. Each of these elements holds two pieces of information, the number of seats remaining and the location of the first passenger.

The second array called *passenger* holds all the passengers. If all seats on all flights are taken, there will be *capacity = 22* passengers. Hence *passenger* will need a maximum of *capacity* locations. Each element of the *passenger* array contains two pieces of information, the passenger's name and the location of the next passenger, if any.

The *passenger* array must be declared as an array of records in order to contain two different data types:

> **type** *entry:*
> > **record**
> > > *name:* **string** *(20)*
> > > *link:* **int**
> > **end record**
> **var** *passenger:* **array** *1..capacity* **of** *entry*

This will designate element *j* of *passenger* to contain two parts:

> *passenger(j).name* and *passenger(j).link*

Before any events happen, the free locations must be linked together. Arrange that each *passenger(j).link* contains a value *j + 1*, except *passenger(capacity).link* which contains a *0* as end of the list.

A variable *available* contains the location of the head of this chain of available locations. For the example given above, *available* contains *10* and *passenger* could have these values:

passenger(1)
  name Hamacher
  link 6

passenger(2)
  name Boulton
  link 5

passenger(3)
  name Ham
  link 8

passenger(4)
  name Hehner
  link 3

passenger(5)
  name Lehman
  link 0

passenger(6)
  name Farkas
  link 7

passenger(7)
  name McNaughton
  link 0

passenger(8)
  name Wilson
  link 9

passenger(9)
  name Vranesic
  link 0

passenger(10)
  name
  link 11

.
.
.

passenger(22)
  name
  link 0

The reservation system is to accept four types of transactions:

Type 1 is a request for a reservation. The data entry contains the code word *res*, name of the passenger, and the flight number.

Type 2 is a request to cancel a reservation. The data entry contains the code word *can*, name of passenger, and the flight number.

Type 3 is a request to display the number of seats remaining on a specified flight. The data entry contains the code word *seats* and a flight number.

Type 4 is a request to display a passenger list for the flight indicated. The data entry contains the code word *list* and a flight number.

Each type of transaction is to be handled by a procedure. *Passenger, flight* and *available* are global variables; all other variables are local to the procedure in which they are used. Here are descriptions of the procedures:

add(who,number). Adds passenger *who* to flight *number*. If that flight is filled, a message is displayed to that effect. The procedure *add* uses a location in *passenger* and must update *available*.

cancel(who,number). Cancels the reservation made in the name of *who* on flight *number*. The location in *passenger* is returned to the free storage pool. The *available* list must be updated.

info(number). Displays the number of seats remaining on flight *number*.

display(number). Displays a passenger list for flight *number*.

The data should simulate a real reservation system in that input of types 1, 2, 3, 4 should be intermixed. It would seem reasonable to assume that most cancellations would be made by persons holding reservations. However, people being what they are, you should not assume too much. In order to get your system off the ground, several reservation entries should be first.

Write and test each procedure as a main procedure before putting the procedures together. Write *display* first and call it from *add* or *cancel* to help in debugging. Be sure to test unusual situations as well as the obvious ones.

Chapter 17

POINTERS AND COLLECTIONS

The previous chapter introduced data structures and showed how linked lists can be built up using arrays with integers as links. We will now introduce new language features, called pointers and collections, that are convenient and efficient for building linked lists. We will show how data structures such as trees are represented using these new features.

COLLECTIONS COMPARED TO ARRAYS

An **array** is a data structure whose elements are located by indexes that are typically integers. For example, the indexes for array *a* are *1, 2,* and *3*:

> **var** *a*: **array** *1..3* **of** *elementType*
> **var** *i: 1..3*   % *An index for array a*

A **collection** is similar in that it is a data structure whose elements are located by indexes, but now the indexes must be declared to be **pointers**:

> **var** *c:* **collection of** *elementType*
> **var** *p:* **pointer to** *c*   % *An index for c*

If *elementType* is **string**, then elements of *a* and *c* can be assigned values this way:

> *a(i)* := *"Hello"*
> *c(p)* := *"Goodbye"*

The main difference between arrays and collections is that an array has a fixed number of elements (*a* has three elements), and a collection has a changing number of elements. The elements of a collection are created (allocated) using a statement called **new**, and they are deleted (de-allocated) by a statement called **free**.

CREATING AND DELETING ELEMENTS OF COLLECTIONS

When a collection is declared, it starts out empty, containing no elements. The **new** statement creates a new element of the collection:

new *c, p*   *% Create element of collection c*

This finds space for a new element of collection *c* and sets pointer *p* to locate this space. The **new** statement requires that the pointer variable *p* be declared as a **pointer** to collection *c*. Note that the declaration of *p* does not automatically create an element of the collection. To delete the element located by *p*, we use:

free *c, p*   *% Delete element of c*

Once this element has been freed, *p* no longer locates an element of *c*, so *p* cannot be used as an index of *c*.

We now combine these statements into an example in which we create an element of *c*, set it to "*Andropov*", assign its value to variable *s*, and then delete the element.

```
type  elementType: string
var  c: collection of  elementType
var  p: pointer to  c
new  c, p                        % Create element of c
c(p) := "Andropov"               % Set value of element
...
var  s: string := c(p)           % Access the element
...
free  c, p                       % Delete the element
```

Generally we use collections and pointers in more interesting ways than this; we commonly use them to build linked lists.

USING POINTERS IN LINKED LISTS

In the last chapter we showed how to use arrays to implement linked lists. Collections are used in a similar way, but they provide an advantage over arrays: with collections we create elements only as we need them. By contrast, all elements of an array are created at the point of the array's declaration, and we cannot increase or decrease their number.

We will re-write the procedure named *insertData* from the last chapter to illustrate the use of collections. This procedure inserts new data values into an ordered list. The procedure will be modified in two ways. First, we will use records instead of parallel arrays named *data* and *link* (this was discussed in the last chapter). Second, we will use a collection of these records.

We show the declaration of the collection, named *node* and its record; these declarations contain two new language features, called **forward** and *nil*, which we will explain.

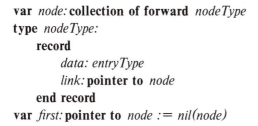

var *node:* **collection of forward** *nodeType*
type *nodeType:*
   record
      data: entryType
      link: **pointer to** *node*
   end record
   var *first:* **pointer to** *node* := *nil(node)*

The keyword **forward** appears in the declaration of the collection to indicate that *nodeType*'s declaration occurs following the declaration of *node*. Ordinarily, Turing requires declaration-before-use, meaning an identifier cannot be used before its declaration. Declaration-before-use is not possible with linked lists involving collections because the collection declaration refers to its record type and also the record contains a pointer referring to the collection. This vicious circle is resolved by use of the **forward** keyword in the collection declaration.

The pointer called *first* is initialized to be *nil(node)*. This is a special pointer value that is used to indicate that the pointer does not currently locate an element of the collection. In the last chapter, we used a constant called *null* set to zero for this purpose when our links were integers.

Here is our new version of the *insertData* procedure:

```
% Insert new data into linked list
procedure insertData (entryData: entryType)
    var entry: pointer to node
    new node, entry   % Obtain storage element for new data
    node (entry).data := entryData   % Place data in element
    % See if new data goes first in list
    if first = nil(node) or entryData < node (first).data then
        node (entry).link := first
        first := entry
    else
        % Find place to insert new data
        var previous: pointer to node := first
        var next: pointer to node := node (first).link
        loop
            exit when next = nil(node) or
                entryData < node (next).data
            previous := next
            next := node (next).link
```

```
        end loop
        % Adjust links to make insertion
        node(previous).link := entry
        node(entry).link := next
    end if
end insertData
```

As you can see, this procedure has the same form as that of the previous chapter. The only changes are (1) the **new** statement allocates the new element, (2) *null* is now written as *nil(node)*, and (3) each reference to the *data* and *link* arrays is replaced by a reference to the *node* collection. The *deleteData* procedure in the previous chapter can be re-written using these same changes, and by de-allocating elements using the **free** statement.

IMPLEMENTING A TREE USING POINTERS

The previous chapter introduced the tree data structure and showed how it can be used to keep data in order. We will now show how trees can be conveniently implemented by using pointers and collections. We will develop a program that reads lines of text, enters these lines in alphabetic order into the tree and finally prints these lines in alphabetic order.

Here are the declarations and the main part of our program:

```
% The "linesort" program
%   Read lines from a file, then print them in sorted order.
var node: collection of forward nodeType
type nodePointer: pointer to node
type nodeType:
    record
        data: string     % Holds one line of data
        left, right: nodePointer     % Locates sub-trees.
    end record
var root: nodePointer := nil(node)  % Tree starts empty

...the enterLine and printLines procedures go here...

%     The data structure used is a binary tree built using collections.
% Successive lines are inserted as new leaves in the tree.
% Read and enter lines; then print all lines.
const fileNo := 1
var line: string
loop
    exit when eof(fileNo)
    get : fileNo, line:*  % Read next line
```

```
      enterLine (line)     % Insert line into binary tree
   end loop
   printLines(root)   % Print all lines in tree
```

The tree consists of nodes, each of which has a *data* field to contain the text line, as well as pointer fields called *left* and *right*. The *left* pointer locates the left sub-tree of the node, unless *left* is equal to *nil(node)*. The *right* pointer is similar. The *root* pointer locates the first node in the tree; it is initialized to *nil(node)* because the tree is originally empty.

The main part of the program repeatedly calls the *enterLine* subprogram to build up the tree a node at a time. Each node will contain one line and the tree will be in alphabetic order from left to right. The *printLines* subprogram traverses the tree from left to right, printing out the lines in alphabetic order.

ENTERING DATA INTO THE TREE

The algorithm for "Adding to a Tree" was given in the previous chapter. The idea is that we find the place to add new data by starting at the tree's root and following links down the tree. At each node, we go left if the new data is to precede this node and right otherwise. When this leads us to a link that is null, we know that this is the link that is to be set to locate the new data. Here is the subprogram.

```
procedure enterLine(line: string )  % "line" is inserted into tree
    var L: nodePointer
    new node, L     % Allocate then fill in new node L
    node(L).data := line
    node(L).left := nil(node)
    node(L).right := nil(node)
    if root = nil(node) then
        root := L     % Attach first node
    else
        var p: nodePointer := root
        loop      % Search for place to attach new node
            const nilNode := nil(node)
            bind var n to node(p) % Shorten name to n
            if line < n.data then
                if n.left = nilNode then
                    n.left := L  % Attach new node here
                    exit
                else
                    p := n.left   % Search left sub-tree
                end if
```

```
            else
                if n.right = nilNode then
                    n.right := L  % Attach new node here
                    exit
                else
                    p := n.right  % Search right subtree
                end if
            end if
        end loop
    end if
end enterLine
```

Notice that we have used a **bind** declaration to shorten the name of *node(p)* to *n*. We used the keyword **var** in the **bind** because *n* is to be assigned to. Each time through the loop, *n* is bound to a new node of the tree. In list processing, it is fairly common to have multiple accesses to a particular node. We bind to the node to shorten the program and to indicate to the compiler that it should try to generate efficient code to access the node.

PRINTING THE LINES IN THE TREE

The tree can be listed in alphabetic order by a recursive subprogram (see last chapter). For a given node, the subprogram (1) prints the lines in the left subtree, (2) prints the node's line, and (3) prints the lines of the right subtree. Since the left and right subtrees are themselves trees, the subprogram calls itself recursively to print these subtrees. This can be written as:

```
% Recursive procedure that prints lines in tree,
%   moving from left to right in the tree
procedure printLines(p: nodePointer)
    if p not = nil(node) then
        printLines(node(p).left)  % Print left subtree
        put node(p).data   % Print this node
        printLines(node(p).right)  % Print right subtree
    end if
end printLines
```

The complete program can now be assembled by inserting the *enterLine* and *printLines* into the main program.

The program can be expanded in a number of useful ways. For example, it could be modified so there is only one entry in the tree for identical lines, so the alphabetic listing prints only lines which are distinct from each other. Another enhancement would be to use only part of the line, say characters 12 through 24, to do the ordering.

The *enterLine* procedure could be generalized to handle nodes of the form:

type *nodeType:*
    record
        key: keyType
        ...other fields of the node...
        left, right: nodePointer
    end *record*

The *key* field is used for ordering the nodes and other fields contain various information associated with the node.

IMPLEMENTATION OF POINTERS AND COLLECTIONS

Pointers and collections provide a facility for creating and destroying data items; these items are elements of collections. The elements must have storage allocated for them in the computer's memory. The part of the memory where storage is allocated is called the **heap**. The heap consists of a set of currently allocated collection elements together with unused space left over to be used for further allocations. When the **new** statement is executed, part of the unused space is set aside to represent the new element. The **free** statement converts an active element back into unused space.

Since the heap is only so big, it may eventually run out of space. For example, we can execute this loop only so long before our program fails:

type *t:* **array** *1..10000* **of int**
var *c:* **collection of** *t*
var *p:* **pointer to** *c*
loop   % *Repeated allocations without freeing*
    new *c, p*   % *Allocate 10,000 more integers*
    ...
end loop

This loop is not very clever, because it keeps allocating more and more elements of *c*, but never frees any of them.

The problem of running out of space in the heap is called **heap exhaustion**. When the **new** statement cannot allocate space for a collection element, because of heap exhaustion, the associated pointer is set to nil. For example, these statements attempt to create an element and test to see if this was successful.

new *c, p*
if *p* = *nil(c)* **then**   % *Was element created?*
    ...

In many programs, we do not make this test, because we simply assume that there is enough space in the heap to handle the problem at hand.

In Turing it is not allowed to declare collections inside subprograms. This restriction is imposed so that there is never the possibility of a collection disappearing, along with the space allocated to it, when the subprogram returns to its point of call.

PROBLEMS WITH POINTERS

The obvious and efficient way to represent a pointer in a computer is as a memory address. This address is actually an integer that locates the element in the computer's memory. An address is efficient because it can be directly followed to find the element. Unfortunately this implementation can cause serious difficulties in two situations. The first is the case of an uninitialized pointer, which may contain an arbitrary address. Assigning a value to the (non-existent) element located by this pointer is very dangerous, because the value will update some arbitrary part of memory, corrupting seemingly unrelated data or programs.

The second situation is caused by **dangling pointers**. We say a pointer is dangling if it seems to locate an element but the element has been freed, as happens here with q:

> **var** c: **collection of string**
> **var** p, q: **pointer to** c
> **new** c, p
> $q := p$ % *Now q and p locate same element*
> ...
> **free** c, p % *Delete element located by p*

After p's element has been freed, q still seems to locate the deleted element. The space for p's element may be allocated for some unrelated purpose. If we try to use q, as in:

> $c(q) :=$ "*Big surprise!* "

The string assigned to $c(q)$ may modify seemingly unrelated data.

The Turing compiler developed at the University of Toronto provides checks that detect the use of uninitialized and dangling pointers, so these are not dangerous. We say that this implementation of Turing is **faithful** to the definition of the Turing language, because any undefined behavior such as use of a dangling pointer is necessarily detected.

This checking, like other checking such as seeing that array indexes are in range, requires extra time and space at run time. When the compiler is instructed to generate highly efficient code, these checks are omitted; as a result, run-time problems such as dangling pointers, uninitialized variables and out-of-bounds subscripts go undetected. It is unwise to omit these run-time checks, except in heavily used programs where performance is critical.

CHAPTER 17 SUMMARY

This chapter has introduced pointers and collections and has shown how they can be used to build linked lists. The following important terms were discussed.

Collection — a set of elements. The set starts out empty. For example, collection *c* whose elements are strings is declared by:

> **var** *c:* **collection of string**

Pointer — an index to locate an element of a particular collection. A pointer *p* to collection *c* is declared by:

> **var** *p:* **pointer to** *c*

Allocate — create a new element of a collection. This is accomplished by the **new** statement:

> **new** *c, p*   % *Create element of c to be located by p*

De-allocate — delete an element of a collection. This is accomplished by the **free** statement:

> **free** *c, p*   % *Delete element of c located by p*

Nil pointer — the pointer that explicitly locates no element. This sets *p* to be the nil pointer for collection *c:*

> *p := nil(c)*

Uninitialized pointer — a pointer that has not been assigned a value. Note that an uninitialized pointer does not locate an element of a collection and is not a nil pointer.

Dangling pointer — a pointer that seems to locate an element of a collection, but the element has been freed using a different pointer.

forward — the element type of a collection must be declared to be **forward** if this type contains a pointer to the collection, for example:

> **var** *node:* **collection of forward** *nodeType*
> **type** *nodeType:*
> > **record**
> > > *data: dataType*
> > > *next:* **pointer to** *node*
> > **end record**

The **forward** keyword secifies that *nodeType*'s declaration will be found following *node*'s declaration.

Heap — the storage used to represent elements of collection.

Pointers to the same collection *c* can be compared for equality and assigned. If *p* and *q* are equal then they locate the same element or else they are both nil. After *q := p, q* locates the same element as *p* (or is also nil). After *c(q) := c(p)*, the element located by *q* has the same value as the element located by *p*.

CHAPTER 17 EXERCISES

1. Rewrite the *deleteData* procedure of Chapter 16 using pointers.

2. Using pointers, computerize the Fly-By-Nite airline company described in exercise 1 of Chapter 16.

3. Consider the *printLines* procedure given in this chapter. How can it be modified to print the lines in backwards order, that is, from Z to A rather than from A to Z?

4. Define a collection called *person* whose elements are records with fields for the person's name, sex, father, spouse, first-born, and younger sibling. These last four fields are pointers to the same collection. Assuming that elements of the collections have been appropriately interconnected using these pointers, write four procedures which accept a pointer to an element and (a) output the person's children, (b) output the person's ancestors, (c) output the person's descendants, and (d) output the person's patriarchal descendent family tree.

5. Write a program that reads in lines of a file, sorts them and prints them in order, deleting multiple copies of identical lines. Use the same program developed in this chapter, but modify the *enterLine* procedure to ignore repeated copies of a particular line.

6. Write a program that reads in lines and divides each line into words. A word is defined as a sequence of letters surrounded by non-letters. Print a cross reference, which is an alphabetic listing of the words, where each word is followed by a list of the line numbers where the word occurred.

Chapter 18

MODULES

This chapter introduces a programming construct called a **module**. This construct is similar to a subprogram in that it is used for dividing a program into parts. A module is commonly used to collect together variable declarations with the subprograms that operate on these variables.

The module construct is a relatively new invention; it does not appear in programming languages such as Fortran, PL/1, and Pascal. It first appeared in the Simula language, and is available in newer languages such as Clu, Euclid, Ada, and Turing. (A module is called by various names; in Simula, it is called a **class**, in Clu it is a **cluster**, and in Ada it is a **package**.)

Before introducing modules, we will review the purpose of subprograms.

USE OF SUBPROGRAMS

In previous chapters, we have shown how subprograms are used for separating a program into smaller units. This separation helps us to construct programs out of parts, where each part (subprogram) can be separately designed and tested. This is called the divide-and-conquer strategy for programming.

We can often save subprograms and use them in future programs. For example, in the chapter introducing subprograms, we developed the *intDollar* function that converts integers to dollar amounts.

The step-by-step instructions that make up a program are called an algorithm. When we write a subprogram, we are giving a name to an algorithm; later we use this name to represent the action performed by the algorithm. For example, the name *intDollar* represents the algorithm of transforming an integer such as *216* to a dollar string such as *$2.16*.

We say *intDollar* is an **abstraction**, because it allows us to consider that *intDollar* is carried out in a single step even though it actually requires several steps. We use abstractions to help us write complex programs. With large programs, it is impossible to keep in mind all the individual actions that are to be carried out. Only by thinking in terms of abstractions rather than always in terms of individual actions are we able to develop large, reliable programs.

Just as subprograms provide abstractions for algorithms, modules provide abstractions for data. In this chapter we will develop a module called *ledger* that we will use to record and look up information. We will have an operation called *enter* that makes an entry into the ledger and an operation called *lookup* that looks up entries in the ledger. When we program the *ledger* module, we will write variable declarations and subprograms. But when we write the rest of the program, which uses *ledger*, we will ignore these declarations and subprograms. Instead we will use this abstraction: there is an object called a ledger that allows us to make entries and later look them up.

AN EXAMPLE MODULE

We will give an example program that keeps track of lost and found items. It will contain a module which will act as a ledger for the lost and found items. When an item is reported to be found, we enter it into the ledger. When an item is reported to be lost, we look up in the ledger to see if it has previously been reported to be found.

Our program will be interactive and will start by outputting:

This program keeps track of lost and found items.
Was an item lost or found (l or f)?

The program expects us to type simply *l* or *f* or if we prefer, *lost* or *found*. If we type *f* or *found*, the program outputs:

Give name of lost or found item

If we found a cat, we type:

cat

Then the program outputs:

Give one line description of found cat

We might type:

Black and white. About 6 months old. Phone 489–9681

The program records this information. It is now ready for another report of a lost or found item, so again it outputs:

Was an item lost or found (l or f)?

Suppose that a person has lost a dog, so the person types *l* or *lost*. The program responds with:

Give name of lost or found item

So the person types:

dog

Assuming no dogs have been reported found, the program outputs

Sorry, no report of found dog

Then the program asks for the next report of a lost or found item. If we report that we have lost a cat, the program outputs:

Description of found cat

Black and white. About 6 months old. Phone 489−9671

We have simplified the program to keep it small. We have no way of deleting an entry once the owner of a lost item has re-claimed it. Also, if too many entries are made, the program fails without warning. Worse yet, if several of the same kind of items are found, for example several cats are found, our lookup operation will always locate only the oldest entry. These flaws will be removed later in this chapter in a more realistic program, but right now we want to keep things simple.

We will now show how a module can be used to represent a ledger in which found items are recorded and looked up. We will represent each entry as a **record** with two fields. The first field gives the name of the item and the second field gives its description:

```
type entryType:
    record
        name: string (25)   % Name of found item
        description: string
    end record
```

The entries in the ledger will be held in an array named *entries.*

```
const ledgerSize := 100   % Maximum number of entries
var entries: array 1..ledgerSize of entryType
var numberEntries: 0..ledgerSize := 0  % How many entries
```

The first entry will be put in *entries (1)*, the second in *entries (2)*, and so on. Each lookup is performed by sequentially searching the array from its beginning. The entries will be kept in order of arrival. An explanation follows the listing of the program. Here is the program.

```
      % The "lost" program
      % Simplified program to keep track of lost and found items
      % Module for recording and looking up items
1     module ledger
2         export (enter, lookup, entryType)
```

```
3              type entryType:
4                  record
5                      name: string (25)
6                      description: string
7                  end record

8              const ledgerSize := 100  % Maximum number of entries
9              var entries: array 1..ledgerSize of entryType
10             var numberEntries: 0..ledgerSize := 0  % How many entries

11             procedure enter(entry: entryType)
12                 numberEntries := numberEntries + 1
13                 entries(numberEntries) := entry
14             end enter

15             procedure lookup(var query: entryType,
16                 var found: boolean )
17                 found := false   % Start by assuming no such entry
18                 for i: 1..numberEntries
19                     if query.name = entries(i).name then
20                         query.description := entries(i).description
21                         found := true
22                         exit
23                     end if
24                 end for
25             end lookup

26         end ledger

           % Use ledger for handling lost and found reports
27         put "This program keeps track of lost and found items"
28         loop   % Infinite loop handling each report of a lost or found item
29             put "Was item lost or found (l or f)?"
30             var lostOrFound: string
31             get lostOrFound:*  % Read line
32             put "Give name of lost or found item"
33             var report: ledger.entryType  % Use type exported from ledger
34             get report.name  % Read name of item
35             if lostOrFound(1) = "f" then   % "f" for "found"
                   % Handle report of found item
36                 put "Give one line description of found ", report.name
37                 get report.description:*      % Read line giving description
```

```
38              ledger.enter(report)      % Enter report into ledger
39          elsif lostOrFound(1) = "l" then    % "l" for "lost"
                  % Handle report of lost item
40              var found: boolean
41              ledger.lookup(report, found)    % Look up in ledger
42              if found then
43                  put "Description of found ",report.name, skip, report.description
44              else
45                  put "Sorry, no report of found ", report.name
46              end if
47          end if
48      end loop
```

As you can see in this program, the *ledger* module occupies lines 1 through 26. Line 2 gives the list of identifiers declared inside the module that are to be accessible outside the module. Since *lookup* is in this **export** list, we can call the *lookup* procedure from outside the module. This is done in line 41, which is:

ledger.lookup(report, found)

This line indicates that we are calling the *lookup* procedure, which is exported from the *ledger* module, passing the parameters *report* and *found.* Since *ledgerSize, entries* and *numberEntries* are declared inside the module, but are not exported, they can only be accessed inside the module.

We will now explain the use of the **boolean** parameter declared in line 16. This parameter to *lookup* is called *found*; it is a **var** parameter that is set to indicate whether the query item has been reported to be found. After calling *lookup* in line 41, an **if** statement tests to see whether *found* has been set to **true**. A variable such as *found* that is set to be **true** or **false** by an operation like *lookup* is said to be a **flag**. We use a flag to return the answer to a simple question such as: "Is there an entry for dog in the ledger?".

Our program would work exactly the same if we deleted lines 1 and 26, and deleted "*ledger* ". from each of lines 33 *(ledger.entry)*, 38 *(ledger.enter)*, and 41 *(ledger.lookup)*. These deletions would leave a legal program that does not have a module in it. But this program would be a poorer program because it would be more difficult to understand. We would no longer be able to easily recognize the parts that represent the ledger. In large programs, it is essential to be able to isolate program parts (modules and subprograms) and treat them as abstractions; otherwise the design, testing, and updating of the program becomes overwhelmingly complex.

DETAILS ABOUT MODULES

Each module in a Turing program has the form:

module *moduleName*
    import (*...names declared outside the module*
                that are accessed inside of it...)
    export (*...names declared inside the module*
                that are to be accessed outside of it...)
    ...declarations and statements inside the module...
  end *moduleName*

The module's name appears following the keywords **module** and **end**. The identifiers declared inside the module, such as *ledgerSize* and *lookup* are the names of **fields** of the modules. This is analogous to records, which also have fields. The fields that are to be accessible outside the module are given in the **export** list. Outside of the module, there is no way to access unexported fields. Outside of the module each access to an exported field must be preceded by the module's name and a dot. For example, outside the *ledger* module, the exported identifier *entryType* must appear as *ledger.entryType.*

The names of subprograms, types, and constants can be exported. One of the purposes of modules is to limit access to variables; for this reason, it is not allowed to export variables.

Any identifiers accessed in the module but declared outside the module must be given in the **import** list. The *ledger* module does not access any outside identifiers, so it does not have an **import** list. If an outside variable is to be changed by an assignment statement inside the module, it must be preceded by **var** in the import list, for example

    import (**var** *x*) *% Module assigns a value to x*

There can be several modules in a program. If module *N* calls procedure *P* exported from module *M*, then *N* must import *M* as **var**, as in:

    module *M*
      export *(P)*
       ...
    end *M*
    module *N*
      import (**var** *M*) *% Module N uses module M*
       ...
      M.P % Module N call procedure P of module M
       ...
    end N

The use of **import** and **export** lists provides **controlled scope** of identifiers; this means that the programmer controls what names can be accessed where by writing these lists.

Turing allows modules to be nested inside modules, as in:

> **module** *R*
>
>   ...
>
>   **module** *S*
>
>   ...
>
>   **end** *S*
>
>   ...
>
> **end** *R*

It is not allowed to **export** a module from a module, so *S* is **hidden** inside *R*. A module cannot be nested inside a subprogram or inside a statement.

A Turing program is executed from its top to its bottom. When a module is encountered, its statements and declarations are executed. This is said to initialize the module. For example, the *ledger* module is initialized by setting *ledgerSize* to *100* and *numberEntries* to *0*. The procedures *enter* and *lookup* are not executed during initialization because they are not called in the module.

CONTROL OF GLOBAL VARIABLES

In the *ledger* module *numberEntries* is global to the *lookup* subprogram because it is declared outside of *lookup*. If *numberEntries* was declared inside of *lookup* then it would be created (or re-created) at each call to *lookup* and discarded each time *lookup* returns to its point of call. This arrangement would not be acceptable because the value of *numberEntries* must be maintained across calls to *lookup*. This is the reason that *numberEntries* is a global variable.

In a large program, there are generally many global variables that must keep their values across subroutine calls. In a programming language like Pascal where there are no modules, these global variables are accessible to much of the program. This is unfortunate because it is hard to keep track of these accesses.

With modules this problem is neatly solved. Each set of global variables is **clustered** together in a module with the subprograms that manipulate these variables. We can easily tell from inspecting the program where a variable can be accessed. We have only to see what module (if any) contains the variable and where the variable is imported.

ALIASING AND MODULES

We consider a value to be **aliased** if it can be changed by one name and accessed by another. For example, if the assignment $x := 2$ changes y then we have an alias; y must be another name for x. Turing makes aliasing impossible by various restrictions. The anti-aliasing restriction for modules is illustrated in the following module that imports variable x.

```
var x: int
module M
    export (P)
    import (x)
    procedure P(var y: int )
        ...
    end P
    ...
end M
M.P(x)    % Not allowed
```

Since module M imports variable x, we are not allowed to pass x as a **var** (or reference) parameter to exported procedure P. This restriction guarantees that x and y cannot be aliased.

BLACK BOXES AND INFORMATION HIDING

A module provides a means of packaging together data and subprograms, and thereby restricting access to the data. In the case of *ledger*, the only way the *entries* variable can be accessed from outside the module is via the *enter* and *lookup* procedures. As a result, we can think of the module as a **black box** with two buttons on it. The buttons are labelled *enter* and *lookup*. To use this black box, we press one of these buttons to either insert information into the box or to request information from it. We consider the black box to be an abstraction, and most of the time we are not concerned about the individual declarations or statements inside the box.

Since the contents of the box cannot be directly accessed, we say that there is **information hiding**. We have hidden the array called *entries* inside the module. An advantage of information hiding is that it allows us to safely update details inside a module without fear that other parts of the program will be affected. For example, suppose we want to change *ledgerSize* to 200. Since *ledgerSize* is not exported from the module, we know that there are no direct dependencies on this value outside the module.

A more interesting example of a change to the module is the situation in which we decide to organize the data in the ledger in an entirely different fashion. To speed up the *lookup* operation, we could arrange the entries into a binary tree with links between entries. We can confidently do this re-organization, knowing that none of the rest of the program depends on details inside the module. The idea is that as long as the exported parts of the module continue to accomplish their purposes, the details of implementation do not matter. The ability to update one part of a program without causing failures in other parts is vital in large programs. This updating is called **program maintenance**.

A MORE REALISTIC PROGRAM

We will now give a more realistic version of our program that handles reports of lost and found items. Our *ledger* module will have new exported procedures called *findNext* and *delete*. We use *findNext* to access successive reports of found items, so we can find all reports for a given kind of item, for example, all reports of found cats. We can use *delete* to remove the last inspected report from the ledger, so a reclaimed item can have its entry removed.

To make *lookup* and *findNext* easier to program, we are keeping the ledger entries in alphabetic order based on the name of the item. Whenever a new report is made, its place in the ordering is found and then room is made for the report by moving down the existing entries beyond it. We might have used a linked list but we did not.

The new program explicitly handles the problem of too many entries in the ledger. The old program ignores this problem and as a result fails badly when an attempt is made to increase *numberEntries* beyond *ledgerSize*. In the new program, a flag (a **var boolean** parameter) is set by the *enter* procedure to indicate whether there was room for the report in the ledger.

In the new program we have separated the *ledger* module into a different source file. This file is copied into the main program by the construct:

> **include** *"ledger"*

We will show the *ledger* module, but first here is the main program.

```
% The "lost2" program.
% This program handles reports of lost and found items
%   It uses a "ledger" module that records
%   found items, which are later looked up
%   when items are reported to be lost
include "ledger"   % Copy ledger module here
put "This program keeps track of lost and found items"
loop    % Infinite loop handling each report of a lost or found item
    put "Was item lost or found (l or f)?"
```

```
var lostOrFound: string
get lostOrFound:*    % Read line
var report: ledger.entryType
if lostOrFound(1) = "f" then    % "f" for "found"
    % Handle report of found item
    put "Give name of found item"
    get report.name:*
    put "Give one line description of found",report.name
    get report.description:*    % Read line giving description
    var overflow: boolean
    ledger.enter(report, overflow)
    if overflow then
        put "Sorry, no more room. Item not recorded"
    end if
elsif lostOrFound(1) = "l" then    % "l" for "lost"
    % Handle report of lost item
    put "Give name of lost item"
    get report.name:*
    var found: boolean
    ledger.lookup(report, found)
    loop    % Repeatedly output entries for this item
        % Just did a "lookup" or a "findNext" operation
        if not found then
            put "Sorry, no report of found", report.name
            exit
        end if
        put "Description of found", report.name,
            skip, report.description
        put "Should entry be deleted (y or n)?"
        var yesOrNo: string
        get yesOrNo:*
        if yesOrNo(1) = "y" then
            ledger.delete  % Delete this entry
            exit
        end if
        put "Do you want to look further (y or n)?"
        get yesOrNo:*
        exit when yesOrNo(1) = "n"
        ledger.findNext(report, found)    % Start loop again
    end loop
end if
end loop    % End of "lost2" program
```

The *ledger* module, which is copied into this main progam, is stored in a separate file as follows:

% The "ledger" module allows items to
% be entered, looked up and deleted.
% Each item has a name whose type
% allows it to be compared with other names.
%   The following subprograms are exported
% from the ledger:
%   enter — records an item of "entryType" in the ledger
%   lookup — attempts to find an item in the ledger
%   findNext — finds the next entry following the one
%   just inspected
%   delete — deletes the just inspected item

```
module ledger
        export (enter, lookup, findNext, delete, entryType)
        % Each entry in the ledger has a name field
        % and a description field
        type entryType:
            record
                name: string (25)
                description: string
            end record


        const ledgerSize := 100
        var entries: array 1..ledgerSize of entryType
        var numberEntries: 0..ledgerSize := 0     % Ledger starts empty
        var activeEntry: 0..ledgerSize := 0    % Initially, no active item
        invariant 0 <= activeEntry and activeEntry <= numberEntries
            % Whenever the module is not executing, the activeEntry
            % is either null (0) or locates an actual report


        % Make new entry into ledger
        procedure enter(entry: entryType, var overflow: boolean)
            if numberEntries = ledgerSize then
                overflow := true
            else
                overflow := false
                % Find where to make entry then make space
                var i: int := 1
                    loop
                        exit when i > numberEntries or
```

$$entry.name < entries(i).name$$
$$i := i + 1$$

end loop
% Make room by sliding down entries
% Copy from bottom to top, so no entries are lost
for decreasing *j: numberEntries..i*
   entries(j + 1) := entries(j)
end for
entries(i) := entry % Copy into vacated spot
numberEntries := numberEntries + 1
end if
end *enter*

% Look up an item.   Desired key has been set in entry.name
procedure *lookup*(**var** *entry: entryType,* **var** *found:* **boolean** *)*
  % Start by assuming that search will fail.
  activeEntry := 0
  found := **false**
  for *i: 1..numberEntries   % Search for name*
    if *entry.name = entries(i).name* **then**
      activeEntry := i
      found := **true**
      entry := entries(i)
      exit
    end if
  end for
end *lookup*

% Access next entry (prior entry was accessed here or by "lookup")
procedure *findNext*(**var** *entry: entryType,* **var** *found:* **boolean** *)*
  pre *activeEntry* **not** *= 0*
  found := (activeEntry < numberEntries)
  if *found* **then**
    activeEntry := activeEntry + 1
    entry := entries(activeEntry)
  else
    activeEntry := 0
  end if
end *findNext*

% Remove active entry from ledger
procedure *delete*

pre *activeEntry* **not** *= 0*
% Move up entries to close up space for deletion
for *i: activeEntry + 1..numberEntries*
  entries(i − 1) := entries(i)
end for
numberEntries := numberEntries − 1
activeEntry := 0
 end *delete*
end *ledger*

This new version of the *ledger* module uses a variable called *activeEntry* to locate the report successfully located by the *lookup* or *findNext* procedures. The *findNext* and *delete* procedures assume that *activeEntry* actually locates such a report; this assumption is documented in the **pre** conditions of *findNext* and *delete*.

Following the declaration of *activeEntry* is the module's **invariant** assertion. This is an optional assertion that documents constraints on the module's data. The idea is that the **invariant** describes what is required for the module's data to be self consistent. In the case of this module the requirement is that *nextEntry* is either null (zero), or locates an actual report in the ledger. A module's **invariant** must be true following its initialization and whenever it is entered or left.

CHAPTER 18 SUMMARY

This chapter has introduced the programming language construct called a module. Modules are particularly useful for programming in the large, that is when writing programs that are hundreds or thousands of lines long. Some programming languages, such as Basic, are useful for programming in the small, for programs of a few dozen lines, but are poor for large programs because they do not provide subprograms and modules.

Subprograms allow us to name parts of an algorithm and to consider that the subprogram is executed in one abstract step. Modules allow us to implement black boxes that hide implementation details. The following important terms were discussed in this chapter.

export − A module exports the names of its fields that are to be accessible outside of the module. An exported field may be a constant, a type, or a subprogram. Variables may not be exported.

import − A module imports names of externally declared items that are to be used inside the module.

Information hiding − Limiting access to items such as variables that are referenced by more than one procedure. This can be done by isolating these variables and procedures in modules.

invariant — A module can have an **invariant** assertion. This assertion is to be true after initialization of the module and whenever an exported subprogram is called.

CHAPTER 18 EXERCISES

1. Write a message passing program that accepts messages directed to certain people. It also receives queries to see if messages have been left for a person. Here is a sample dialogue:

   Computer: Are you sending or receiving (s or r)?
   Alice: sending
   Computer: Who are you sending to?
   Alice: George
   Computer: Give message (one line long)
   Alice: Please buy cat food today.

   Later we might observe:

   Computer: Are you sending or receiving (s or r)?
   George: receiving
   Computer: What is your name?
   George: George
   Computer: There is a message for you: Please buy cat food today.

2. It is never absolutely necessary to use modules, because we can use global declarations instead. Explain why modules are important although they are not absolutely necessary.

3. A previous chapter presented data structures such as stacks. Give a module that implements a stack using exported subprograms named *push* and *pop*. Give another implementation of your *stack* module with a different internal organization. For example, your first module may represent the stacked items in an array while the second may use a linked list.

4. Write a general purpose module that implements a FIFO queue of items whose type is *entryType*. This type is imported into the module. The module exports two subprograms: *enqueue* (put item on end of queue) and *dequeue* (takes item from front of queue).

Chapter 19

SCIENTIFIC CALCULATIONS

Most of the applications that we have discussed so far in this book are connected with the use of computers in business or in the humanities. We do business applications on computers because of the large numbers of each calculation that must be done. A single payroll calculation is simple, but if a company has thousands of employees, computer processing of payroll is warranted. Computers were originally developed with scientific and engineering calculations in mind. This is because many scientific and engineering calculations are so long that it is not practical to do them by hand, even with the help of a pocket calculator.

Often the scientific laws describing a physical situation are known in the form of equations, but these equations must be solved for the situation of interest. We may be designing a bridge or aircraft or an air-conditioning system for a building. A computer can be used to calculate the details of the particular situation.

Another important use of computers in science is to find equations that fit the data produced in experiments. These equations then serve to reduce the amount of data that must be preserved. Science as a word means knowledge. The object of scientific work is to gather information about the world and to systematize it so that it can be retrieved and used in the future. There is such a large amount of research activity now in science that we are facing an **information explosion**. We have talked about retrieving information from a **data bank** and computers will undoubtedly help us in this increasingly difficult and tedious job. But the problem of **data reduction** is of equal importance.

In this chapter we will try to give some of the flavor of scientific calculations, but we will not be including enough detail for those people who will need to work with them. We will give only an overview of this important use of computers.

EVALUATING FORMULAS

To solve certain scientific problems we must substitute values into formulas and calculate results. For example, we could be asked to calculate the distance traveled by a falling object after it is dropped from an airplane. A formula that gives the distance in meters traveled in time t seconds, neglecting air resistance, is

$$d = 4.9t^2$$

Here the constant *4.9* is one-half the acceleration due to gravity. Here is a program to compute the distance at the end of each second of the first *10* seconds after the drop:

```
% The "fall" program
% Output table of distance fallen versus time
var  distance: real
% Label time-distance table
put "time": 12, "distance"
for time: 1..10
    distance := 4.9 * time ** 2
    put time: 2, distance: 18
end for
```

The output for this program is

time	distance
1	4.9
2	19.6
3	44.1
4	78.4
5	122.5
6	176.4
7	240.1
8	313.6
9	396.9
10	490

This example outputs a table of values of *distance* for different times. Calculation of tables is an interesting and historic scientific use of computers. Scientific calculations are usually done using **real** variables. In the output the distances and times are given with up to 7 digits, although a maximum of 4 appears here. If 7 were required, not all these digits would be **significant**; the constant 4.9 in the formula is only expressed with two digits. We must realize then that only about two digits of the calculated distance traveled are significant.

In Turing these calculations are carried out in the computer keeping roughly 14 digits, but this does not imply that they are meaningful. Even if the constant in the formula were entered to 14-digit precision, we would not necessarily have 14 significant digits in the answer. Because computers represent **real** numbers only to a limited precision, there are always what are called numerical or **round-off** errors. These are not mistakes you make but are inherent in the way that **real** numbers are represented in the computer. When two **real** numbers are multiplied, the product is rounded off to the same precision as the original numbers; no more digits in the product would be significant. As calculations proceed, the rounding process can erode the significance even of some of the digits that are maintained. We usually quote numerical errors by saying that a value is, for example,

$$19.25 \pm 0.05$$

This means that the value could be as high as 19.30 or as low as 19.20. If the error were higher, say 0.5 instead of 0.05, then the values could range between 19.75 and 18.75. In this case the fourth digit in the value is certainly not significant, and you would say instead that the value was

$$19.2 \pm 0.5$$

Or we might round it up instead of truncating the insignificant digit, and write

$$19.3 \pm 0.5$$

The estimation of errors is an important job that is done by **numerical analysts**. If you are doing numerical calculations, you should be aware of the fact that answers are not exact but have errors.

PREDEFINED MATHEMATICAL FUNCTIONS

Scientific calculations require mathematical functions that are not commonly used in business calculations. For many of these functions, programs have already been written for Turing; they are predefined in the compiler. For example, suppose for our falling-body calculation we wanted to compute the times when the body reached different distances. To calculate the time, given the distance, we use this form of the same formula:

$t =$ the square root of $(d / 4.9)$

Now we need to be able to calculate a square root. This can be done by using the built-in function for square root, which is called *sqrt*. We would write in the program:

time := sqrt(distance/4.9)

Other predefined functions available to Turing for scientific calculations are connected with trigonometry. They include *sin* and *cos*. These give the values of the sine and cosine, when the argument of the function is in radians. The function *arctan(x)* gives the angle in radians whose tangent is *x*. The natural logarithm is obtained by using *ln*, the exponential by using *exp*. The appendix lists all these functions.

GRAPHING A FUNCTION

Frequently a better understanding of a scientific formula can be had if you draw a graph of the function. In the first example of this chapter we evaluated a function at regular intervals. It is possible to use these values to plot a graph on the screen. We could, for instance, plot a distance-time graph for the falling object.

When you draw a graph of *x* versus *y* you usually make the *x*-axis horizontal and have the *y*-axis vertical. The values of *x*, which is the independent variable, increase uniformly; the corresponding values of *y* are obtained by substituting *x* into the function *y=f(x)*. When we plot a graph using the display screen the lines of output text are uniformly spaced, so we will use the distance between lines to represent the uniform interval between the *x*'s. This means that the *x*-axis will be vertical and the *y*-axis horizontal.

We represent the *y*-value corresponding to the *x* of a particular output line by displaying an asterisk in the position that approximates its value. We use 31 columns to represent the range of *y*'s. If the lowest *y*-value that we must represent is *yMinimum* and the highest is *yMaximum*, then the 31 output positions must represent a range of

$$yRange = yMaximum - yMinimum$$

To find the position for a value *y* we compute an integer variable *yPosition* from

$$yPosition := round(30*(y - yMinimum)/yRange) + 1$$

The value 1 is added to put *yMinimum* in the first position. We are assuming *yRange* is not zero so that we can divide by it.

To form a string of characters for display, we first create a string variable called *basicLine* that holds a string of blanks. We put an *x*-axis on our graph if it is in the proper range. To do this we place a vertical bar in the line of blanks. The axis is placed in the position where a zero value of *y* would be placed. The axis does not appear at all if 0 is less than *yMinimum* or greater than *yMaximum*. Here is the program segment for forming the *basicLine*. Here instead of 31 output positions we assume a number given by a constant *width*. Then it can be easily changed if we want a wider or narrower graph.

basicLine := *repeat*(" ", *width*)   % *String of blanks*
zeroPlace := *round*((*width*− *1*)*(*0*− *yMinimum*)/*yRange*) + *1*
if *zeroPlace* > =*1* **and** *zeroPlace* < =*width* **then**
     basicLine := *basicLine*(*1*..*zeroPlace* − *1*) + " |" +*basicLine*(*zeroPlace*+*1*..*)
end if

For each line we set *yLine* to *basicLine* with the *y* position changed to an asterisk. This is done by

$$yLine := basicLine(1..yPosition - 1) + "*" + basicLine(yPosition + 1..*)$$

We do not display a *y*-axis, but we list the *x*-values corresponding to each line opposite the line.

A PROCEDURE FOR PLOTTING GRAPHS

Here is the complete procedure for plotting a graph from *n* pairs of **real** values of *x* and *y* stored in arrays of those names. The values of *x* are uniformly spaced. The actual names of the variables to be plotted will be given as arguments *xName* and *yName*, which are of type **string**. The calling statement would be of the form

$$graph(x, y, n, xName, yName)$$

We will call a procedure to find *yMaximum* and *yMinimum*. It will be called *minMax*.

```
% Find smallest and largest in table
procedure minMax(value: array 1..* of real , n: int,
    var  minimum, maximum: real )
    minimum := value(1)
    maximum := value(1)
    for i: 2..n
        if  value(i) < minimum then
            minimum := value(i)
        elsif  value(i) > maximum then
            maximum := value(i)
        end if
    end for
end minMax
% Procedure to plot a graph
procedure graph(x, y: array 1..* of real, n: int,
        xName, yName: string)
    const  width := 31
```

```
    var yMinimum, yMaximum: real
    % Find range of y to be plotted
    minMax(y, n, yMinimum, yMaximum)
    const yRange := yMaximum − yMinimum
    % Form string of width blanks
    % Place x-axis mark in basicLine
    var basicLine: string (width) := repeat(" ", width)
    const zeroPlace := round((width− 1)*(0− yMinimum)/yRange) + 1
    if zeroPlace > =1 and zeroPlace < =width then
        basicLine := basicLine(1..zeroPlace− 1)+" |" +basicLine(zeroPlace+1..*)
    end if
    % Label graph
    put "GRAPH OF", yName, " VERSUS", xName
    put "MINIMUM OF", yName, yMinimum: 10: 2
    put "MAXIMUM OF", yName, yMaximum: 10: 2
    % Prepare and output lines of graph
    for i: 1..n
        const yPosition := round((width− 1)*(y(i)− yMinimum)/yRange) + 1
        const yLine := basicLine(1..yPosition− 1)+" *" +basicLine(yPosition + 1..*)
        put x(i): 5: 2, repeat(" ", 8), yline
    end for
end graph
```

USING THE GRAPH PROCEDURE

We now give the program that can be used to plot the function of x,

$$y = x^2 - x - 2$$

between the values $x = -2$ and $x = 3$. We plot it at intervals of x that are 0.2 wide. There are 26 points in all. Here is the program:

```
    % The "curve" program
    % Plot the function y = x**2− x− 2
    const interval := 0.2
    const points := 26
    var x, y: array 1..points of real
    (copy graph procedure here)
    % Compute values for x and y arrays
    for i: 1..points
        x(i) := − 2 + (i− 1)*interval
        y(i) := x(i)*x(i)− x(i)− 2
    end for
    graph(x, y, points,"X", "Y")
```

You will notice that as the graph crosses the *x*-axis the vertical bar is replaced by an asterisk. It crosses twice, at

$$x = -1.00 \quad \text{and at}$$
$$x = 2.00$$

We say that $x=-1$ and $x=2$ are the roots of the equation

$$x^2-x-2=0$$

The function (x^2-x-2) becomes zero at these values of x. This graphical method is one way of finding the roots of an equation. We will look later at another way of finding roots that is numerical rather than graphical.

```
GRAPH OF Y VERSUS X
MINIMUM OF Y      -2.24
MAXIMUM OF Y       4.00
-2.00                         |                             *
-1.80                         |                         *
-1.60                         |                    *
-1.40                         |              *
-1.20                         |   *
-1.00                        *
-0.80                    *    |
-0.60                 *       |
-0.40              *          |
-0.20           *             |
 0.00         *               |
 0.20       *                 |
 0.40      *                  |
 0.60      *                  |
 0.80      *                  |
 1.00       *                 |
 1.20         *               |
 1.40           *             |
 1.60             *           |
 1.80                *        |
 2.00                        *
 2.20                         |  *
 2.40                         |       *
 2.60                         |          *
 2.80                         |             *
 3.00                         |                  *
```

FITTING A CURVE TO A SET OF POINTS

In the last sections we have seen how to compute a set of points of corresponding x and y values from a formula and then to plot a graph of these points. In some scientific experiments we measure the value of a variable y as we change some other variable x in a systematic way. The results are displayed by plotting x and y. If there is a theory that relates the values of x to y in a formula or equation, then we can see how well the results fit the theoretical formula.

One way would be to compute the values of y for each x from the formula. The measured values could be called y (experimental) and the calculated ones y (theoretical). The differences between corresponding values

y (experimental) $-$ y (theoretical)

are called **deviations** of experimental from theoretical values.

We have spoken so far as if it were possible to compute the proper theoretical value that corresponds to each experimental value. For example, here is the formula for v, which is the velocity of an object at time t, given that its initial velocity is *vInitial* and its acceleration is a.

$v = vInitial + a*t$

If we measured the velocity of an object that has a uniform acceleration we could plot a graph between v and t. Theoretically, the graph should be a straight line, but the experimental points are scattered. It is possible to draw a line by eye that is placed so that the deviations of points from the line are small. Since some deviations, v (experimental) $-$ v (theoretical), are positive and some negative their sum might be small even though individual deviations were large. To get a good fit we minimize the sum of the squares of the deviations which is always positive. We choose as the best straight line the one that makes the sum of the squares of the deviations the least.

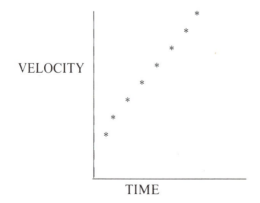

VELOCITY

TIME

This is called **least squares fitting** of a curve (here a straight line) to experimental points. This process can be done very efficiently by a computer. Most computer installations provide standard procedures for least squares fitting, so that scientists do not have to write their own.

Sometimes no theoretical curve is known. We can still fit our data to an equation. We choose an equation that has a form resembling our data. If there is no theory we say it is an **empirical** fit, meaning that it is an equation based on the observations.

SOLVING POLYNOMIAL EQUATIONS

The graph that we plotted as an example was of the function

$$y = x^2 - x - 2$$

This is a **polynomial** function of x. The places where the graph crosses the x-axis are the **roots** of the equation

$$x^2 - x - 2 = 0$$

This is a second-degree equation since the highest power of the unknown x is the second power. It is a **quadratic equation**. There are general formulas for the roots of a quadratic equation. For the equation

$$ax^2 + bx + c = 0$$

the two roots $x1$ and $x2$ are given by the formulas

$$x1 = (-b + \sqrt{b^2 - 4ac})/(2a) \quad \text{and}$$

$$x2 = (-b - \sqrt{b^2 - 4ac})/(2a)$$

Most students of mathematics know these formulas. If the quantity $(b^2 - 4ac)$ inside the square root sign is positive, all is straightforward. If it is negative, then the formula requires us to find the square root of a negative number, and we say the roots are **complex**. This means, in graphical terms, that the curve does not cross, or touch, the x-axis anywhere. It is either completely above or completely below the x-axis. There is no use looking for values of x where the function is zero.

Here is a procedure for finding the roots of a quadratic equation.

```
% Find roots of a*x*x + b*x + c = 0
procedure roots(a, b, c: real)
    const test := b**2 - 4*a*c
    if test >= 0 then
        const sqRoot := sqrt(test)
```

```
        const root1 := (− b + sqRoot)/(2*a)
        const root2 := (− b− sqRoot)/(2*a)
        put "Roots are ", root1: 14, root2: 14
    else
        put "Roots are complex"
    end if
end roots
```

In this procedure the formulas for finding the roots do not provide values that are accurate under various circumstances. For example, if *root1* is nearly zero because *b* and *sqRoot* are very close in value, a better approximation to it can be obtained by working out *root2* and using the assignment:

$$root1 := c/(a*root2)$$

to compute *root1*. This relationship holds in general so it can always be used. Can you see why it is true?

For equations that are polynomial in *x* of degrees higher than two, the method for finding the roots is not as easy. For an equation of degree three or four, there is a complicated formula for the roots. For larger degrees there are no formulas and we must look for the roots by a **numerical method**.

The secret of any search is first to be sure that what you are looking for is in the right area, then to keep narrowing down the search area. One method of searching for roots corresponds to the binary search we discussed in Chapter 13. First we find two values of *x* for which the function has different signs. Then we can be sure that, if it is continuous, the graph will cross the *x*-axis at least once in the interval between these points. The next step is to halve the interval and look at the middle. If there is only one root in the interval, then in the middle the function will either be zero, in which case it is the root, or it will have the same sign as one of the two end points. Remember they have opposite signs. We discard the half of the interval that is bounded by the middle point and the end with the same sign and repeat the process. After several steps we will have a good **approximation** to the location of the root. We can continue the process until we are satisfied that the error, or uncertainty, in our root location is small enough. There is no point in trying to locate it more accurately than the precision with which the numbers are stored in the computer.

SOLVING LINEAR EQUATIONS

Computers are used to solve sets of linear equations. If we have two unknowns, we must have two equations to get a solution. We can solve the set of equations

$$x - y = 10$$
$$x + y = 6$$

to get the result $x = 8$, $y = -2$. To solve the equations we first eliminate one of the unknowns. From the first equation we get

$$x = y + 10$$

Substituting into the second eliminates x. It gives

$$(y + 10) + y = 6 \quad \text{or} \quad 2y = -4 \quad \text{or} \quad y = -2$$

Then substituting back gives

$$x = -2 + 10 \quad \text{or} \quad x = 8$$

This process of elimination can be carried out a step at a time for more equations in more unknowns. Each step lowers the number of unknowns by one and the number of equations by one. A computer program can be written to perform this job, and can be used to solve a set of linear equations. What we must provide is the coefficients of the unknowns and the right-hand sides of the set of equations. A common method is called the **Gauss elimination method**.

COMPUTING AREAS

Another numerical method that is relatively easy to understand is the calculation of areas by the **trapezoidal method**. Suppose we have a curve of $y = f(x)$ and we want to find the area between the curve and the x-axis and between lines at $x = x1$ and $x = xn$.

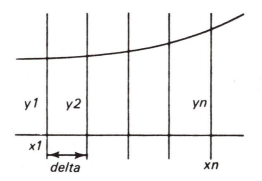

We will divide the distance between *x1* and *xn* into intervals of size *delta*. In the drawing we have shown four intervals. The area of the first section, thinking of it as a trapezoid, is

   (y1 + y2)*delta/2

The total area under the curve is approximated by the sum of all the trapezoids. The total area of the trapezoids is

   (y1 + y2)*delta/2 + (y2 + y3)*delta/2 + ...
            (y(n − 1)+yn)*delta/2

If we factor out *delta* the formula becomes

   ((y1 + yn)/2 + y2 + y3 + ... + y(n − 1))*delta

This is half the sum of *y1* and *yn* plus the sum of the other *y*'s multiplied by the width of the trapezoids. As *delta* is made smaller, the sum of the areas of the trapezoids comes closer and closer to the area under the curve. It is a better and better approximation. There is, however, a limit to the accuracy that can be obtained, due to the precision of the **real** numbers. Here is a program segment to compute the area if the *y*'s are stored in an array:

```
sum := (y(1) + y(n))/2
for i: 2..n − 1
    sum := sum + y(i)
end for
area := sum*delta
```

CHAPTER 19 SUMMARY

This chapter has given an introduction to the use of computers in scientific calculations. Generally, these calculations are done using **real** numbers. The scientist needs to know the accuracy of the final answers. The answers may be inaccurate because of:

Measurement errors — the original data was collected by measuring physical quantities, such as length or speed. These measurements can never be perfect and an estimate of the measurement error should be made.

Round-off errors by the computer — a given computer stores **real** numbers with a particular precision. Calculations using **real** numbers will be no more accurate than the number of digits of precision provided by the computer. They could even be less accurate due to the cumulative effect of round-off. (Note: sometimes the programmer can choose between single-precision **real**, giving typically 6 digits of accuracy and double-precision **real**, giving typically 14 digits accuracy. Turing uses double-precision **real**.)

Truncation errors in repeated calculations — some calculations, such as searching for the roots of a polynomial equation, produce approximations that are successively closer to the exact answer. When the repeated calculation stops, we have a truncation error, which is the difference between the final approximation and the exact answer (ignoring errors due to measurement and round-off).

The number of digits of accuracy in a particular answer is called its number of **significant figures**. The scientist needs to know that the computer produces a particular answer with enough significant figures for his purposes.

Turing provides predefined functions that are useful in solving scientific or mathematical problems. The function *sqrt* takes the square root of a non-negative number. The functions *sin, cos,* and *arctan* operate on or return angles in radians. The function *ln* takes the natural logarithm of a number, and *exp* raises *e* to a specified power.

This chapter presented the following typical scientific and mathematical uses of computers.

Evaluating formulas — a computer can produce tables of numbers, for example tables of navigational figures used on sailing boats.

Graphing functions — a computer can plot a particular function using the display screen.

Fitting a curve to a set of points — data points from an experiment can be read by a program and used to determine an equation (a curve) that describes the data.

Solving polynomial equations — a polynomial equation such as

$$x^3 + 9x^2 + 6x - 23 = 0$$

can be solved by a program that reads the coefficients (1, 9, 6 and -23).

Solving linear equations — a set of equations such as

$$2x + 9y = 7$$

$$10x - 4y = 2$$

can be solved by a program that reads the coefficients of the unknowns (2, 9, 10 and -4) and the right sides of the equations (7 and 2).

Areas under curves — a program can find the area under a given curve by using the heights of the curve at many points. Essentially, the program slices the area into narrow strips and adds up the areas of the strips. This process is sometimes called **numerical integration** or **quadrature**.

CHAPTER 19 EXERCISES

1. One jet plane is flying 1083.7 kilometers per hour; another jet plane, chasing it from behind, is flying 1297.9 kilometers per hour. What is the relative speed of the second plane, that is, how fast is it catching up to the first plane? The speed of the first plane is known to an accuracy of ±5 km/hr and the speed of the second is known to an accuracy of ±0.5 km/hr. How accurately can we calculate the relative speed? How many significant figures are there in the first plane's speed, the second plane's speed and the relative speed?

2. Use the graphing procedure given in this chapter to plot the function *sin(x)* for *x* varying from zero to three in steps of one tenth.

3. Use the graphing procedure given in this chapter to plot the function *x* sin(x)* for *x* varying from 0 to 12 in steps of 0.25.

Chapter 20

NUMERICAL METHODS

In the last chapter we outlined some of the important types of calculations used in scientific and engineering computing. In any calculations, for example those for evaluating functions such as the trigonometric functions sin and cos or finding the area under a curve, the calculation can be carried out to varying degrees of accuracy. Usually the more calculating you do, the more accurate the answer you get. But some methods are better than others; for the same amount of work you get greater accuracy. We will, for instance, be looking at a way of finding areas under curves that is usually superior to the trapeziodal rule described in the last chapter. As well we will show a general method of solving linear equations and a method for least squares fitting of a straight line to a set of experimental points. But first we will look at an efficient way of evaluating a polynomial.

EVALUATION OF A POLYNOMIAL

In doing numerical calculations we should be concerned with getting the best calculation we can for the least cost in terms of computer time. This is one of the concerns of people who design what are called numerical methods. They are not just concerned about getting an answer but about whether the cost of getting the answer can be decreased.

As an example of how different methods giving apparently the same result can have different costs, we will look at the calculation of the value of a polynomial. We will look at a third-degree polynomial and then generalize the result later for a polynomial of degree n. A third-degree polynomial has the form

$$y(x) = a3\ x^3 + a2\ x^2 + a1\ x + a0$$

One way of evaluating this is

$$y = a3^*x^*x^*x + a2^*x^*x + a1^*x + a0$$

In this evaluation there are 6 multiplications (count the asterisks) and 3 additions. For a fourth-degree polynomial there would be 10 multiplications and 4 additions. For an nth—degree polynomial there would be $n + (n-1) + (n-2) + ... + 1 = n(n + 1)/2$ multiplications and n additions.

Now we will look at a different method of evaluating the third-degree polynomial. It is

$$y = ((((a3)*x + a2)*x + a1)*x + a0)$$

Here there are 3 multiplications and 3 additions. (Just count the asterisks.) For an nth-degree polynomial there would be n multiplications and n additions. This method is called **Horner's rule** and is certainly much more efficient, particularly for polynomials of higher degree.

We will now write a function subprogram that will evaluate a polynomial of degree n by this method given that the coefficients of the powers of x namely the a's are stored in a one-dimensional array. Here is a program segment that would work for the third-degree polynomial of our example.

```
sum := a(3)
for decreasing i: 2..0
    sum := sum*x + a(i)
end for
```

If we extend this now to work for an nth degree polynomial we would write

```
sum := a(n)
for decreasing i: n − 1..0
    sum := sum*x + a(i)
end for
```

The complete function subprogram would be

```
% Function to evaluate polynomial of degree n
function poly(a: array 0..*of real, x: real, n: int): real
    var sum: real
    sum := a(n)
    for decreasing i: n − 1..0
        sum := sum*x + a(i)
    end for
    result sum
end poly
```

ROUND-OFF ERRORS

Since real numbers are represented in a computer by finite strings of bits, each operation such as a multiply, usually introduces a slight error. This error is called a round-off error. The last bit in the string may be inexact. In decimal notation, if the answer fraction 0.132762 is to be represented by a string of decimal digits of length 4, then the four digits will be either .1327 or .1328. The string may simply be chopped off after the 4th digit, which is called **truncating** or **chopping**, or we can pick the closest 4 digit approximation. This latter method is better and is the method that you usually are thinking of if you ask that a number be rounded off.

As numbers are combined in the arithmetic operations of addition, subtraction, multiplication and division, the round-off error may increase. We say that a further error is **generated**. As operations continue, the generated error may grow and is said to be a **propagated error**.

In adding or subtracting two numbers the error in the sum, or difference is equal to the sum of the errors in the two numbers. Suppose for instance that the number 0.132762 is represented as the 4-digit string 0.1328. The error in this representation due to rounding off is 0.000038. If the number 0.521689 is represented as 0.5217 the error is 0.000011. The sum of the numbers will be 0.6545 as compared with the result of adding the two 6-digit representations which gives 0.654451. The error in the sum is 0.000049 which is the sum of 0.000038 and 0.000011.

In multiplication the **relative** (or **percentage**) **error** introduced in the product is equal to the sum of the relative (or percentage) errors of the two factors. In division the relative error of the quotient is the difference between the relative errors of the dividend and divisor. In any event all arithmetic operations serve to propagate errors due to rounding.

We found that Horner's rule was more efficient for evaluating polynomials than the straightforward method because there were fewer multiplications. Now we can see that it is also more accurate since the propagation of round-off error is less when there are fewer arithmetic operations. This is why we can say that it is a better method; it is more accurate and costs less.

LOSS OF SIGNIFICANT FIGURES

We have seen that arithmetic operations result in errors and these cause the rounding due to the finite representations of real numbers in a computer to grow larger. The number of digits in our final result that are significant gradually decreases as errors are propagated.

There are more drastic ways of losing significant figures. One place where this occurs is in the situation where two nearly equal numbers are subtracted. When 0.3572 is subtracted from 0.3581 the answer is 0.0009 which is normalized to 0.9???e-03. The digits that are written as question marks could be anything; only the 9 is significant. We had 4 significant figures in each of the original numbers and now we have only 1 significant figure in the difference. One way to cope with this loss of precision is to avoid calculations of this sort. Often by regrouping or resequencing operations the offending subtraction can be eliminated. If it is not possible then it may be necessary to work to greater precision, say double precision, during the part of a calculation where this can occur. Loss of significant figures can also occur when divisors are small or multipliers large.

EVALUATION OF INFINITE SERIES

Many mathematical functions can be represented by an infinite series of terms to be added. For example,

$$\exp(x) = 1 + (x/1!) + (x^2/2!) + (x^3/3!) + ...$$

$$\sin(x) = (x/1!) - (x^3/3!) + (x^5/5!) - ...$$

$$\cos(x) = 1 - (x^2/2!) + (x^4/4!) - ...$$

$$\log(1+x) = (x/1) - (x^2/2) + (x^3/3) - ...$$

The series for sin and cos are for angles x in radians. The series for *log(1+x)* is valid only for values of x whose magnitudes are less than 1.

If we evaluate the infinite series for say *sin(x)* for a value of $x=pi/4$ we would get terms that alternately are positive and negative and decrease in magnitude as successive terms are calculated. Here is a program that outputs the value of the sum of the sine series up to a given term as well as the value of the latest term added for eight terms.

```
% Compute series for sin(x) term by term
% The "sinSeries" program
const pi := 3.141593
```

```
const x := pi/4
const sqrx := x*x
put "sin(x)": 30, "term"
var term: real := x
var sine: real := term
for i: 1..8
    put sine: 12: 6: 2, term: 30: 6: 2
    term := -1*(term*sqrx)/(2*i*(2*i + 1))
    sine := sine + term
end for
put " Value of sine using predeclared function sin is",
    sin(pi/4): 13: 6: 2
```

The output for this program is

sin (x)	term
7.853982e−01	7.853982e−01
7.046527e−01	−8.074554e−02
7.071431e−01	2.490396e−03
7.071065e−01	−3.657623e−05
7.071068e−01	3.133620e−07
7.071068e−01	−1.757250e−09
7.071068e−01	6.948463e−12
7.071068e−01	2.041030e−14

Value of sine using predeclared function sin is 7.071068e−01

You can see that the terms become progressively smaller right from the start. This is because x is less than 1. The ratio of the one term to the next term is $x^2/(2i(2i+1))$. This ratio becomes smaller as i becomes larger. The terms are decreasing faster and faster. Terms after the 5th do not make any difference. This series for $sin(x)$ can be used even when x is greater than 1. Here is the output if we run the previous program again with the statement $x:=pi/2$ instead of $x:=pi/4$ and output the value of $sin(pi/2)$ which is 1.

sin (x)	term
1.570796e +00	1.570796e +00
9.248322e−01	−6.459643e−01
1.004525e +00	7.969267e−02
9.998431e−01	−4.681758e−03
1.000004e +00	1.604413e−04
9.999999e−01	−3.598848e−06
1.000000e +00	5.692181e−08
1.000000e +00	−6.688046e−10

Value of sine using predeclared functions sin is 1.000000e +00

This time the terms do not decrease as rapidly; but they are not affecting the result after the 6th term. The accuracy obtained from the evaluation of a fixed number of terms depends on the value of the parameter x.

If the series is stopped after 3 terms the value of sine differs from the true value of *sin(pi/2)* which is $0.100000e+01$ by $0.0004525e+01$ which is 4/10 of 1 percent. We say that this error is partly due to truncating the series. If truncation occurs after 4 terms the error is $0.0001569e+01$ which is 1/10 of 1 percent. The more terms we calculate, the smaller is the **truncation error**. By taking sufficient terms we can make the truncation error as small as we want.

One way of deciding how many terms of a series are enough is to stop when the absolute value of the most recent term is less than a certain amount. The amount we usually choose is such that it will not change the value of the sum in a noticeable way. It is useless to evaluate more terms because they do not matter.

Even when we have evaluated enough terms so that the contribution of the last term is insignificant, there still remain errors due to round off. In our example, the round-off error would be present even in the first term of the series; as each term is added another round off occurs. These errors may tend to cancel each other; sometimes the number is rounded up, sometimes down. It is possible that all errors are in the same direction so that the total possible error introduced in this way grows larger with the number of terms. We must expect the worst. The round-off error in the sine of *pi/4* seems to be 0.0000003, that in sine of *pi/2* seems to be 0.0000007. In each case the last figure output is dubious.

One way of avoiding the accumulation of round-off errors is to work in double precision. (Turing calculations are always done in double precision.) In double precision each number is represented by a string of bits that is twice as long as in single precision. The round-off error will then accumulate in the least significant bits of the double precision number. When the result is finally reduced to single precision, a single round off occurs.

A relationship between the functions sine and cosine may be used to improve the accuracy of the result for a given number of terms in the series. This relationship is

$$sin(x) = cos((pi/2)-x)$$

This means that for angles greater than *pi/4* but less than *pi/2* we can compute the sine by using the series for cosine with the argument *((pi/2)-x)*. This will be equal to or less than *pi/4* and comparable accuracy can be obtained using the same number of terms in the series.

When a fixed number of terms has been decided on, say six, the evaluation of the series becomes the evaluation of a polynomial. We can take advantage of the efficiencies of Horner's method. In the series for sine and cosine not every power of x is present so the polynomial is really like one in x^2 rather than x. For example, the series for sine to 5 terms can be written as

$$\sin(x) = ((((x^2/9!) - (1/7!))x^2 + (1/5!))x^2 + 1)x$$

The coefficients $(1/9!)$, $(1/7!)$, and $(1/5!)$ can all be evaluated once and for all and stored as constants in the program.

All values of angles greater than *pi/2* must be reduced to be related to either the sin or cos series for the range of x less than or equal to *pi/4*. This is called **range reduction**.

ROOT FINDING

In the last chapter we looked at one method for finding the value of x where a polynomial in x has a zero value. This same method applies to any function of one variable, say $f(x)$. If there are two values, say *x1* and *x2*, of x at which *f(x)* has opposite signs then, provided the function is continuous, there must be at least one point in between these values where the function has a zero value. We described a search technique that halved the interval between the given values of x and determined in which half the zero of the function lay. This process can then be repeated in a manner similar to a binary search.

This **interval-halving method** can be improved upon and numerous other methods for finding zeros, or roots, of a function of one variable have been devised. The purpose of these methods is to provide a faster way of homing in on a root once it has been located between two values of x. A technique called the **secant method** uses, instead of the mid-point, the point at which a line drawn between the point *(x1, f(x1))* and *(x2, f(x2))* cuts the x-axis. This will be at a point x given by solving the equation

$$f(x2) / (x2 - x) = f(x1) / (x - x1)$$

or $x = (f(x1)x2 + f(x2)x1) / (f(x2) + f(x1))$

If you have studied analytical geometry you can see this from the diagram.

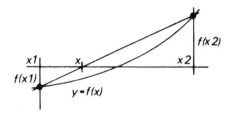

This process is repeated using the point x as a replacement for either $x1$ or $x2$. The choice depends on which gives a value to the function opposite to the value at x. As the iteration proceeds the interval is always being narrowed down.

Both the interval-halving method and the secant method will converge on the root. The rate of the convergence depends on the particular function whose zero is being sought. The rate of convergence can sometimes be improved at the cost of the guarantee of convergence. In the secant method, instead of using one of the end points all the time, two intermediate points can be used. Of course, there may not be a zero between these points but the search interval is much smaller.

A method called the **Newton-Raphson method** is useful for simple functions, like polynomials, whose slopes can be computed using calculus. The iteration formula for approximating the root is

$x(n+1) = xn - f(xn)/s(xn)$

where $x(n+1)$ is the approximation to the root at the $(n+1)$th iteration, xn is the nth approximation, $f(xn)$ is the value of the function at xn, and $s(xn)$ is the value of the slope of the function at xn.

For those who have studied calculus, if, for example,

$f(x) = 3x^2+2x+1$ then
$s(x) = 6x+2$

$s(x)$ is the derivative of $f(x)$.

The Newton-Raphson method has very rapid convergence, but convergence is not always guaranteed.

SUBPROGRAM FOR ROOT FINDING

We will give a subprogram *solve* which uses the interval-halving method. It is perhaps slow, but safe. This is an example of a subprogram identifier being used as a parameter of another subprogram. For the function evaluations in *solve* we use a **parametric function** *func*. The parameter *epsilon* stands for the Greek letter epsilon. In mathematics, we use epsilon to stand for the small difference between an approximation and a true value. We will use as a stopping condition the fact that two successive approximations to the root differ from each other by less than *epsilon*. When you use the *solve* function you must decide what accuracy you want. Of course there is no use asking for greater accuracy than is permitted by the finite representation of the numbers. Note the use of the *sign* predefined function that returns $+1$ for positive arguments, -1 for negative, and 0 for zero.

```
% Find roots of func(x)=0 by interval halving
function solve(left,right,epsilon: real, function func(x: real): real): real
    var x1: real := left
    var x2: real := right
    var root: real
    const signLeft := sign(func(left))
    loop
        root := (x1 + x2)/2
        exit when abs(x2 − x1) < = epsilon
        if signLeft = sign(func(left)) then
            x1 := root
        else
            x2 := root
        end if
    end loop
    result root
end solve
```

We will now use this procedure to find the zero of

$$quad(x) = x^2 - x - 2$$

that is between x=0 and x=3 to an accuracy of 0.00005.

```
% Find one root of quad(x)=x*x − x − 2
% The "zero" program
function quad(x: real): real
    result (x − 1)*x − 2
end quad
(include declaration of solve here)
put "Zero of quadratic is ", solve(0, 3, 5e− 5, quad)
```

The output for this program is

Zero of quadratic is 1.9999987

Notice that the polynomial is being evaluated by Horner's method. We do not need to use this kind of method of root finding for a quadratic but it illustrates the method in a case where we can compute the correct answer which is *2.000000.*

NUMERICAL INTEGRATION

In calculus, we find that the area under a curve can be calculated by evaluating the definite integral of the function that represents the curve between the two limiting values of the independent variable. Not every function can be integrated analytically, but a numerical approximation can be obtained for any continuous function. In the last chapter we presented the trapezoidal rule for calculating areas under curves; the function is evaluated at uniformly spaced intervals between the limiting values and the function values are used to find the area. The accuracy of the result improves as smaller intervals are chosen and more function evaluations made.

For the same number of function evaluations it is possible to have an integration formula that combines the values to give a better approximation to the area.

One formula which is usually better than the trapezoidal formula is called **Simpson's rule**. The trapezoidal formula assumes that each little slice of the area has the shape of a trapezoid; Simpson's rule assumes that the curved boundary of two adjacent slices has the shape of a parabola (a second-degree polynomial). It uses the area under such a parabola that can be found using calculus to give a way of finding the area under the curve. The area must be divided into an even number of slices. The area of any pair of slices is the slice width *delta*, multiplied by one-third of the sum of the values of the function at the outside together with four times the value in the middle. If the complete area is divided into 2 pairs of slices then the area is

$$delta * (f(x1) + 4*f(x2) + 2*f(x3) + 4*f(x4) + f(x5)) / 3$$

You can see how to extend this for more pairs of slices.

We will write a program to compare the accuracy of the result obtained with the same number of function evaluations (slices) using the trapezoidal rule and Simpson's rule. We will calculate the area for a simple curve so that a calculus result can give the exact area for comparison. We will compute the area under the curve

$f(x) = sin(x)$

between the values of $x=0$ and *pi*. From calculus we know the answer should be 2.0000000. We will use 6 slices so that *delta* will be *pi/6*.

```
% The "integrate" program
% Compare Simpson's and trapezoidal rule
const pi := 3.141592
var f: array 1..7 of real
const delta := pi/6
% Evaluate sin(x) at 7 values of x
for i: 0..6
    f(i+1) := sin(i*delta)
end for
% Compute area by trapezoidal rule
const middle := f(2) + f(3) + f(4) + f(5) + f(6)
const trap := delta * (f(1) + 2*middle + f(7)) / 2
% Compute area by Simpson's rule
const even := f(2) + f(4) + f(6)
const odd := f(3) + f(5)
const simp := delta*(f(1) + 4*even + 2*odd + f(7)) / 3
put "Trapezoidal method gives ",trap
put "Simpson's  method gives ",simp
```

Here is the output

Trapezoidal method gives 1.954097
Simpson's   method gives 2.000863

You can see that the error in the trapezoidal method is 0.045903, that in Simpson's rule is 0.000863. This shows that Simpson's rule is a superior one here; the error is smaller.

LINEAR EQUATIONS USING ARRAYS

We have looked at the problem of solving two linear equations in two unknowns. We do not use computers to solve such simple systems. But computers are useful when we have many equations in many unknowns. In handling these problems we store the coefficients of the unknowns in an array. If we had four equations in four unknowns the equations might be written as

$$a(1,1)x1+a(1,2)x2+a(1,3)x3+a(1,4)x4=b1$$
$$a(2,1)x1+a(2,2)x2+a(2,3)x3+a(2,4)x4=b2$$
$$a(3,1)x1+a(3,2)x2+a(3,3)x3+a(3,4)x4=b3$$
$$a(4,1)x1+a(4,2)x2+a(4,3)x3+a(4,4)x4=b4$$

where *a* is a two-dimensional array of the coefficients. We can write the *b*'s, the right-hand sides of these equations, as part of the *a* array by letting *b1=a(1,5), b2=a(2,5)* and so on. To solve the equations, we must reduce these equations in turn to three equations in three unknowns, two equations in two unknowns, and then one equation in one unknown. This method eliminates all the unknowns except one. Then by substituting back you can find the value of all unknowns. If the array of coefficients was of the form

a(1,1) a(1,2) a(1,3) a(1,4) a(1,5)
0   a(2,2) a(2,3) a(2,4) a(2,5)
0   0   a(3,3) a(3,4) a(3,5)
0   0   0   a(4,4) a(4,5)

then we could see from the last line that *x4=a(4,5)/a(4,4)*. Then using this we could substitute back into the equation represented by the second last line namely

$$a(3,3)x3 + a(3,4)x4 = a(3,5)$$

and solve for *x3*, and so on to get *x2* and *x1*.

What we have to do is move from the original array of coefficients to the one with all the zeros in the lower left corner. We do this by dividing each element of the first row by *a(1,1)* and storing it back in the same location. This makes the new value of *a(1,1)* a one. Next multiply this row by *a(2,1)* and subtract it from each element of row two, storing the result back in the same location. The new value of *a(2,1)* will be zero. The process will eventually result in an array with zeros in the lower left.

Certain problems of loss of precision can arise if the element that is currently to be reduced to 1 is small. This element, referred to as the **pivot element**, should be as large as possible. Various ways of rearranging the array can help prevent difficulties but trouble is always possible.

LEAST SQUARES APPROXIMATION

Very often in scientific experiments, measurements of a quantity *y* are made at various values of an independent variable *x*. It may be known from theory that the relationship between *y* and *x* is a linear one, for example

$$y = ax + b$$

The various corresponding values of *x* and *y* can be plotted on a graph; there would be a number of points, say *n*. A straight line drawn through any two of these points would not pass exactly through the others. We want to choose the values of the constants *a* and *b* so that they define a straight line in such a way that the sum of the squares of deviations of the actual points from the straight line is a minimum, that is, the sum of squares is least. For the *i*th point, say at x_i, y_i, the deviation squared is

$$(y_i - (a*x_i + b))^2$$

We want the minimum so we use calculus and set the derivatives with respect to the variables equal to zero. We can differentiate a sum of squares of this type partially with respect to *a* and *b*, the values that can be varied, and set the derivatives equal to zero. This gives two equations. One is the sum of *n* terms of the form

$$y_i - (a*x_i + b)$$

set equal to zero. The value of *i* goes from 1 to *n*. The other is the sum of *n* terms of the form

$$(y_i - (a*x_i + b))*x_i$$

set equal to zero. These two equations can be written as two equations in two unknowns, *a* and *b*. These are

$$c_1*a + c_2*b = c_3$$
$$c_4*a + c_5*b = c_6$$

where c_1 is the sum of values x_i with *i* going from 1 to *n*; c_2 is *n* and c_3 is the sum of values y_i with *i* going from 1 to *n*; c_4 is the sum of x_i*x_i from 1 to *n*, c_5 the sum of x_i from 1 to *n*, and c_6 the sum of x_i*y_i from 1 to *n*. The solution to the two equations can easily be found once they are formed.

This same technique can be used for points that in theory lie on a higher degree curve than a straight line but the calculation is more complex.

MATHEMATICAL SOFTWARE

We have been describing a few of the simpler numerical methods used in scientific calculations. Over the years these methods have been improved and made more reliable, more efficient, and more accurate. Nowadays we usually rely on a packaged program for carrying out this type of calculation. We call the program packages **mathematical software**, to distinguish them from the programs that operate the system or compile programs. These latter are called systems software and compilers respectively.

Mathematical software packages exist for almost every standard numerical calculation. All that you must do is to find out how to call them in your program, and what their limitations are. Every piece of software should be documented so that you do not need to read it to be able to use it. You must know what each input parameter of the subprogram is and what range of values is permitted. You must know also how the output is stored so that you can use it.

Frequently software packages are stored in the secondary memory of the computer and may be included in your program by using special control statements in your program.

One of the great things about science is that we build on the work of others and using subprograms prepared by others is good scientific practice. Of course these subprograms must meet the highest standards.

CHAPTER 20 SUMMARY

In this chapter we have been examining numerical methods for evaluating polynomials and infinite series, calculating areas under curves, solving systems of linear equations, and obtaining least squares approximations. We were concerned particularly with certain properties of the methods.

Efficiency of a method — the amount of work, as measured in number of basic arithmetic operations required to obtain a certain numerical result. Horner's rule for polynomial evaluation is more efficient than the straightforward method. It is more efficient because it requires fewer multiplications.

Horner's rule — a method for computing the value of a polynomial that is efficient. The polynomial

$$y = 5x^2 + 2x + 3$$

is evaluated by the Turing statement which represents Horner's rule

y := (5*x + 2)*x + 3

rather than

y := 5*x*x + 2*x + 3

Round-off error — error in real numbers introduced because a computer represents the number by a finite string of bits. When real numbers are added or subtracted the round-off error of the sum or difference is the sum of the round-off errors of the two individual numbers. In multiplications the relative errors add.

Generated error — round-off errors produced due to arithmetic operations. The fewer the arithmetic operations the smaller the cumulative round-off error generated.

Propagated error — generated round-off errors that grow as calculations proceed.

Significant digits — digits in the representation of a real number that are not in error. Numbers are often quoted with a final decimal digit that may be in error by as much as unity. Digits that are not significant should not be quoted in an answer.

Loss of significant digits — this may occur as the result of subtraction of nearly equal numbers.

Infinite series — many mathematical functions such as *sin, cos, exp*, and *log* can be written as a sum of an infinite series of terms. These series may be used to evaluate the functions. Because the terms in the series eventually decrease in magnitude, a good approximation can be obtained by stopping the addition after a certain number of terms.

Rate of convergence — the ratio of the magnitude of two adjacent terms of an infinite series. For *sin(x)* the ratio is $x^2/(2i(2i+1))$. If x is less than 1 then this ratio is always less than one. If x is greater than 1 the terms might initially get larger but eventually get smaller. A series cannot converge if the term ratio never becomes less than 1.

Double precision — keeping twice the basic number of bits to represent a number in the computer. Calculations carried out to double precision maintain a larger number of significant figures.

Interval-halving method — for finding a root of an equation $f(x)=0$ by a method similar to binary search. The method is guaranteed to converge on a root since the root is always kept between the end points of the interval and the interval is constantly decreasing in size.

Secant method — a method that sometimes has better convergence properties than interval halving for finding a root of an equation.

Newton-Raphson — a method for finding a zero of a function whose derivative can be computed. Convergence is rapid but not guaranteed.

Stopping criterion — the size of error that is to be tolerated in a result due to truncating such as in evaluating an infinite series term by term or iterating to find a root.

Numerical integration — approximation of the value of the definite integral which represents the area between the curve and the *x*-axis between two limits.

Simpson's rule — for numerical integration, assumes each pair of slices of area under a curve is bounded by a parabola. The trapezoidal method assumes each slice is bounded by a straight line. Simpson's rule often gives greater accuracy for the same number of slices (function evaluations).

Array of coefficients — for linear equations. This is manipulated so as to be transformed into an array that is triangular, that is, has zero elements on the lower left of the diagonal. This is accomplished by operations such as multiplying a row by a constant and subtracting one row from another. Neither of these operations alters the values of the unknowns.

Back substitution — evaluating the unknown once the transformed set of linear equations can be represented by a triangular array.

Least squares approximation — finding an equation to represent experimental information so that the sum of the squares of the deviations is a minimum. We investigated the case of fitting a straight line to a set of experimental points.

Mathematical software — prefabricated subprograms embodying good numerical methods for getting standard results. The software should be documented to alert the user to the accuracy to be expected, the cost of the result, and any limitations that must be respected.

CHAPTER 20 EXERCISES

1. Write a function subprogram that will compute the sine of an angle whose value in radians is between *0* and *pi/2*. Use the series for sine for angles between *0* and *pi/4* and for cosine between *pi/4* and *pi/2*. Use the same number of terms in each series. Test your program and compare the results with those obtained by using the predeclared function *sin*. Try varying the number of terms in the series.

2. Compute the value of *exp(1)* using the series. Find the values as each term is added up to a maximum of 8 terms.

3. Use the predeclared function for *exp(x)* to tabulate values of this function for *x* going from -10 to $+10$. Sketch the graph of the function for this range. You may choose to use the program for graph plotting on the screen.

4. Use the interval-halving subroutine to find a root of the equation

    2x − tan(x) = 0

    given that there is at least one between 0 and *pi* radians.

5. Use Newton's method of finding roots to find a root of the polynomial

    $$x^4 + 6x^2 - 1 = 0$$

6. Use Simpson's rule to find the area under the curve

    $$y = x^2 - 2x - 1$$

    from *x=0* to 3. Does it matter how many slices you have? Test this.

7. Write a procedure that keeps doubling the number of slices in an area calculation using Simpson's rule until two successive results for the area under a curve agree to within an accuracy *epsilon*. Make sure you do not have to reevaluate the function at places already computed.

8. Compare Simpson's rule and the trapezoidal rule for finding areas under a curve for *y=exp(x)* between *x=0* and *x=1*. Do you know the answer from calculus?

9. Write a procedure that will solve a set of *n* equations in *n* unknowns. Do not include any form of pivoting. Would you expect this to be a good piece of mathematical software?

10. Write a procedure that will solve two linear equations in two unknowns. Do you encounter any problems about loss of accuracy with such a small system of equations? What happens when there is no solution, for example, if the two equations represent parallel lines?

11. Write a procedure that accepts two arrays *x* and *y* of *n* values that represent *n* points and outputs the equation of the straight line that gives a minimum value to the sum of the square of the deviations of the points from the straight line.

Chapter 21
PROGRAMMING IN OTHER LANGUAGES

In this book we have been presenting structured programming in the high-level language Turing. Turing was designed in 1982 by R.C. Holt and J.R. Cordy of the Computer Systems Research Group at the University of Toronto. The first Turing compiler was operative in early 1983. The language was developed in response to inadequacies of the language Pascal, but is a Pascal-like language. There are a number of extended Pascal dialects, such as UCSD Pascal, but even these do not get over some of its problems, particularly for scientific computing. Pascal was introduced in 1971 by Niklaus Wirth. It has enjoyed great acceptance because it had a well-defined syntax and relatively few language constructs. It was well suited to accompany the move to structured programming, and could be implemented on microcomputers. Pascal has influenced the design of a number of other high-level languages such as Euclid. It grew out of the development of Algol-W which was an extension of Algol 60. Algol 60 was a language designed with the hope that it might be a universal language for scientific computing. Cobol was a language designed for business data processing. Cobol stands for COmmon Business Oriented Language; it is used very widely in business applications of computers. As it stated in the official Cobol report "Cobol is an industry language and is not the property of any company or group of companies; or of any organization or group of organizations".

PL/1, or Programming Language One, was designed in an attempt to combine the capabilities of Algol, Fortran, and Cobol. Unfortunately it was too extensive a language and its compilers needed larger computers. Several successful subsets of PL/1 have been devised with their appropriate compilers. These include PL/C from Cornell University and SP/k from the University of Toronto.

Fortran, the earliest of the common high-level languages, has had many improvements made in it since it was presented in 1956. Some of these improvements were incorporated in Standard Fortran, or Fortran

66, by the American National Standards Institute. And further improvements are contained in Fortran 77.

As new languages appear older programming languages are often extended to incorporate the improvements. Many are nonetheless attracted to make a change to the new language. We believe that Turing is the ideal general programming language for the '80s. It is a powerful language but one that is very straightforward, with minimal eccentricities. It has benefitted from its predecessors even from languages such as Basic.

In this chapter we will be looking at these different languages so you can see that, once you have learned to program in one, it would not be difficult to program in another. You will have learned the fundamentals of programming and can quickly adapt to a different language.

PL/1, PASCAL, AND FORTRAN 77

We cannot present very much of the syntax of the PL/1, Pascal, or Fortran 77 languages in this book but we will compare them with Turing by way of a single example program. This will give you an idea of the similarities among these four languages. The example has been chosen to demonstrate the two kinds of loops: the counted loop and the conditional loop. A series of data entries is to be read, each containing, in the first 8 columns right-justified, the cost in cents of a certain item, then a blank column and, in the next two columns, the expected lifetime in years of the item. The program reads these entries, until the end-of-file entry with a lifetime of 99 years is reached. For each entry it calculates and outputs a table, with an appropriate label, giving the balance at the end of each year for the item after the depreciation has been subtracted. This is done for the lifetime of the item. The balance in the last year will be close to zero, if it is not precisely zero.

Thus for input data

500.00 5

the computer should output

```
COST=   500.00 LIFE=  5
  1  400.00
  2  300.00
  3  200.00
  4  100.00
  5    0.00
```

We have been using little letters for our Turing programs as is done in many Pascal programs this makes our program easy to type and easy to read. It is more common to program PL/1 or Fortran in capital letters so our programs and output for these other languages will be given that way.

Also many systems using Fortran or Cobol operate in a batch mode rather than interactively. Programs must then have some entry such as $JOB preceding them and data is preceded by an entry such as $ENTRY or $DATA. We have not needed these in our Turing programs but if we operated in a batch environment we would have.

The four programs have their lines numbered so we can make reference to them. Some lines are left blank so that corresponding parts of the program are on the same line number. First of all here is the Turing program for doing the job. We are using variable identifiers that are at most 6 characters long because they are so limited in Fortran.

```
1
2        % The "example" program
3        % This is a comment
4        var life: int
5        var cost, deprec, balnce: real
6        loop
7            get cost, life
8            exit when life = 99
9            put "  COST= ", cost: 8: 2, " LIFE= ", life: 2
10           deprec := cost/life
11           balnce := cost
12
13           for year: 1..life
14               balnce := balnce-deprec
15               put year: 2, balnce: 8: 2
16
17           end for
18       end loop
```

Here is a Fortran 77 program for doing the same job.

```
1   $JOB      FORTRAN 77
2
3 C THIS IS A COMMENT
4         INTEGER LIFE,YEAR
5         REAL COST,DEPREC,BALNCE
6         READ 50,COST,LIFE
7    50   FORMAT(F8.2,1X,I2)
8    80   IF(LIFE.EQ.99)GO TO 250
9         PRINT 90,'COST= ',COST,' LIFE= ',LIFE
10   90   FORMAT(' ',A6,F8.2,A7,I2)
11        DEPREC=COST/LIFE
12        BALNCE=COST
13        DO 150 YEAR=1,LIFE
14            BALNCE=BALNCE-DEPREC
15            PRINT 100,YEAR,BALNCE
16   100      FORMAT(' ',I2,F8.2)
17   150      CONTINUE
18        READ 200,COST,LIFE
19   200  FORMAT(F8.2,1X,I2)
20        GO TO 80
21   250  CONTINUE
22      STOP
23      END
24   $ENTRY
     500.00  5
     480.00  3
       0.00 99
```

We will compare these two programs and the ones on the next two pages line by line. Line 1 is the job control entry used for batch processing which is different for different operating systems in the way the job identification is given. As well there may be a different character used immediately after the $JOB to indicate different compilers. We have not shown such a line for Turing. In line 2 we have the heading that is necessary for all PL/1 and Pascal programs. In Pascal, *example* is a name the programmer has chosen, but the rest is all standard. A Fortran program requires no such introductory line. The Turing language does not require such a line but in this book we have used a comment to record the file name for the program. Line 3 shows how comments are handled. Lines 4 and 5 give the declarations of variables. Fortran uses the keywords INTEGER and REAL, like Pascal, for what PL/1 calls FIXED and FLOAT. By this time you have probably noticed that PL/1 statements are

terminated by a semicolon. This is so they could all be run together on the same line. Pascal statements are **separated** by a semicolon. Fortran must be placed properly on lines or the compiler would be very confused. Turing needs no such punctuation but, with the exception of comments which must be terminated by the end of a line, the lines may all be run together. The compiler can cope.

Both PL/1 and Fortran 77 have more formatting control for the input statement than does Pascal. The formatted input statement in PL/1 is GET EDIT. In PL/1 the list of format items is in parentheses after the list of output items and is in the same statement. In Fortran, a separate FORMAT line gives the format items. We have split the single PL/1 statement into two lines to show the parallelism. In Pascal we have *readln*.

Here is the program written in Pascal.

```
1      $job 'Pascal'
2      program example(input,output);
3          (* this is a comment *)
4          var life,year:integer;
5              cost,deprec,balnce:real;
6          begin
7              readln(cost,life);
8              while life<> 99 do
9                  begin
10                     writeln(' COST= ',cost:8:2,' LIFE= ',life:2);
11                     deprec:=cost/life;
12                     balnce:=cost;
13                     for year:=1 to life do
                           begin
14                             balnce:=balnce-deprec;
15                             writeln(year:2,balnce:8:2)
16
17                         end;
18                     readln(cost,life)
19
20                 end
21
22          end.

$data
          500.00  5
          480.00  3
            0.00  99
```

Here is the program written in PL/1

```
1      $JOB ID='PL/1'
2      EXAMPLE:PROCEDURE OPTIONS(MAIN);
3          /* THIS IS A COMMENT */
4          DECLARE(LIFE,YEAR)FIXED;
5          DECLARE(COST,DEPREC,BALNCE)FLOAT;
6          GET EDIT(COST,LIFE)
7              (F(8,2),X(1),F(2));
8          DO WHILE(LIFE^=99);
9              PUT SKIP EDIT('COST= ',COST,' LIFE= ',LIFE)
10                 (A(6),F(8,2),A(7),F(2));
11             DEPREC=COST/LIFE;
12             BALNCE=COST;
13             DO YEAR=1 TO LIFE;
14                 BALNCE=BALNCE-DEPREC;
15                 PUT SKIP EDIT(YEAR,BALNCE)
16                     (F(2),F(8,2));
17                 END;
18             GET EDIT(COST,LIFE)
19                 (F(8,2),X(1),F(2));
20             END;
21
22         END;
23
24     $DATA
           (same data as before)
```

In line 8 we have the beginning of the conditional loop (line 6 in Turing). In Fortran the **termination condition** is given after the IF. In Turing it is after the **exit when** of line 8. In PL/1 the **continuation condition** is given after the DO WHILE. The one condition is the opposite of the other. The relational operator that we would write in Fortran as .NE., we write in PL/1 as ¬= and in Pascal we use < >.

In the output labelling in lines 9 and 10, the SKIP in PL/1 does the same thing as the ' ' in the FORMAT of Fortran, namely starts the printing on a new line. In Pascal using *writeln* instead of *write* does this.

In line 13 a counted loop begins. Notice that in PL/1 as in Pascal or Turing there is no need to say at the start of the loop where the loop ends. The compiler is perfectly capable of deciding when it reaches an end. In line 20 the end of the conditional loop is signified (in line 18 of Turing); control is automatically returned to line 8 in PL/1 or Pascal and explicitly returned in Fortran by the GO TO 80. In PL/1, END is all that is necessary to terminate the program. Note that it has a semicolon following it and not, as in Pascal, a period. Fortran has STOP before END. A Turing program needs no special instruction at its end.

ALGOL 60

We will now show a program written in Algol to produce the same result as we showed in Turing, Pascal, Fortran 77, and PL/1. The actual dialect is that of Algol-W.

ALGOL-W

```
1     $JOB   ALGOL-W
2        BEGIN
3           COMMENT THIS IS A COMMENT;
4           INTEGER LIFE,YEAR;
5           REAL COST,DEPREC,BALNCE;
6           READ(COST,LIFE);
7
8           WHILE(LIFE¬=99)DO
9             BEGIN WRITE('COST= ',COST,' LIFE= ',LIFE);
10
11             DEPREC:=COST/LIFE;
12             BALNCE:=COST;
13             FOR YEAR:=1 UNTIL LIFE DO
14                BEGIN
15                   BALNCE:=BALNCE-DEPREC;
15                   WRITE(YEAR,BALNCE)
16
17                END;
18             READ(COST,LIFE)
19
20          END
21
22       END
23
24       $DATA
```

This program is closer to Pascal than to the PL/1 and Fortran programs already given. It has the keyword BEGIN as a header and this is also used to begin the body of the conditional loop in line 9 and the indexed loop in line 14. Each BEGIN has its corresponding END. There is no input or output formatting at all in Algol-W, so we use the unformatted READ and WRITE. You probably can see that these four languages have many similarities. The assignment statement of Turing, Pascal, and Algol uses ":=" instead of "=" as do PL/1 and Fortran.

For a while Algol 60 enjoyed considerable popularity partly because it was hoped that it might become an international standard language, not linked to any specific machine manufacturer. (Fortran had originated with IBM.) Two other virtues that it enjoyed were that it supplied control structures that permitted well-structured programs and, perhaps less important, that its syntax had been defined in a formal way.

Fortran has maintained its prominence over the years and, ever since Fortran 66, is no longer connected with just one manufacturer. Its syntax is formally described by the American National Standards Institute (X3.9-1978). The fact that Fortran 77 now has an IF...THEN...ELSE helps structured programming. Its new character handling ability (which Algol-W had) enlarges its usefulness. And format-free input and output (which Algol-W had) makes it easier for the beginner.

COBOL

A complete Cobol program consists of a number of different divisions which permit great flexibility in the use of the various input-output components of a computer system. These are called the IDENTIFICATION, ENVIRONMENT, and DATA divisions. Some compilers, such as Watbol from the University of Waterloo allow a beginning Cobol programmer to by-pass these divisions by using a standard assignment for files, card reader, and printer. We will just show the remaining part of a Cobol program which consists of the WORKING STORAGE SECTION and the PROCEDURE DIVISION. These are the parts that correspond to our other programs. The WORKING STORAGE SECTION contains the parts that are in declarations and format specifications. Variables and formats are described in terms of pictures (PIC). In the PIC description a 9 indicates a digit, an X any character, and a V a decimal point. A picture described as

PIC 9(6)V99

is of a number with 6 digits to the left of the decimal point and 2 digits to the right. The name FILLER is used for blanks in a record or print line. Like Turing and Pascal, Cobol has records. PL/1 also has records but

Fortran does not. The record name is defined at level 01, the fields at level 02. Although our example does not show it, a record may be moved from one place to another as a unit.

Cobol was intended to provide business people with very readable programs, a goal that we applaud, but sometimes as a programmer it gets monotonous writing out all the keywords in a Cobol sentence. There are alternatives; for instance, the sentence

> SUBTRACT DEPREC FROM BALNCE.

could be written as

> COMPUTE BALNCE=BALNCE−DEPREC.

and then it would look like our other languages.

Each Cobol sentence ends with a period. The corresponding line numbers of the other programs are given along the left margin.

COBOL Program

```
        DATA DIVISION.
        FILE SECTION.
        FD  INPUT-FILE
              LABEL RECORD OMITTED.
        01    INPUT-RECORD.
5             02    COST              PIC 9(6)V99.
              02    FILLER            PIC X.
4             02    LIFE              PIC 99.
              02    FILLER            PIC X(69).
        FD  PRINTER
              LABEL RECORD OMITTED.
        01    PRINT-LINE              PIC X(133).
        01    OUTPUT-RECORD.
15-16         02    FILLER            PIC X.
              02    YEAR              PIC 99.
              02    BALNCE            PIC 9(6).99.
        WORKING-STORAGE SECTION.
        01    OUTPUT-LABEL.
9-10          02    FILLER            PIC X(7) VALUE ' COST= '.
              02    COST              PIC 9(6).99.
              02    FILLER            PIC X(7) VALUE ' LIFE= '.
              02    LIFE              PIC 99.
        01    VARIABLES.
4-5           02    YEAR              PIC 99.
              02    DEPREC            PIC 9(6)V99.
```

```
              02   BALNCE                    PIC 9(6)V99.
2        PROCEDURE DIVISION.
              OPEN INPUT INPUT-FILE, OUTPUT PRINTER.
6-7           READ INPUT-FILE
                  AT END MOVE HIGH-VALUE TO LIFE OF INPUT-RECORD.
8             PERFORM OUTER-LOOP
                  UNTIL LIFE OF INPUT-RECORD EQUALS HIGH-VALUE.
              CLOSE INPUT-FILE, PRINTER.
22            STOP RUN.
         OUTER-LOOP.
9-10          MOVE CORR INPUT-RECORD TO OUTPUT-LABEL.
              WRITE PRINT-LINE FROM OUTPUT-LABEL.
11            DIVIDE LIFE OF INPUT-RECORD INTO COST OF INPUT-RECORD
                  GIVING DEPREC ROUNDED.
12            MOVE COST OF INPUT-RECORD TO BALNCE.
13            PERFORM INNER-LOOP
                  VARYING YEAR OF VARIABLES FROM 1 BY 1
                  UNTIL YEAR OF VARIABLES IS GREATER THAN
                  LIFE OF INPUT-RECORD.
18-19         READ INPUT-FILE
                  AT END MOVE HIGH-VALUE TO LIFE OF INPUT-RECORD.
         INNER-LOOP.
14            SUBTRACT DEPREC FROM BALNCE.
15-16         MOVE CORR VARIABLES TO OUTPUT-RECORD.
              WRITE OUTPUT-RECORD.
```

In the PROCEDURE DIVISION it is necessary to OPEN the input and output devices and at the end to CLOSE them before STOP RUN. HIGH-VALUE is a keyword meaning a value beyond the normal range of a variable similar to putting 99 for LIFE in the Fortran or PL/1 programs to indicate the end-of-file. A loop body is listed separately under a paragraph name. For example, the outer conditional loop, called OUTER-LOOP, is invoked by the sentence

        PERFORM OUTER-LOOP
            UNTIL LIFE OF INPUT-RECORD EQUALS HIGH-VALUE.

The body of this loop is listed after the paragraph heading.

        OUTER-LOOP.

In the outer loop the counted inner loop is invoked by

        PERFORM INNER-LOOP
            VARYING YEAR OF VARIABLES FROM 1 BY 1
            UNTIL YEAR OF VARIABLES IS GREATER THAN

LIFE OF INPUT-RECORD.

and the inner loop body is listed after the paragraph name

INNER-LOOP.

There is no doubt that the Cobol program is longer and wordier, but Cobol is still the most commonly used language for business data processing.

CHAPTER 21 SUMMARY

In this chapter we have been comparing Turing with some other high-level programming languages. These were Pascal, PL/1, Fortran 77, Algol 60, and Cobol. It is clear that the fundamentals of programming learned in Turing make it relatively easy to learn other languages. But the Turing language has benefitted from our experience with the other languages; it has a simplicity and a power that recommends it.

The following important terms were introduced.

Incompatible — dialects of the same basic programming language are incompatible if programs that are correct in one dialect are incorrect in another. Fortran was standardized to minimize incompatibilities among the various Fortran compilers. Pascal is well standardized because it was carefully defined. There are certain versions of Pascal in which there are extensions to the language. UCSD Pascal is an extended Pascal.

Compatible subset — a portion of a more extensive language that does not contain all the constructs present in the larger language but may contain some restrictions on the use of the language not enforced in the main language.

Extensions - constructs that are added to a language thus making the extended language incompatible with the original language. Fortran 77 added a number of extensions to Fortran 66. Fortran 66 programs are compatible with Fortran 77 but not vice versa.

Portable — a program is portable if it can be run on different computers. One way of making programs portable is to write them in a high-level language such as Turing, Pascal, or Fortran 77 for which there exists a precise definition.

PL/1 — short for Programming Language One, a programming language developed to contain the constructs necessary for both scientific applications and business data processing.

Algol 60 — a programming language that many hoped would become an international standard language for scientific computing. In its dialect Algol-W, the ability to handle characters and have format-free input-output was added. Pascal evolved from this language.

CHAPTER 21 EXERCISES

1. Translate the following Turing program segment to Pascal, Algol, PL/1, and Fortran 77.

   > **if** *a*> =*b* **then**
   >   *a := 5*
   >   **put** *b*
   > **end if**

2. Find any three complete programs or subprograms in other chapters of this book, each at least 15 lines long, and try to translate them to Pascal, Algol 60, PL/1, and Fortran 77. List any questions about these three languages that arise in trying to make the translations. If you have any of these compilers available try running the program.

3. Why are statement labels not needed in the Turing, Pascal, Algol, and PL/1, programs that we have shown.

4. Find a textbook giving Cobol programs and see if you can read and understand some of them.

5. Various compilers respond to program syntax errors in different ways. Try purposely making a few errors in programs for Pascal, PL/1, or Fortran 77 to see what response you get from the compiler. How does it compare with your Turing compiler?

6. Consult a textbook on PL/1 and list three features of the language that you did not know about after reading this chapter.

Chapter 22

ASSEMBLY LANGUAGE
AND MACHINE LANGUAGE

In this book we have presented programming in terms of the Turing language. Turing is a **high-level language**; it provides us with a convenient means for directing a computer to do work. The computer cannot execute Turing programs directly; it can only execute programs in machine language, a **low-level language**. Before a Turing program can be executed by a computer, the program must be **translated** or **compiled** to machine language. In this chapter we will explain how a computer carries out instructions. We will present features of machine languages and their associated assembly languages.

MACHINE INSTRUCTIONS

In Chapter 2 we gave a brief introduction of machine language. We explained that the instructions a computer can execute are much more basic than Turing statements. These **machine instructions** use a special location, called the **accumulator**, when doing arithmetic or making assignments. For example, the assignment of j to i, written as the Turing statement

$i:=j$

could be translated to the instructions

load	*j*	(copy j into the accumulator)
store	*i*	(copy the accumulator into i)

As another example, the Turing statement

$i := j + k$

could be translated into the three instructions

load	*j*	(copy j into the accumulator)
add	*k*	(add k to the accumulator)
store	*i*	(copy the accumulator into i)

Different kinds of computers have different machine languages. Some computers have many accumulators and some have few. Some computers have many instructions and some have few. We will introduce common features of machine languages by inventing a very simple computer. We will call our computer VS, for **very simple** computer. The machine instructions for the VS computer are designed to be convenient for representing programs written in a subset of Turing. The VS computer has never been built; it is just a hypothetical machine that we will use to illustrate points about computer languages. The instructions for the VS computer have the form

> operator operand

for example,

> *store i*

The **operator** of an instruction tells the computer what to do; the **operand** tells the computer what to do it to. After the computer executes one instruction, it continues to the next, unless the executed instruction directs the computer to jump to another instruction or to skip an instruction. We can translate the Turing statements

> **if** $i < = k$ **then**
> $k := i + j$
> **end if**
> $i := j$

into the VS computer instructions

load	*k*	(copy *k* into the accumulator)
skiple	*i*	(if $i < =$ accumulator, skip next instruction)
jump	*m*	(jump to instruction labelled *m*)
load	*i*	(copy *i* into the accumulator)
add	*j*	(add *j* to the accumulator)
store	*k*	(copy the accumulator into *k*)
m : load	*j*	(copy *j* into the accumulator)
store	*i*	(copy the accumulator into *i*)

In this example, *m* is the **label** of an instruction; instructions are labelled so they can be jumped to. In languages like Fortran and Pascal, but not in Turing, there are statement labels and there is a **goto** statement that is analogous to the *jump* machine instruction. In the Pascal language, the following statements are equivalent to the example we just gave:

> **if** $i > k$ **then**
>   **goto** *23;*
> $k := i + j;$
> 23: $i := j$

The **goto** statement was purposely left out of Turing because careless use of it leads to unreadable programs. One of the reasons that low-level languages are inconvenient to use is that they do not directly provide looping constructs, such as **loop...end loop**, and selection constructs, such as **if...then...else...end if**. The programmer must build up these constructs using instructions like jumps and skips. When a Turing program is translated into a low-level language, the loop and selection constructs appear as jumps and skips.

INSTRUCTIONS FOR A VERY SIMPLE COMPUTER

The instruction to output the value in the accumulator is:

putInteger

This instruction needs no operand because the accumulator's value is always output. There is an instruction to output messages:

putString operand

The operand represents a string to be output. There is an instruction that directs the machine to stop executing a program:

halt

The *halt* instruction has no operand.

Altogether the VS computer has nine instructions; most real computers have many more instructions, typically around 100. This table lists the VS instructions.

	Operator	Operand	Action by Computer
1	*load*	variable	Assign variable to accumulator.
2	*store*	variable	Assign accumulator to variable.
3	*add*	variable	Add variable to accumulator.
4	*subtract*	variable	Subtract variable from accumulator.
5	*jump*	label	Jump to labelled instruction.
6	*skiple*	variable	If variable $<=$ accumulator then skip next instructon.
7	*putInteger*	(none)	Output the integer in the accumulator.
8	*putString*	string	Output the string.
9	*halt*	(none)	Halt, the program is finished.

We have purposely kept the VS computer simple by leaving out instructions that might normally be part of the instruction set of a computer. We have left out a whole set of skip instructions, such as *skipgt* (skip when greater than). We left out instructions for doing real arithmetic and for reading data. We left out instructions for manipulating character strings, indexing arrays, and calling and returning from procedures. These additional instructions are important in a real computer; if you like, you can design a super VS computer that includes them.

TRANSLATION OF A TURING PROGRAM

If we use some care in picking our example, we can translate an entire Turing program into VS instructions. This example Turing program requires only the types of instructions available on the VS computer:

High-Level Language		Low-Level Language	
% The "t" program			
var *i:* **int**			
put *"Powers of 2"*		*putstring*	*title*
i := 1		*load*	*one*
		store	*i*
loop	*l1:*	*load*	*eight*
exit when *i> 8*		*skiple*	*i*
		jump	*l2*
put *i*		*load*	*i*
		putInteger	
i :=i+i		*load*	*i*
		add	*i*
		store	*i*
end loop		*jump*	*l1*
	l2:	*halt*	

The first VS instruction in this example has as its operand *title; title* gives the location of the string *Powers of 2.* Similarly, *one* and *eight* give the locations of the values 1 and 8.

MNEMONIC NAMES AND MACHINE LANGUAGE

Up to this point we have written VS instructions using names such as *load, store, i,* and *j*. These names are not present in the machine language that a computer executes; they are replaced by numbers. We will now show how these names can be translated into appropriate numbers.

As you may recall from Chapter 2, the main memory of the computer consists of a sequence of **words**. The words of memory are numbered; the number that corresponds to a particular word is called the **location** or **address** of the word. Words can be used to represent variables. For example, the variables *i, j,* and *k* could be represented by the words with locations 59, 60, and 61. Here we show these three words after *i, j*, and *k* have been assigned the values 9, 0, and 14.

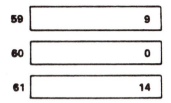

There is no special significance to 59, 60, and 61. We could just as well represent *i, j*, and *k* by locations 42, 3, and 87; the important thing is to remember which location corresponds to which variable.

If *i, j*, and *k* correspond to location 59, 60, and 61, we can write the instructions

        load   *j*
        add   *k*
        store   *i*
as
        load   *60*   (copy contents of word 60 into accumulator)
        add   *61*   (add contents of word 61 to accumulator)
        store   *59*   (copy accumulator into word 59)

The VS instruction operators, *load, store*, and so on, are numbered. The *load* operator is number 1, *store* is 2, *add* is 3, and so on. The names *load, store*, and *add* as used in the VS instructions are **mnemonic names**; a mnemonic name is an easy-to-remember name. We can choose the names of the operands so that they too are easy to remember.

Using the numbers of the operators we can write

        load   *60*
        add   *61*
        store   *59*
as
        1   *60*
        3   *61*
        2   *59*

Instructions that consist only of numbers are in **machine language**. Instructions that contain mnemonic names, such as *load* and *i*, are in **assembly language**.

Assembly Language	Machine Language
load j	*1 60*
add k	*3 61*
store i	*2 59*

As you can see, there is a simple translation from assembly language to machine language. Writing programs in machine language is even more inconvenient than writing programs in assembly language. People almost always prefer assembly language over machine language; they use a program called an **assembler** to translate mnemonic names in assembly language programs to corresponding numeric operators and operands. Although we do not show it here, assemblers allow the programmer to reserve and initialize memory for variables and constants. For example, location 59 would be reserved for *i*, and location 98 could be reserved for *eight* and initialized to 8.

STORING MACHINE INSTRUCTIONS IN WORDS

The values of variables of a program are stored in words of the computer's memory. In a similar manner, the instructions of the program are stored in words of memory. We can use two words to hold each VS instruction; one word for the operator and one word for the operand. Here we show three instructions stored in locations 18 through 23:

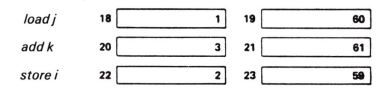

We could have saved space if the VS computer allowed us to pack the operator and operand into a single word. For example, the instruction *1 59* could be packed into a single word as *1059* with the convention that the rightmost three digits are the operand and the other digits are the operator. Instructions for real computers are packed into words to save space, but to keep things simple, the VS computer uses two words for its instructions.

A *jump* instruction has as its operand the label of an instruction. When a *jump* instruction is written in machine language, the label must be a number. The number used is the location of the instruction being jumped to. Here is a translation of assembly language into machine language; the label *l* becomes 48:

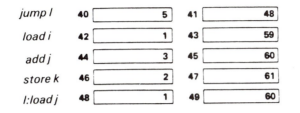

jump *l*	40	5	41	48
load *i*	42	1	43	59
add *j*	44	3	45	60
store *k*	46	2	47	61
l:load *j*	48	1	49	60

Just as the variables and instructions are stored in words in memory, strings such as *Powers of 2* are stored in memory. In real computers this is done by packing several characters into each word. Since mixing characters and numbers is confusing, we will assume that the VS computer has a separate part of its memory used only for strings. Each string is saved in a different location in the special string memory. If the string *Powers of 2* is in location 1 in the special string memory, then we translate the Turing statement

put *"Powers of 2"*

to the machine instruction

    8   1   *(putString title)*

We have now shown how to translate all VS instructions into numbers and thus into machine language. We will return to our program that outputs powers of 2 and will translate it to machine language.

A COMPLETE MACHINE LANGUAGE PROGRAM

We will assume that a VS computer starts by executing the instruction in words 0 and 1. So we will place our machine language instructions in words 0, 1, 2, 3, ... We will continue assuming that variable *i* corresponds to memory location 59. The integer constants 1 and 8 will be represented by memory locations 91 and 98; these locations are initialized to hold the values 1 and 8 before the program is executed. We show the program as it would appear in memory after having executed instructions in locations 0 through 14. Up to this point the program has output

    Powers of   2
    1

The VS computer has an **instruction pointer**, presently set to 16, that locates the next instruction to be executed. When an instruction has no operand, we give it a dummy operand of zero; for example, *halt* becomes 9 0.

STORAGE OF PROGRAM IN COMPUTER

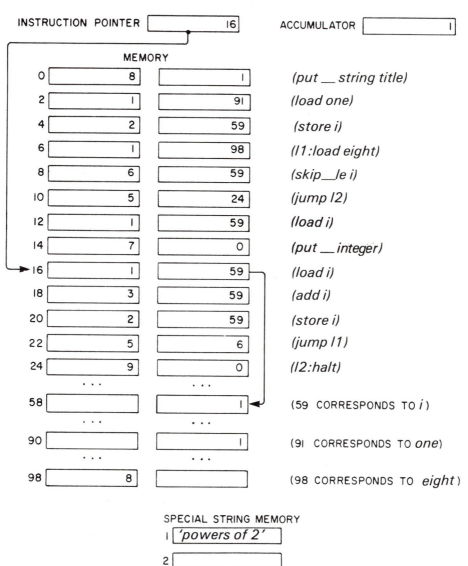

INSTRUCTION POINTER [16]   ACCUMULATOR [1]

MEMORY

0	8	1	*(put __ string title)*
2	1	91	*(load one)*
4	2	59	*(store i)*
6	1	98	*(l1:load eight)*
8	6	59	*(skip__le i)*
10	5	24	*(jump l2)*
12	1	59	*(load i)*
14	7	0	*(put __ integer)*
16	1	59	*(load i)*
18	3	59	*(add i)*
20	2	59	*(store i)*
22	5	6	*(jump l1)*
24	9	0	*(l2:halt)*
...		...	
58		1	(59 CORRESPONDS TO *i*)
...		...	
90		1	(91 CORRESPONDS TO *one*)
...		...	
98	8		(98 CORRESPONDS TO *eight*)

SPECIAL STRING MEMORY

1 [*'powers of 2'*]

2 [ ]

...

SIMULATING A COMPUTER

A VS computer has never been built and undoubtedly never will be built. It might seem that we can never have a VS machine language program executed. But we can, by making an existing computer **simulate** a VS computer. This is done by writing a program, called a **simulator**, that acts as if it is a VS computer. We will discuss later in more detail the importance of simulators in computing, but first we will develop a Turing procedure that is a simulator for the VS computer.

The VS computer has an accumulator, which can be simulated by a variable declared by

> **var** *accumulator:* **int**

It also has a memory containing 100 words, whose addresses are 0 to 99. This can be simulated by an array:

> **const** *memorySize* := *99*
>
> **var** *memory:* **array** *0..memorySize* **of int**

There is a special string memory. Assuming that the VS computer can hold, at most, 10 strings, we can simulate the string memory by another array:

> **const** *numberOfStrings* := *10*
>
> **var** *str:* **array** *1..numberOfStrings* **of string**

We need an instruction pointer to keep track of which instruction is to be executed next.

> **var** *instructionPointer:* **int**

When the VS computer is executing, the instruction pointer has a particular value, say 10, indicating that word 10 contains the operator of the next instruction to be executed. Word 11 contains the operand. If *operator* and *operand* are declared as **int** variables in the simulator, then they should be given values by:

> *operator* := *memory(instructionPointer)*
>
> *operand* := *memory(instructionPointer + 1)*

If the *operator* is 1, meaning *load*, the simulator carries out the *load* machine instruction by executing:

> *accumulator* := *memory(operand)*

If the *operator* is 2, meaning *store*, the simulator carries out the *store* instruction by executing:

> *memory(operand)* := *accumulator*

Similarly, the simulator can carry out the other VS instructions. After each instruction is carried out, the *instructionPointer* is incremented by 2 and *operator* and *operand* are set for the next instruction. When the instruction is a *jump* or *skip*, then *instructionPointer* can be modified so an instruction other than the next sequential instruction will be selected. For example, if the *operator* is 6, for *skiple*, the simulator executes this:

```
if memory(operand) < = accumulator then
    instructionPointer := instructionPointer + 2
end if
```

We will use named constants for each of the VS instructions:

```
const load := 1
const store := 2
    ...
const halt := 9
```

These declarations should be global to the simulator procedure, and we will use

```
const firstInstruction := 0
```

to specify that execution begins with the instruction in words zero and one.

Now we give the complete simulator as a Turing procedure. This procedure assumes that the *memory* and *str* arrays have been declared and initialized.

```
% This procedure simulates a very simple computer
procedure simulator
    var accumulator, operator, operand: int
    var instructionPointer: int := firstInstruction
    loop
        operator := memory(instructionPointer)
        operand := memory(instructionPointer + 1)
        exit when operator = halt
        case operator of
            label load:
                accumulator := memory(operand)
            label store:
                memory(operand) := accumulator
            label add:
                accumulator := accumulator + memory(operand)
            label subtract:
                accumulator := accumulator − memory(operand)
            label jump:
                instructionPointer := operand − 2    % 2 added below
            label skiple:
```

```
          if memory(operand) < = accumulator then
              instructionPointer := instructionPointer + 2
          end if
      label putInteger:
          put accumulator
      label putString:
          put str(operand)
      end case
      instructionPointer := instructionPointer + 2
  end loop
end simulator
```

If you want to run a VS machine language program, you can write a main procedure to put the numbers representing the program and constants into the *memory* array, initialize the *str* array and then call the *simulator* procedure.

USES OF SIMULATORS

We will now discuss some of the uses of simulators. Our simulator for the VS computer can be used to execute VS machine language programs. But it can serve another purpose, too. By reading the *simulator* procedure, you can determine the actions carried out for each VS instruction; if you did not know how a VS computer worked, you could find out by studying its simulator. So not only can the simulator direct one computer to act like another, it can also show how a computer works.

Computer simulators are often used to allow programs written for one machine to execute on another machine. For example, a business may buy a new computer to replace an old computer. After the old computer is removed, programs written for the old computer can be executed by a simulator running on the new machine.

Sometimes a hypothetical computer is designed to help solve some particular problem. This is the case with compilers especially designed to run on small on microcomputers and minicomputers. A hypothetical computer is designed to allow easy translation from high level programs to the hypothetical computer's machine language. The translated programs are executed using a simulator for the hypothetical machine. Other compilers translate programs into the real computer's machine language; then a simulator is not required because the translated program is executed directly by the computer.

CHAPTER 22 SUMMARY

In this chapter we have presented features of machine language in terms of a very simple hypothetical computer called VS. The VS computer has an accumulator that is used for doing calculations. There are VS machine instructions for loading, storing, adding to, subtracting from, and outputting the accumulator. There is a machine instruction for outputting strings. There are instructions for jumping to instructions, skipping instructions and for halting. The nine VS machine instructions were sufficient for the translation of the example Turing program given in this chapter. Real computers typically have many more instructions. The following important terms were discussed:

Word — the computer's main memory is divided into words. Each word can contain a number. In real computers, a word can contain several characters, for example, 4 characters.

Location (or address) — the number that locates a particular word in the computer's main memory.

Operators and operands — most VS machine instructions, such as,

> *load i*

consist of an operator and an operand; these are *load* and *i* in this example. Some instructions have an operator but no operand.

Mnemonic name — a name that helps programmers remember something. For example, *store* is the mnemonic name for VS machine instruction number 2.

Machine language — the purely numeric language that is directly executed by a particular type of computer. Some computer manufacturers sell families of computers, of various sizes and speeds, that all use the same machine language.

Assembly language — programs in assembly language use mnemonic names corresponding to the numeric operators of machine language. They also permit programmers to choose mnemonic names for the operands and labels.

Assembler — a program that translates programs written in assembly language to machine language.

Label — a name that gives the location of a machine instruction or a statement. The *jump* machine instruction, as written in assembly language, transfers control to a labelled instruction. The **goto** statement, available in languages like Fortran and Pascal, but not in Turing, transfers control to a labelled statement.

Simulator — a program that simulates some system such as a computer. A simulator treats a sequence of numbers as a machine language program and carries out the specified operations.

CHAPTER 22 EXERCISES

1. The VS computer described in this chapter does not have an instruction for reading data. Invent an instruction named *getInteger* that reads the next integer in the data into the accumulator. Show how to translate a statement such as

   > **get** *k*

   into VS machine language, as augmented by *getInteger*. Show how the *simulator* procedure given in this chapter can be modified to execute *getInteger* instructions.

2. Translate the following Turing program into VS assembly language and then into VS machine language.

   > **var** *i, j:* **int**
   > *i := 1*
   > *j := 5*
   > **if** *i < = j* **then**
   >   **put** *"i is smaller"*
   > **else**
   >   **put** *"j is smaller"*
   > **end if**

3. What will the following VS assembly language program output? Translate the program to both machine language and Turing.

	load	*zero*
	store	*previous*
	load	*one*
	store	*current*
l1:	*load*	*fifty*
	skiple	*current*
	jump	*l2*
	load	*current*
	add	*previous*
	store	*next*
	load	*current*
	store	*previous*
	load	*next*
	store	*current*

putInteger
jump   *l1*
l2:   *halt*

4.   In this chapter an example program was given that output powers of 2. Have this program executed by the VS simulator given in this chapter. This can be done by writing a main procedure that declares *memory* and *string* arrays, initializes these arrays to hold the machine language version of the example program, and then calls the *simulator* procedure.

5.   Invent new instructions for the VS computer that allow array indexing and procedure call and return.

Appendix: TURING LANGUAGE REPORT

By R.C. Holt and J.R. Cordy

Abstract. This report specifies the Turing language. Turing is a general purpose programming language that is well suited for teaching programming. It is designed to support the development of reliable, efficient programs. It incorporates language features that decrease the cost of program maintenance and that support formal verification.

Turing is designed to be supported by a user-friendly compiler and run-time system of modest size; these should insulate the user from vagaries of the underlying hardware and operating system. Turing is a Pascal-like language and incorporates almost all of Pascal's features. Turing alleviates many difficulties with Pascal; for example, Turing provides convenient string handling, it provides modules, its variant records (unions) are type safe, and it has dynamic parameters and arrays.

Acknowledgements. The design of the Turing language has drawn heavily from previous programming languages and from the advice and help of a number of people. The heaviest debt is to the Euclid family of languages, including Concurrent Euclid, which in turn draws extensively from Pascal.

The language design was greatly helped by concurrent development of its formal semantics, its first compilers and a text book. J.A. Rosselet formally specified the language's context checking using his ADL notation. P.A. Matthews developed Hoare-style proof rules for the language; he also helped implement the run-time support package. J.R. Cordy, R.C. Holt, M.P. Mendell and S.G. Perelgut developed the original Turing compiler for the DEC Vax, based on the Concurrent Euclid compiler, using the S/SL compiler-writing system. S.W.K. Tjiang transported the compiler to the IBM 370.

T.E. Hull encouraged the creation of the language and guided the development of its numeric features. J.N.P. Hume co-authored the text book and helped simplify certain language constructs. E.C.R. Hehner helped clarify and simplify procedures and functions. I.S. Weber managed the computer type-setting of the Turing Report and the text book.

The original development period of Turing, from its inception, to its specification and formalization, to using its text book with compilers in classrooms, was 12 months.

The development was made possible by the financial support of the Canadian Natural Sciences and Engineering Research Council and Bell Northern Research Limited.

CONTENTS OF REPORT

1. INTRODUCTION, TERMINOLOGY AND NOTATION

This report specifies the Turing language. Turing is intended to be a general purpose language, meaning that it is potentially the language of choice for a wide class of applications. Because of its combination of convenience and expressive power it is particularly attractive for learning and teaching. Because of its clean syntax, Turing programs are relatively easy to read and easy to write.

The language improves reliability by disallowing error-prone constructs. It provides numerous compile-time and run-time checks to catch bugs before they cause disaster. These checks guarantee that each Turing program behaves according to the Turing language definition, or else a warning message is printed.

To support maximal efficiency, there is an option to remove run-time checking. This option allows well-tested, heavily used Turing programs to be extremely efficient. Each construct in Turing is designed to have an obvious, efficient implementation on current and future computer hardware.

The Turing language has been formally specified and is designed to support formal verification of program correctness. The design of Turing has eliminated verification and security difficulties of Pascal-like languages. For example, compile-time checks are used to prevent aliasing of variables and side effects in functions. Aliasing due to pointers has been eliminated using the concept of **collections**. Variant records (**unions**) have been made type safe by means of a **tag** statement that explicitly selects among the types of values to be represented.

Perhaps the most important programming construct developed in the last decade is the module or cluster, which enforces information hiding and supports data abstraction. Turing incorporates this feature, with the result that construction of large programs as a set of nearly independent parts is relatively straightforward.

Turing is well suited to interactive programming; it is intended for use on personal computers as well as on traditional main-frame computers.

The language is designed to be easily and efficiently implemented. Experience has shown that a production quality portable Turing compiler can be constructed in a few man-months.

1.1 Terminology and Basic Concepts

This section informally introduces basic terms, such as "scope" and "constant", used in describing the Turing language.

Variables and constants. A *variable* is a named item whose value can be changed by an assignment statement. Example:

```
var i: int        % This declaration creates variable i
i := 10           % This assignment sets i's value to 10
```

This example uses comments that begin with a percent sign (%) and are concluded by the end of the line. Various items such as variables are given names; these names are called *identifiers*.

A *named constant* is a named item whose value cannot change. In the following, *c* and *x* are named constants:

> **const** *c* := *25*
> **const** *x* := *sin(y)**2*   % *y is a variable*

In this example, *c*'s value is known at compile time, so it is a *compile-time* constant (or *manifest* constant). (See also "Compile-Time Expressions"). The value of *x* is computed at runtime; it is a *run-time* constant (or *nonmanifest* constant). Since *x*'s value depends on variable *y*, different executions of the construct containing *x*'s declaration may produce different values of *x*. During the lifetime of each *x*, the value of that particular *x* remains constant, even though *y* may change.

An *explicit* constant (or *literal* constant) is a constant that denotes its own value; for example, following are an explicit integer constant, an explicit boolean constant and an explicit string constant:

> *219*
> **true**
> "*Have a nice day*"

Scope and visibility. The textual lifetime of a named item is called its *scope*. For example, the scope of *z* in the following is the body of the **begin** statement.

> **begin**
> > **var** *z:* **real**
> > ... body of begin statement ...
>
> **end**

A declared item's scope is begun by its declaration and continues to the end of the construct in which the declaration occurs. An item's declaration textually precedes any use of the item (except in those cases in which the identifier is preceded by the **forward** keyword).

The visibility (scope) rules of Turing are basically the same as those of the Algol/Pascal family of languages. This means that a declared item is visible (can be named) throughout its scope, including in subconstructs of the scope.

Most constructs (variables, types, constants, subprograms and modules) cannot be named by an identifer that is already visible. That is, for most constructs, redeclaration of names is disallowed.

Certain constructs (modules) in an item's scope do not automatically inherit the ability to access the item. Modules must explicitly import items that are to be accessed in the body of the construct.

A subprogram may optionally use an **import** list to specify items used in the subprogram's body. Example:

```
1       var i: int
2       procedure increase(increment: int )  % Increase i by increment
3           import (var i)
4           i := i + increment
5       end increase
        ...
6       increase(4)   % Increase i by 4
```

In this example, variable *i* is imported on line 3; *i* is imported **var** (as in **var**iable) indicating that *i* can be changed in the procedure (in line 4). If *i* were imported without the **var** keyword, then *i* could be inspected, but line 4, which changes *i*, would not be allowed. A variable that is imported non-**var** is called a *read-only* variable. If a subprogram does not use an **import** list, it is considered to *implicitly* import any items that it actually references. By contrast, a module is required to explicitly import items accessed in the module's body.

Subprograms. Turing has two kinds of *subprograms*; these are *procedures* and *functions.* A procedure is called by a "procedure call statement". Calls to a function occur in expressions and return a value to be used in the expression.

A subprogram header may contain declarations of *formal parameters*, for example, line 2 of the above example declares *increment* as a formal parameter. Each call to the subprogram must supply *actual parameters* corresponding to the formal parameters; for example in line 6 above, *4* is an actual parameter.

Modules. A *module* is a construct used for packaging items including subprograms and variables. Access to these items is controlled by an *export list.* Example:

```
module stack     % Implement a stack of integers
    export (push, pop) % Entries to stack are push and pop
    var contents: array 1..100 of int
    var top: 0..100 := 0
    procedure push(i: int)
        top := top + 1
        contents(top) := i
    end push
    procedure pop(var i: int )
        i := contents(top)
        top := top - 1
    end pop
end stack
    ...
stack.push(14)   % Push 14 onto the stack
```

Since the module exports only *push* and *pop*, these are the only parts of the module that can be accessed outside of the module. To access an exported item, one prefixes its name by the module's name, as in *stack.push*.

Side effects. If executing a construct changes values of items outside of the construct, we say it has *side effects*. For example, the *increase* procedure given as an example above has the side effect of changing the value of variable *i*. Turing prevents functions from having side effects. The method of guaranteeing that functions have no side effects is by disallowing them from having **var** parameters (these are parameters that can be changed), by disallowing them from importing items **var**, and by disallowing them from directly or indirectly importing procedures that import items **var**.

Since expressions cannot have side effects, all calls to a function with the same values of parameters and of imported variables necessarily return the same value. Example:

> *x := f(24)   % Call function f with 24 as parameter*
> *y := f(24)   % Function f does not import x*

After the execution of these two Turing statements, it is necessarily true that $x = y$.

Aliasing. Given distinct visible identifiers x and y, *aliasing* is said to exist if a change to the value of x would change the value of y. In the following, suppose i and j are aliases for the same variable.

> *i := 1*
> *j := 2*

After execution of these statements, i and j (which are actually the same variable) will both have the value 2. Aliasing causes havoc in formal program verification, and confuses the programmer. For these reasons, Turing bans aliasing. This ban is enforced by placing constraints on those language constructs which allow variables to be renamed. In Turing, the only constructs that rename variables are (1) reference parameters to subprograms and (2) the **bind** construct. Constraints on the use of these two constructs guarantee that once the new identifier is visible, either the old identifier is inaccessible or both identifiers are read-only.

Dynamic arrays. An array is said to be *dynamic* if its size is not known at compile time, i.e., if its bounds are computed at run-time. Turing allows dynamic arrays. Example:

> **get** *n   % Read value into variable n*
> **var** *a:* **array** *1..n* **of real**

This creates an array (really a vector) called *a* of *n* **real** values.

Parameters of subprograms can be dynamic. For example, the following function sums the first *i* elements of an array.

```
1        function sum(b: array 1..* of real, i: int) .real
2            var total: real := 0.0
3            for j: 1..i
4                total := total + b(j)
5            end for
6            result total
7        end sum
             ...
8        x := sum(a,10)
```

Line 8 calls the *sum* function to add up the first 10 elements of array *a*. Line 1 uses "*" as the upper bound of parameter *b* to specify that *b* is to inherit the upper bound of its corresponding actual parameter. The final keyword **real** on line 1 specifies that the function returns a **real** value. Lines 3-5 are a **for** statement; it adds the first *i* elements of array *b* to *total*. Line 6 returns the value of *total* as the value of the function.

Checking and faithful execution. An implementation of the Turing language is said to be *faithful* if it meets the following criteria: the results of executing any Turing program will be determined by the source program together with the Turing specification (this Report) or else execution will abort with a message indicating (1) the reason for the abortion and (2) the location in the program where it was executing at the time of abortion. A *checking* implementation guarantees that execution is faithful. Abortion may occur only because of (1) violation of a particular run-time constraint, such as a subscript out of bounds, or (2) resource exhaustion. In most implementations, the only case of resource exhaustion will be due to a lack of storage space for calling a subprogram; however, in some implementations resource exhaustion may be considered to occur for such reasons as excessive processing time or excessive input/output.

The *run-time constraints* are categorized as (1) mathematical constraints or (2) implementation constraints. The *mathematical constraints* disallow those actions that are clearly meaningless, such as division by zero, subscript out of bounds or a false value in an **assert** statement. *Implementation constraints* disallow actions which have a clear meaning but which are infeasible due to hardware or efficiency reasons, such as: limited range of **int** and limited exponent range of **real**. Note that there are compile-time as well as run-time implementation constraints; limited range of case statement labels is an example of a compile-time implementation constraint.

A *non-checking* implementation of Turing may omit any or all of the run-time checks required for faithful implementation; this lack of checking allows Turing programs to have efficiency comparable to programs written in machine-oriented languages. A non-checking implementation may assume that the user has written his program in such a way that there will be no violations of run-time constraints nor resource exhaustion; these assumptions may be used for improving the quality of generated code. A non-checking implementation should provide documentation of the run-time constraints that are not enforced and of any resource exhaustion that is not detected.

This section has introduced basic terminology and concepts. The remaining sections give the detailed specification of the Turing language.

1.2 Identifiers and Explicit Constants

An *identifier* consists of a sequence of at most 50 letters, digits and underscores beginning with a letter; all these characters are significant in distinguishing identifiers. Upper and lower case letters are considered identical in identifiers and keywords, hence *aa, aA, Aa* and *AA* all represent the same identifier. Keywords and predefined identifiers must not be redeclared (they are reserved words).

An *explicit string constant* is a sequence of zero or more characters surrounded by double quotes. Within explicit string constants, the back slash character (\) is an escape to represent certain characters as follows: \" for double quote, \n or \N for end of line character, \t or \T for tab, \f or \F for form feed, \r or \R for carriage return, \b or \B for backspace, \e or\E for escape, \d or\D for delete, and \\ for back slash. Explicit string constants must not cross line boundaries. Within explicit string constants, the following two characters are disallowed: *eos* and *uninitchar.* The *eos* (end of string) character is an implementation dependent character that an implementation may use to mark the ends of strings. The *uninitchar* is an implementation dependent character that an implementation may use to mark a string that has not been assigned a value.

Character values are ordered by either the ASCII or EBCDIC collating sequence (see "Character Collating Sequence").

An *explicit integer constant* is a sequence of one or more decimal digits optionally preceded by a plus or minus sign.

An *explicit real constant* consists of three parts: (1) an optional plus or minus sign, (2) a *significant digits part* and (3) an *exponent part.* The significant figures part consists of a sequence of one or more digits optionally containing a decimal point. The exponent part consists of the letter e (or E) followed optionally by a plus or minus sign followed by one or more digits. If the significant figures part contains a decimal point then the exponent part is optional. The following are examples of real explicit real constants.

$$2.0 \quad -0. \quad .1 \quad 2e4 \quad -56.1e+27$$

"Separators" may appear immediately following the initial sign of an explicit real or integer constant; see "Comments and Separators".

The *explicit boolean constants* are **true** and **false**.

1.3 Comments and Separators

An *end-of-line comment* begins with the character % and ends at the end of the current line. A *bracketed comment* is any sequence of characters not including comment brackets surrounded by the comment brackets /* and */. Bracketed comments may cross line boundaries.

A *separator* is a comment, blank, tab, form feed or end of line. Programs are free-format; that is, the identifiers, keywords, explicit constants, operators and special characters which make up a program may have any number of separators between them.

1.4 Syntactic Notation

The following syntactic notation is used:

{item} means zero or more of the item
[item] means the item is optional

Be warned: although this report uses braces {...} and brackets [...] as syntactic notation, another use of braces and brackets appears in the appendix "Short Forms". That appendix explains the use of braces and brackets as short forms for **loop** and **if** statements.

Keywords and special characters are given in **boldface**. Nonterminals, e.g., *typeSpecification*, are given in *italics*. The following abbreviations are used:

id for *identifier*
expn for *expression*
typeSpec for *typeSpecification*

2. PROGRAMS AND DECLARATIONS

2.1 Programs

A program consists of a sequence of declarations and statements.

A *program* is:

declarationsAndStatements

A program is executed by executing its declarations and statements.

DeclarationsAndStatements are:

{*declarationOrStatement*}

A *declarationOrStatement* is one of:

    a. *declaration* [;]
    b. *statement* [;]

Each *declaration* or *statement* may optionally be followed by a semicolon.

2.2 Declarations

A *declaration* is one of the following:

    a. *constantDeclaration*
    b. *variableDeclaration*
    c. *variableBinding*
    d. *typeDeclaration*
    e. *subprogramDeclaration*
    f. *moduleDeclaration*

Each declaration creates a new identifier (or identifiers); each new identifier must be distinct from other visible identifiers. That is, redeclaration of visible identifiers is not allowed. The effect of the declaration (its scope) lasts to the end of the construct in which the declaration occurs. This will be the end of the program, the end of a subprogram or module, the end of a **begin**, **loop** or **for** statement, the end of a **then**, **elsif** or **else** clause of an **if** statement, or the end of a **case** statement alternative. An identifier must be declared textually preceding any references to it; the exception to this rule is the form "**forward** *id* ", occurring in **import** lists and in **collection** declarations.

2.3 Constant Declarations

A *constantDeclaration* is one of:

    a. **const [pervasive]** *id* [: *typeSpec*] := *expn*
    b. **const [pervasive]** *id*: *typeSpec*
               := **init** (*initializingValue* {, *initializingValue*})

An *initializingValue* is one of:

    a. *compileTimeExpn*
    b. **init** (*initializingValue* {, *initializingValue*})

Examples:

```
const c := 3
const s := "Hello "     % The type of s is string(5)
const x := sin(y)**2
const a: array 1..3 of int := init (1,2,3)
const b: array 1..3 of int := a
const c: array 1..2, 1..2 of int := init (1,2,3,4)
    % Assigns: c(1,1) := 1; c(1,2) := 2; c(2,1) := 3; c(2,2) := 4
```

A *constantDeclaration* introduces a name whose value is constant throughout the scope of the declaration. The named value is either a *compile-time* constant or a *run-time* constant. See also "Compile-Time Expressions". Named nonscalar values are always considered to be run-time values. The initializing expression in form (a) may be a compile-time or run-time expression, and must be assignable to the constant's type (if present). (See "Type Equivalence and Assignability").

The **init** construct is used only to initialize arrays, records and unions. All values in an **init** construct must be compile-time expressions. Note that **init** may be nested inside **init** to initialize records, unions or arrays that contain other records, unions or arrays. The number of elements inside an **init** construct must equal the number of elements of the type being initialized. For a union, the **init** must contain first the tag value and then the field values corresponding to this tag value (see discussion of union types in "Types and Type Declarations").

Constants declared using **pervasive** are visible in all subconstructs of the constant's scope. Such constants need not be explicitly imported.

2.4 Variable Declarations

A *variableDeclaration* is one of:

a. **var** *id* {,*id*}: *typeSpec* [:= *expn*]
b. **var** *id* {,*id*} := *expn*
c. **var** *id* {,*id*} : *typeSpec* := **init** (*initializingValue* {,*initializingValue*})
d. **var** *id* {,*id*}:
      array *compileTimeExpn..expn* {,*compileTimeExpn..expn*} **of** *typeSpec*
e. **var** *id* {,*id*}: **collection of** *typeSpec*
f. **var** *id* {,*id*}: **collection of forward** *id*

Examples:
      var *j,k:* **int** := *1*   % *j and k are assigned initial value 1*
      var *t* := *"Sample output"*   % *The type of t is* **string**
      var *v:* **array** *1..3* **of string** *(6):=* **init** *("John", "Fred", "Alice")*
      var *n:* **int**
      get *n*
      var *w:* **array** *1..n, 1..n* **of real**   % *n by n matrix of reals*

A *variableDeclaration* creates a new variable (or new variables). Form (a) allows optional initialization by an expression while form (c) allows initialization by an **init** clause (see "Constant Declarations"). In form (b), the variable's type is taken to be the "root" type of the *expn* (see "Type Equivalence and Type Assignability"); this type must not be a dynamic array.

Form (d) allows the declaration of *dynamic* arrays, whose upper bounds are run-time expressions. Each upper bound must be at least as large as its corresponding lower bound. Note that a dynamic array cannot be initialized in its declaration.

Forms (e) and (f) are for declaring collections. A collection is essentially an array whose elements are dynamically created and deleted at runtime. Elements of a collection are referenced by subscripting the collection name with a variable of the collection's pointer type. (See discussion of pointers in "Types and Type Declarations".) This subscripting selects the particular element of the collection located by the pointer variable.

A collection must not be declared in a subprogram. (This restriction is made (1) to avoid the possibility of having a function's value depend on whether space exists for a new element, and (2) to avoid the possibility of resource exhaustion due to unreclaimed space of elements in collections local to subprograms.)

The keyword **forward** is used to specify that the type *id* of the collection elements will be given by a later declaration in the collection's scope. The later declaration must appear at the same level (in the same list of *declarationsAndStatements*) as the original declaration. This allows the declaration of cyclic collections, for example, collections whose elements contain pointers to other elements in the collection. A collection whose element type is **forward** can be used only to declare pointers to it until the type's declaration is given.

Elements of a collection are created and deleted dynamically using the statements **new** and **free**; see "Types and Type Declarations" for an example. The statement "**new** *C,p* " creates a new element in the collection *C* and sets *p* to point at it; however, if because of resource exhaustion the new element cannot be created, *p* is set to the value *nil(c)*. The statement "**free** *C,p*" deletes the element of *C* pointed to by *p* and sets *p* to *nil(C)*. In each case *p* is passed as a **var** parameter and must be a variable of the pointer type of *C*. Suppose pointer *q* is equal to pointer *p* and the element they locate is deleted via "**free** *C,p* ". We say q is a *dangling pointer* because it seems to locate an element, but the element no longer exists. A dangling pointer is considered to be an uninitialized value; it cannot be assigned, compared, used as a collection subscript, or passed to **free**.

The value *nil(C)* is the null pointer for the collection.

Collections themselves cannot be assigned, compared, passed as parameters, bound to, or named by a **const** declaration.

2.5 Variable Binding

A *variableBinding* is:

bind [**var**] *id* **to** *variableReference* {, [**var**] *id* **to** *variableReference*}

A *variableBinding* is used to give a new name to a variable (or a part of a variable). This declares an identifier that is itself considered to be a variable. The new variable is considered to be "read-only" unless preceded by **var** (see "Restrictions on Constants and Read Only Items"). Example:

bind var *x* **to** *a(i)*, *y* **to** *r.j*

This declares *x* and *y*, which are considered to be variables; *y* is read-only. Changing the value of *i* during the scope of the **bind** does not change the value denoted by *x*. Variable *a* is inaccessible and *r* is read-only until the end of the scope of the **bind**.

A **module** must not contain as one of its fields a *variableBinding*. (This restriction is made to prevent re-entry into the scope of an existing **bind**.)

Turing does not allow aliasing. Hence, the "root" identifier of the *variableReference* (the first identifier in the reference) of a **var bind** becomes invisible for the scope of the binding. Even though the root identifier is invisible, it cannot be redeclared in its scope. See also "Restrictions Preventing Aliasing". To allow binding to different parts of a variable, each root identifier remains visible to the end of the list of bindings in the *variableBinding*. The new identifiers do not become visible until the end of this list. Bindings that are **var** to different parts of the same variable must be non-overlapping.

3. TYPES

3.1 Types and Type Declarations

A *typeDeclaration* is:

> **type [pervasive]** *id: typeSpec*

A *typeDeclaration* gives a name to a type. The type name can subsequently be used in place of the full type definition.

Named types may optionally be declared **pervasive**. Type names declared using **pervasive** are visible in all subconstructs of the scope in which they are declared. Such types need not be explicitly imported.

A *typeSpec* is one of:

       a. *standardType*
       b. *compileTimeExpn* **..** *compileTimeExpn*
       c. **enum** (*id* {*, id*})
       d. **array** *indexType* {*, indexType*} **of** *typeSpec*
       e. **set of** *baseType*
       f. *recordType*
       g. *unionType*
       h. *pointerType*
       i. *namedType*

The *standardTypes* are:

> **int**
> **real**
> **boolean**
> **string** [(*compileTimeExpn*)]

The standard types are implicitly declared pervasive in the outermost scope.

The optional compile-time expression in a string type is a strictly positive integer value giving the string's maximum length. If the string's maximum length is omitted, it is given a standard default, which will be at least 255. Example:

> **var** *s:* **string** *:= "Hello there"*

An implementation may limit the allowed values for maximum lengths; this limit will be at least *255*. Parameters can be declared to be *dynamic* strings, with maximum lengths declared as "*"; see "Subprograms".

A *scalar type* is an integer, real, boolean, enumerated type, set type, subrange or pointer. The *nonscalar types* are: strings, arrays, records, and union types.

An *index type* is a subrange, enumerated type or a named type which is an index type. Index types can be used as array subscripts, as selectors (tags) for **case** statements and **union** types, and for base types of **sets**.

Form (b) is a subrange type. The two expressions give the lower and upper bounds of the range of values of the type. The two expressions must be both integers or both of the same enumerated type. The lower bound must be less than or equal to the upper bound. Example:

> **var** *i : 1..10 := 2* % *i can be 1,2 ... up to 10*

Form (c) is an enumerated type. The values of an enumerated type are distinct, contiguous and increasing. See definitions of the *ord, succ* and *pred* functions in "Predefined Functions". Example:

> **type** *color:* **enum** *(red,green,blue)*
> **var** *c: color := color.green*
> **var** *d: color := succ(c)* % *d becomes blue*

The values are denoted by the name of the enumerated type followed by a dot followed by an identifier; example: color.green. Enumerated types and their subranges are index types.

Form (d) is an **array** type. Each *indexType* must be a subrange type, an enumerated type or a named type which is an *indexType*. Note that variables and parameters can be declared to be *dynamic* arrays, with run-time upper bounds; see "Subprograms". A dynamic array type must not be given a name. Each *indexType* gives the range of a subscript. The *typeSpec* gives the type of the elements of the array.

Elements of an array may be referenced using subscripts (see "Variables and Constants") and themselves used as variables or constants. Arrays may be assigned (but not compared) as a whole.

Form (e) is a **set** type. The *baseType* of the set must be an *indexType*. An implementation may limit the number of items in a *baseType*; this number will be at least *31*. A variable of a set type is assigned as values subsets of the entire set. See "Set Operators and Set Constructors". Example:

> **type** *smallSet:* **set of** *0..2*
> **var** *s: smallSet := smallSet(0,1)* % *s contains 0 and 1*

A *recordType* is:

> **record**
>   *id* {, *id*} : *typeSpec*
>   {*id* {, *id*} : *typeSpec*}
> **end record**

Variables declared using a **record** type have the fields given by the declarations in the *recordType*. Fields of a record may be referenced using the dot operator (see "Variables and Constants") and themselves used as variables or constants. Record variables may be assigned (but not compared) as a whole.

A **union** type (or variant record) is like a record in which there is a runtime choice among sets (called alternatives) of accessible fields. This choice is made by the **tag** statement, which deletes the current set of fields and activates a new set.

A *unionType* is:

> **union** [*id*]: *indexType* **of**
>   **label** *compileTimeExpn* {, *compileTimeExpn*} : {*id* {, *id*}: *typeSpec*}
>   {**label** *compileTimeExpn* {, *compileTimeExpn*} : {*id* {, *id*}: *typeSpec*} }
>   [**label** : {*id* {, *id*}: *typeSpec*}]
> **end union**

Example:

> **type** *vehicle:* **enum** (*passenger, farm, recreational*)
> **type** *vehicleRecord:*
>   **union** *kind: vehicle* **of**
>   **label** *vehicle. passenger:*
>   *cylinders: 1..16*
>   **label** *vehicle.farm:*
>   *farmClass:* **string** *(10)*
>   **label**:   % *No fields for "otherwise" alternative*
>   **end union**
> **var** *v: vehicleRecord :=* **init** *(vehicle.farm, "dairy")* % *Set tag and farmClass*
> ...
> **tag** *v, vehicle.passenger*   % *Activate passenger alternative*
> *v.cylinders := 6*

The optional identifier following the keyword **union** is the name of the *tag* of the union type. If the identifier is omitted, the tag is still considered to exist, although a non-checking implementation would not need to represent it at run time.

Each compile-time expression following **label** is called a *label value*. These values must be distinct in a given union type. Each label value must be assignable to the tag's type, which is an index type. Each labeled set of declarations is called an *alternative*. The final optional alternative with no label expressions is called the *otherwise alternative*.

An implementation may limit the range of the tag's type; its range, from the minimum label value to the maximum inclusive, will be at least 256.

The fields and tag of a union may be referenced using the dot operator (see "Variables and Constants"), and the fields can be used as variables or constants. Access or assignment to a field of an alternative is allowed only when the tag's value matches one of the alternative's label values (or matches none of the union's label values for the otherwise alternative). A checking implementation checks for this match at each access or assignment to a field. A tag cannot be assigned to and must not be the object of a **var bind** nor passed to a **var** parameter. A union's tag value is changed using the **tag** statement (see "Statements"). In a checking implementation, the **tag** statement will actually change (uninitialize) any existing field values. A non-checking implementation will not necessarily change the fields. Note that **union** types under a checking implementation are "type safe"; so, changing the tag will *not* automatically change values of one alternative to be values of another alternative. A union's tag can be changed by assigning to the entire union.

The identifiers declared as fields of a record, tag and fields of a union type, or values of an enumerated type must be distinct from each other. However, they need not be distinct from other visible identifiers. Fields of records and unions must not be dynamic arrays.

A *pointerType* is:

> **pointer to** *collectionId*

Variables declared using a *pointerType* are pointers to dynamically created and deleted elements of the specified collection; see "Variable Declarations". Pointers are used as subscripts of the specified collection to select the element to which they point. The selected element can be used as a variable or constant. Pointers may be assigned, compared for equality and passed as parameters. Example:

```
var list: collection of forward node
type node:
    record
        contents: string (10)
        next: pointer to list
    end record
var first: pointer to list := nil(list)
```

> **var** *another:* **pointer to** *list*
>
> ...
>
> **new** *list, another*   *% Create new list element*
> *list (another).contents :=* " *Belgium* "
> *list (another).next := first*
> *first := another*

A *namedType* is:

> [*moduleId .*] *typeId*

The typeId must be a previously declared type name. Type names exported from a module are referenced using the dot operator.

3.2 Type Equivalence and Assignability

This section defines the terms *type equivalence* and *type assignability*. Roughly speaking, an actual parameter can be passed to a **var** formal parameter only if their types are equivalent, and a value can be assigned to a variable (or a value passed to a non-**var** parameter) only if the value's type is assignable to the variable's type. Type equivalence is always determined at compile time; assignability sometimes cannot be determined until run time (when the target type is a subrange).

Two types are defined to be *equivalent* if they are

(a)   the same standard type,

(b)   subranges with equal first and last values,

(c)   arrays with equivalent index types and equivalent component types,

(d)   strings with equal maximum lengths,

(e)   sets with equivalent base types, or

(f)   pointers to the same collection; in addition,

(g)   a declared type identifier is equivalent to the type it names, with the exception of **opaque** types (exported from modules).

Outside of the exporting module M an **opaque** type with identifier T is not equivalent to any other type. The exported type $M.T$ is distinct from any other type that M exports or imports. A value of type $M.T$ can be assigned, but cannot be compared, subscripted, or field selected, and cannot be an operand to an operator. All that can be done with a value of an opaque type is to assign it or to pass it as a subprogram parameter. See "Modules" for an example using **opaque** types.

Each textual instance of a type definition for an enumerated, record or union type creates a new type that is not equivalent to any other type definition.

The **int** type is not considered to be equivalent to any integer subrange. The **string** type without explicit maximum length is not considered to be equivalent to any **string** type having an explicit maximum length.

The *root* type of any integer expression is **int**, that of any enumerated value is the defining enumerated type, that of any string expression is **string** (without specified maximum length), and that of any other value is the value's type. Note that the root type of an integer subrange is **int** and that of an enumerated subrange is the original **enum** type.

A value is *assignable* to a type (called the target type) if (1) the value's root type is equivalent to the target's root type or (2) the value is an integer and the target is **real**. These two requirements are enforced at compile time. In case (1) there is also a runtime requirement that (a) a value assigned to a target subrange is contained in the subrange, and (b) a value assigned to a target string does not exceed the target's maximum length. In case (2) the integer is implicitly converted to real. Throughout the language, wherever a real expression is required, an integer expression is allowed and is converted to real via an implicit call to the predefined function *intreal.*

The type of an expression passed to a **var** parameter must be equivalent to the formal's type. The type of an expression passed to a non-**var** (constant) parameter must be assignable to the formal's type. A dynamic actual array parameter (a parameter with run-time computed upper bounds) can be passed only to a formal array parameter with * declared for upper bounds. Similarly a dynamic actual string parameter can be passed only to **string(*)**. See also the discussion of *parameterType* in "Subprograms". Dynamic strings can be assigned, but dynamic arrays cannot. In an assignment *v := e*, a variable initialization, or **const** declaration, or an initialization **init** *v := e*, *e* must be assignable to *v* and neither *v* nor *e* can be dynamic arrays. Examples:

> **type** *smallint: 0..10*
> **var** *i: smallint*
> **var** *j: 1..100*   % *Variable j is assignable to i when in range 0..10*
>
> **type** *smallarray:* **array** *0..10* **of real**
> **var** *a:* **array** *smallint* **of real**   % *Equivalent to smallarray*
>
> **type** *rec:*
>   **record**
>   *f:* **string**
>   *g:* **real**
>   **end record**
> **var** *r1: rec*
> **var** *r2: rec*
> **var** *r3:*   % *Not equivalent to r1 and r2*
>   **record**
>   *f:* **string**

> *g:* **real**
> **end record**

Variables *i* and *j* have the same root type (**int**), so one can be assigned to the other, given that the assigned value is in the target's declared range. Array *a*'s type is equivalent to the type *smallarray*, so *a* could be assigned to a variable or passed to a formal parameter of type *smallarray*. The types of *r1* and *r2* are equivalent and one can be assigned to the other. However, *r3*'s type is not equivalent to the type of *r1* and *r2*.

4. SUBPROGRAMS AND MODULES

4.1 Subprograms

A *subprogram* is a procedure or a function.

A *subprogramDeclaration* is one of:

    a. *subprogramHeader*
        [*importList*]
        subprogramBody

    b. **forward** *subprogramHeader*
        import ([[**var**] [**forward**] *id* {, [**var**] [**forward**] *id* }])

    c. **body procedure** *id*
        subprogramBody

    d. **body function** *id*
        subprogramBody

A *subprogramHeader* is one of:

    a. **procedure** [**pervasive**] *id*
        [(*parameterDeclaration* {, *parameterDeclaration*})]

    b. **function** [**pervasive**] *id*
        [(*parameterDeclaration* {, *parameterDeclaration*})] [*id*] : *typeSpec*

A **pervasive** subprogram is implicitly imported into all subconstructs of the current scope (including into the subprogram's body). A subprogram that imports variables or modules (**var** or non-**var**, directly or indirectly) must not be pervasive.

A procedure is invoked by a procedure call statement, with actual parameters if required. A function is invoked by using its name, with actual parameters if required, in an expression. If a subprogram *P* has no parameters, a call to it does not require parentheses, i.e., the call is of the form "*P*" and not "*P()*".

A procedure may return explicitly by executing a **return** statement or implicitly by reaching the end of the procedure body. A function returns via a **result** statement (see "Statements").

Subprograms may optionally take parameters, the types of which are defined in the header. The parameters can be referred to inside the subprogram using the names declared in the header. Parameters to a procedure may be declared using **var**, which means the parameter is considered to be a variable inside the procedure. Parameters declared without using **var** are considered to be constants. Functions are not allowed to have any side effects and cannot have **var** parameters.

The identifiers declared in a parameter list must be distinct from each other. However, they need not be distinct from any other visible identifiers.

A *parameterDeclaration* is one of:

    a. [**var**] *id* {, *id*} : *parameterType*
    b. *subprogramHeader*

Form (a) is used to declare formal parameters that are **var** (variable) or non-**var** (constant). An actual parameter that is passed to a **var** formal must be a variable whose type is "equivalent" to the formal's type. An actual parameter that is passed to a non-**var** formal parameter must be a value that is "assignable" to the formal's type. (See "Type Equivalence and Assignability".)

A *reference* parameter is any non-scalar or **var** parameter. Parameters that are not reference parameters are called *value* parameters; a value parameter is any scalar non-**var** parameter. See "Restrictions Preventing Aliasing" for constraints on the use of **var** and reference parameters. Example:

```
function odd(i: int): boolean     % i is a value parameter
    result  (i mod  2) not =  0
end odd
```

Example:

```
var messageCount: int := 0
procedure putMessage(msg: string)   % msg is a reference parameter
    messageCount := messageCount + 1
    put "Message number", messageCount, ":", msg
end putMessage
```

The second kind of *parameterDeclaration*, form (b), specifies a *parametric subprogram.* The corresponding actual parameter must be a subprogram identifier. The actual parameter subprogram must have parameters and result type equivalent to those of the formal parameter. Parametric subprograms are called like other subprograms. Declaring a parametric subprogram as **pervasive** has no effect. Example:

```
% Find zero of parametric function f
function findZero (function f(r: real ): real,
    left,right,accuracy: real ): real
    pre sign(f(left)) not = sign(f(right)) and accuracy > 0
    var L: real := left
    var R: real := right
    var M: real
    const signLeft := sign(f(left))
    loop
        M := (R + L)/2
        exit when abs(R− L) < = accuracy
        if signLeft = sign(f(M)) then
            L := M
        else
            R := M
        end if
    end loop
    result M
end findZero
```

A *parameterType* is one of:

    a.   *typeSpec*
    b.   **array** *compileTimeExpn* **..** * {, *compileTimeExpn* **..** *} **of** *typeSpec*
    c.   [**array** *compileTimeExpn* **..** * {, *compileTimeExpn* **..** *} **of**] **string** (*)

In forms (b) and (c), the upper bounds of the index types of a *dynamic* array parameter are declared as * in which case any array whose element type and index types' lower bounds are equivalent to the parameter's can be passed to the parameter. In form (c), the maximum length of a *dynamic* string is declared as *. For **var** parameters or arrays of strings, the maximum length is taken to be that of the actual parameter. For non-array, non-**var** formal parameters, the type **string**(*) is taken to mean simply **string**. Note that multiple parameters declared using one dynamic parameter type do not necessarily have the same upper bounds and string maximum lengths; instead each parameter inherits the sizes of its actual parameter. The upper bounds and maximum lengths of dynamic parameters can be accessed using *upper*, see "Attributes".

An *importList* is:

    import ([[**var**] *id* {, [**var**] *id*}])

If a subprogram has an **import** list, it uses this to specify identifiers visible outside the subprogram that are to be visible in the subprogram's body. Identifiers not in the list will not be visible in the body. Pervasive identifiers need not be imported (they are implicitly imported). If a subprogram does not have an **import** list, it is considered to implicitly import identifiers that textually appear in its body. An implicitly imported identifier is considered to be imported **var** if it is assigned to, bound to **var**, passed to a **var** parameter, or acted on by a **tag**, **new** or **free** statement inside the subprogram. The identifier is also considered to be imported **var** if (1) it names a module and (2) a procedure of this is called in the subprogram. Modules also have **import** lists, and these have the same meaning as in subprograms with the following difference: a module with no explicit **import** list is considered to have this **import** list:

> **import** ()

Only identifiers that name variables or modules can be imported **var**. (See "Restrictions on Constants and Read Only Items.")

Functions are not allowed to have side effects and cannot import anything **var**. This restriction is transitive; hence a function cannot import a procedure that directly or indirectly imports anything **var**. Input/output is considered to be a side effect; hence functions cannot use **get** or **put** statements; they must not directly or indirectly call procedures that use these statements or that call the predefined procedures. A parametric procedure that is passed as an actual parameter to a function must not directly or indirectly import anything **var** or directly or indirectly use the **get** and **put** statements or the predefined procedures.

An identifier must not be repeated in an **import** list. It is permissible to import pervasive identifiers and predefined identifiers.

When a subprogram *P* is passed as a parametric subprogram to subprogram *Q*, any variables imported **var** directly or indirectly by *P* are considered to be **var** parameters passed to *Q*. Any variables imported directly or indirectly non-**var** by *P* are considered to be read-only reference parameters passed to *Q*. This is done to prevent potential aliasing as a result of the call.

The *result type* of a function is given by the *typeSpec* that follows the function's (optional) parameter declarations. The expression in a function's **result** statement must be assignable to the function's result type. Note that the result type can be a nonscalar, but must not be a dynamic array or dynamic string. The optional identifier preceding this *typeSpec* is the name of the function's result. This identifier can only be referenced in the function's **post** assertion.

A *subprogramBody* is:

> [**pre** *booleanExpn*]
> [**init** *id* := *expn* {, *id* := *expn*}]
> [**post** *booleanExpn*]
> *declarationsAndStatements*
> **end** *id*

The identifier following **end** must be the name of the subprogram. The **pre** expression must be true when the subprogram is called; the **post** expression must be true when returning.

The **init** clause defines constants (the identifiers to the left of each assignment operator :=). These can only be accessed in **post**, **assert** and **invariant**.

A **forward** subprogram is a subprogram whose **body** declaration will be given later in its scope. (This is the only situation in which the keyword **body** is used as a prefix for a subprogram declaration.) The **body** declaration must appear at the same level (in the same list of *declarationsAndStatements*) as the **forward** declaration. The prefix **forward** in an **import** list can be applied only to subprograms. The use of **forward** in an **import** list refers to a subprogram declared later in the same list of *declarationsAndStatements*. Before a subprogram can be called, its header as well as headers of subprograms directly or indirectly called by it must have appeared. A function must not call a **forward** procedure. (This restriction is imposed to simplify checks for side effects in functions). **Forward** subprograms allow subprograms to be mutually recursive. Example of mutual recursion:

```
% Evaluate an input expression e of the form t { + t } where
%    t is of form p { * p} and p is of form ( e ) or explicit real constant
% For example, the value of 1.5 + 3.0 * ( 0.5 + 1.5 )"halt" is 7.5

var token: string

forward procedure expn(var eValue: real)
    import (forward term, var token)

forward procedure term(var tValue: real)
    import (forward primary, var token)

forward procedure primary(var pValue: real)
    import (expn, var token)

body procedure expn
    var nextValue: real
    term(eValue)        % Evaluate "t "
    loop        % Evaluate "{ +t}"
        exit when token not = "+"
        get token
        term(nextValue)
        eValue := eValue + nextValue
    end loop
end expn

body procedure term
    var nextValue: real
    primary(tValue)        % Evaluate "p "
```

```
loop                % Evaluate "{*p}"
    exit when token not = "*"
    get token
    primary(nextValue)
    tValue := tValue * nextValue
end loop
end term

body procedure primary
    if token = "(" then
        get token
        expn(pValue)      % Evaluate "(e)"
        assert token = ")"
    else
        pValue := strreal(token)     % Evaluate "explicit real"
    end if
    get token
end primary

get token      % Start by reading first token
var answer: real
expn(answer)     % Scan and evaluate input expression
put "Answer is:", answer
```

The declaration of a subprogram or module must not appear inside a subprogram or statement.

4.2 Modules

A module defines a package of variables, constants, types, subprograms, and sub-modules. The interface of the module to the rest of the program is defined by its **import** and **export** clauses.

A *moduleDeclaration* is:

```
module [pervasive] id
    [importList]
    [export ([opaque] id {, [opaque] id} ) ]
    [pre booleanExpression]
    declarationsAndStatements
    [invariant booleanExpression]
    declarationsAndStatements
    [post booleanExpression]
end id
```

A module declaration is executed (and the module is initialized) by executing its declarations and statements. See "Terminology and Basic Concepts" for an example of a module.

The identifier following the **end** of a module must be the module's name.

A module can be **pervasive** only if it does not import (directly or indirectly) any variables (whether **var** or non-**var**). A pervasive module is implicitly imported into all subconstructs of the scope of the module's name (not including the module itself); this implicit importation is **var** except for importation into functions, where it is non-**var**.

The *importList* gives identifiers visible outside the module that are to be visible inside the module. See the description of **import** clauses in "Subprograms".

Exported identifiers are identifiers declared inside the module which may be accessed outside the module using the dot operator. Unexported identifiers cannot be referenced outside the module. Only subprograms, constants and types can be exported. Variables and modules must not be exported. The **opaque** keyword can be used only to prefix names of types. Outside the module an **opaque** type is distinct from all other types; see "Type Equivalence and Assignability". An identifier must not be repeated in an **export** list. Example:

```
module pervasive Complex     % Implements complex arithmetic
    export (opaque value, constant, add, ... other operations ...)
    % The "value" type is opaque, so information about the representation
    % of complex values is hidden in this module
    type pervasive value:    % "Value" is visible throughout module
        record
            realPt, imagPt: real
        end record

    function constant(realPt, imagPt: real ): value
        var answer: value
        answer.realPt := realPt
        answer.imagPt := imagPt
        result answer
    end constant

    function add(L,R: value): value
        var answer: value
        answer.realPt := L.realPt + R.realPt
        answer.imagPt := L.imagPt + R.imagPt
        result answer
    end add

    ... other operations for complex arithmetic go here ...
end Complex
```

> **var** *u,v: Complex.value := Complex.constant(1.0, 2.0)*
> **var** *w: Complex.value := Complex.add(u,v)*

See "Restrictions Preventing Aliasing" for constraints on reference parameters in calls to enter a module.

The module's **pre** expression must be true when execution of the module declaration begins. The **post** expression must be true when the initialization of the module (execution of its declaration) is finished. The **invariant** expression must be true whenever execution is outside of the initialized module. The initialization of the module must make the **invariant** expression true, and it must be true whenever an exported subprogram is called or returns. The **invariant** expression must not reference any variables or modules imported into the module, nor any functions that directly or indirectly import these. The **invariant** clause must appear before the declarations of exported subprograms.

Module declarations may be nested inside other modules but must not be nested inside subprograms. A module must not contain as one of its declarations a *variableBinding*.

4.3 Restrictions on Constants and Read Only Items

A variable or module is read-only in a subprogram or module into which it is imported non-**var**. An identifier declared non-**var** in a **bind** construct is also read-only. Exported procedures of a read-only module cannot be called.

All components of a constant are considered constant, and all components of read-only variables are considered read-only.

Constants and read-only variables are restricted as follows. They cannot be assigned to, bound to **var**, further imported **var**, or passed to **var** parameters. A constant or read-only union cannot be the object of a **tag** statement. A read-only collection cannot be the object of a **new** or **free** statement.

4.4 Restrictions Preventing Aliasing

Given distinct visible identifiers x and y, *aliasing* is said to exist if a change to the value of variable x would change the value of y. Aliasing is possible only when variables are renamed. In Turing, renaming of variables occurs in only two constructs: reference parameters and **bind**. Aliasing is prevented by placing restrictions on these two constructs.

(Note that variables imported by a parametric subprogram *P* are considered to be parameters to the subprogram to which *P* is passed; see "Subprograms".)

To explain these restrictions, we first define the terms "direct importing" and "indirect importing". A subprogram or module *directly* imports the items in its **import** clause. (A subprogram that does not have an explicit

import clause is considered to have an implicit **import** clause giving the identifiers it accesses; see "Subprograms".) Each item is imported non-**var** (which means read-only for imported variables and modules) or **var**.

A subprogram or module *P indirectly* imports all items that are directly or indirectly imported by items directly imported into *P*. The direct and indirect imports of a read-only module are all considered to be non-**var**.

Aliasing due to the first construct (reference parameters) is prevented by restrictions (a) and (b). Restriction (a): a (part of) a variable is not allowed to be passed to a **var** parameter if the called subprogram or module has another means of accessing (the same part of) the variable. This access can occur in two ways. The first is by a direct or indirect import of the variable by the called subprogram or module. The second is by passing (an overlapping part of) the same variable to another reference parameter in the same call. Restriction (b): (part of) a variable is not allowed to be passed to a *reference* parameter if the called subprogram or module has another means of *changing* (the same part of) the variable. The possibility of changing the variable can occur in two ways. The first is by a direct or indirect **var** import of the variable by the called subprogram or module. The second is by passing (an overlapping part of) the same variable to a **var** parameter in the same call.

Aliasing due to the second construct (**bind**) is prevented by restrictions (c) and (d). Restriction (c): a **var bind** of *y* to *x* makes *x* invisible for the scope of *y*, and a non-**var bind** of *y* to *x* makes *x* read-only for the scope of *y*. Restriction (d): a **var bind** to *x* disallows calls to subprograms or modules that directly or indirectly import *x*, and a non-**var bind** to *x* disallows calls to subprograms or modules that directly or indirectly import *x* **var**.

Function calls never cause aliasing because functions cannot import variables **var** (either directly or indirectly) and cannot have **var** parameters.

5. STATEMENTS AND INPUT/OUTPUT

5.1 Statements

A *statement* is one of:

    a. *variableReference* := *expn*
    b. [*moduleId* .] *procedureId* [(*expn* {, *expn*})]
    c. **assert** *booleanExpn*
    d. **return**
    e. **result** *expn*
    f. **if** *booleanExpn* **then**
          declarationsAndStatements
      {**elsif** *booleanExpn* **then**
          declarationsAndStatements}

[**else**
  declarationsAndStatements]
end if

g. **loop**
  [**invariant** *booleanExpn*]
  declarationsAndStatements
  end loop

h. **exit** [**when** *booleanExpn*]

i. **case** *expn* **of**
  label *compileTimeExpn* {, *compileTimeExpn*} : *declarationsAndStatements*
  {**label** *compileTimeExpn* {, *compileTimeExpn*} : *declarationsAndStatements* }
  [**label** : *declarationsAndStatements*]
  end case

j. **begin**
  declarationsAndStatements
  end

k. **new** *collectionId, variableReference*

l. **free** *collectionId, variableReference*

m. **for** [**decreasing**] [*id*] : *expn..expn*
  declarationsAndStatements
  [**invariant** *booleanExpn*]
  end for

n. **tag** *variableReference, expn*

o. **put** [: *streamNumber*,] *putItem* {, *putItem*} [..]

p. **get** [: *streamNumber*,] *getItem* {, *getItem* }

A declaration inside an **if**, **loop**, **case**, **for** or **begin** statement must not be for a module or subprogram; all other kinds of declarations, including **bind**, are allowed.

Form (a) is an assignment statement. The expression is evaluated and the value assigned to the variable. The expression must be assignable to the variable type; see "Type Equivalence and Assignability".

Form (b) is a procedure call. An exported procedure is called outside the module in which it was declared using the dot operator. See "Subprograms" and "Modules".

Form (c) is an **assert** statement. The boolean expression must be true whenever the **assert** statement is executed. A checking implementation evaluates the assertion at runtime and aborts the program if it is false.

Form (d) is a **return** statement, which causes immediate return from a program or a procedure. A program or procedure returns either via a **return** statement or implicitly by reaching the end of the program or procedure. Functions and module bodies must not contain **return** statements.

Form (e) is a **result** statement, which must be contained in a function and causes immediate return from the function giving the function's value. The **result** expression must be assignable to the result type given in the function's header. Execution of a function must conclude by executing a **result** statement and not by reaching the end of the function.

Form (f) is an **if** statement. The boolean expressions following the keyword **if** and each **elsif** are successively evaluated until one of them is found to be true, in which case the statements following the corresponding **then** are executed. If none of the expressions evaluates to true then the statements following **else** are executed; if no **else** is present then execution continues following the **end if**.

Form (g) is a **loop** statement. The statements within the loop are repeated until terminated by one of its **exit** statements or an enclosed **return** or **result** statement. The boolean expression in the **invariant** must be true whenever execution reaches it; a checking implementation will abort if it is false.

Form (h) is a loop **exit**. When executed, it causes an immediate exit from the nearest enclosing **loop** or **for** statement. The optional boolean expression makes the exit conditional. If the expression evaluates to true then the exit is executed, otherwise execution of the loop continues. An **exit** statement can appear only inside **loop** and **for** statements.

Form (i) is a **case** statement. The optional final clause with no expression between **label** and : is called the *otherwise clause*. The case expression is evaluated and used to select one of the alternative labels. The statements which follow the matching label value are executed. If the case expression value does not match any of the label values then the otherwise clause is executed. If no otherwise clause is present, the case expression must match one of the label values. When execution of the selected alternative is completed, execution continues following the **case** statement.

Each label value must be assignable to the root type of the case expression; see "Types and Type Declarations". The type of the case expression must be an **int** or an index type. Label expressions must be compile-time expressions. The values of all label expressions in a given case statement must be distinct.

An implementation may limit the range of case label values to insure efficient code; this range, from the minimum label value to the maximum, will be at least 256.

Form (j) is a **begin** statement. **Begin** statements are used to group local declarations.

Forms (k) and (l) are **new** and **free** statements for creating and deleting elements of a **collection** (see "Variable Declarations").

Form (m) is a **for** statement. The statements enclosed in the **for** statement are repeated for the specified range, or until the loop is terminated by one of its **exit** statements or an enclosed **return** or **result** statement. The range is given by the value of the two expressions at the time the **for** statement is entered. The types of the two values must be of the same index type or of type **int**. For the first iteration, *id* has the left expression's value; for successive iterations, *id* is increased by one (or decreased if **decreasing** is present), until in the last iteration *id* equals the right value. If the left value exceeds the right (or is less than the right when **decreasing**), there are no iterations. For each repetition, *id* is set to a new value in the range; these are contiguous values that are increasing, unless **decreasing** is specified in which case they are decreasing. The **for** statement is a declaration for *id*, which must be distinct from other visible identifiers. The scope of *id* is from the beginning to the end of the **for** statement. If the *id* is not present, the **for** statement behaves the same, except that the value corresponding to the *id* cannot be accessed. For each repetition, *id* is a constant and its value cannot be changed. The boolean expression in the **invariant** must be true whenever execution reaches it; a checking implementation will abort if it is false.

Form (n) is a **tag** statement. The variable of the statement must be a union. The union's tag is changed to be the value of the expression, which must be assignable to the tag's type. See "Types and Type Declarations" for an example of usage.

5.2 Input and Output

Statement forms (o) and (p) are **put** and **get** statements, which are used to read/write items to/from streams (sequential files of characters). Each *streamNumber* is a non-negative integer expression. Omitting the stream number from these statements results in the default input stream for **get** and the default output stream for **put**. (See also "Predefined Procedures" for *open* and *close*, which are used to associate streams with stream numbers.) The written or read items must be strings or numbers (integer or real). The default input and output streams cannot be selected using a streamNumber. There is a run-time constraint that a particular stream can be read from or written to but not both.

Since functions cannot have side effects, they are not allowed to contain **get** and **put** statements or to directly or indirectly call procedures that contain **get** or **put** statements.

A *putItem* is one of:

    a. *expn* [: *widthExpn* [: *fractionWidth* [: *exponentWidth*]]]
    b. **skip**

From left to right in a **put** statement, either the first expression of the *putItem* is appended to the output stream, or **skip** starts a new line. A new line is also started at the end of the list of *putItems*, unless the list is followed by "..", in which case this new line is not started. The ".." leaves the current line so it can be completed by other **put** statements.

If the *widthExpn* is omitted, then the value is printed in a field just large enough to hold the value. The *fractionWidth* and *exponentWidth* are allowed only for integer and real values.

For string value s, integer value i and real value r, the *putItems* given on the left are defined by the string *putItems* on the right.

s: w	*s + repeat(blank, w-length(s))*
i	*intstr(i, 0)*
i: w	*intstr(i, w)*
r	*realstr(r, 0)*
r: w	*realstr(r, w)*
r: w: fw	*frealstr(r, w, fw)*
r: w: fw: ew	*erealstr(r, w, fw, ew)*

See "Predefined Functions" for definitions of the functions used on the right. Following are example **put** statements with their output.

Statement	Output	Notes
put *24*	24	
put *1/10*	0.1	Trailing fraction zeros omitted
put *100/10*	10	Decimal point omitted
put *5/3*	1.666667	Assumes *fwdefault* = 6
put *sqrt(2)*	1.414214	
put *4.86*10**9*	4.86e9	Exponent printed for $>= 1e6$
put *121: 5*	bb121	Width of 5; blank shown as "b"
put *1.37: 6: 3*	b1.370	Fraction width of 3
put *1.37: 11: 3: 2*	bb1.370e+00	Exponent width of 2
put *"O'Brian"*	O'Brian	
put *"X = ", 5.4*	X=5.4	
put *"XX": 4, "Y"*	XXbbY	Blank shown here as "b"

The **get** statement reads from a stream.

A *getItem* is one of:

    a.   *variableReference*
    b.   **skip**
    c.   *variableReference: **
    d.   *variableReference: widthExpn*

Form (a) supports *token-oriented* input, forms (b) and (c) support *line-oriented* input, and form (d) supports *character-oriented* input. In form (a) the *variableReference's* root type must be integer, real or string, while forms (c) and (d) allow only strings. The value read into a string must not contain an *eos* or *uninitchar* character (see "Identifiers and Explicit Constants").

Form (a) first skips *white space* (defined as the characters blank, tab, form feed, and new line); then it reads the next characters as a token. A token consists of either (1) one or more non white space characters, up to but not including either a white space character or end of file, or else (2) if the token's first character is a quote ("), then it is an explicit string constant. (See also "Identifiers and Explicit Constants".) Explicit string constants can only be input for string *variableReferences.* When the *variableReference* is a string, the value of the explicit string constant or else the characters of the token, are assigned to the variable. If it is an integer, the predefined function *strint* converts the token to an integer before assigning to the variable. Analogously for reals, *strreal* converts the token to real before assigning it to the variable. It is an error to use form (a) if no token remains in the stream.

In form (b), the **skip** option skips white space, stopping when encountering non-white space (a token) or end of file. This option is used to detect whether further tokens exist in the input; if no more tokens exist in the input, all characters of the file are skipped and the *eof* predefined function becomes **true**. The following input stream:

    Alice 216 "World champion"

is used in this example:

> **var** *name, fame:* **string**
> **var** *time:* **int**
> **get** *name, time, fame*
> *% name = "Alice", time = 216 and fame = "World champion"*

Example:

> *% Read and sum a non-empty sequence of numbers*
> **var** *sum:* **real** *:= 0.0*
> **var** *x:* **real**
> **loop**
>   **get** *x,* **skip**   *% After reading x, skip to eof or next token*
>   *sum := sum + x*
>   **exit when** *eof*   *% eof is explained in "Predefined Functions"*
> **end loop**
> **put** *"Sum is:", sum*

Form (c) reads the rest of the characters of the present line (not including the trailing new line character) and assigns them to the *variableReference.* The trailing new line character is read and discarded. (Note: it may be that the final line of a stream is not terminated by a new line character; in this case form (c) reads the remaining characters.) It is an error to use form (c) if no characters remain in the stream (if *eof* is true for the stream).

Form (d) is similar to form (c) except (1) at most *widthExpn* (a non-negative integer) characters are read, (2) the new line character at the end of a line is part of the string assigned to the *variableReference,* and (3) attempting to read past the end of stream is allowed and returns zero characters. Examples:

    var *s,t,u:* **string**
    get *s: **   *% Reads input line, discarding final new line character*
    get *t:20* *% Reads at most 20 characters; t may end with "\n"*
    get *u:1*   *% Reads next char (or null string for eof)*

Example:

    % Read and print stream a line at a time
    var *line:* **string**
    loop
        exit when *eof*
        get *line:** *% Read line*
        put *line*
    end loop

Example:

    % Read and print stream a character at a time
    var *c:* **string** *(1)*
    loop
        exit when *eof*
        get *c: 1* *% "\n" is read into c at end of line*
        put *c ..* *% Lines are ended when c="\n"*
    end loop

6. REFERENCES AND EXPRESSIONS

6.1 References

The syntax for *reference* includes variable references and constant references, as well as function calls, values of enumerated types, and attributes. A *variableReference* is a *reference* that denotes a variable or part of a variable.

A *reference* is:

    [*moduleId* **.**] *id* {*componentSelector*}

A *componentSelector* is one of:

    a. (*expn* {**,** *expn*})
    b. **.** *id*

Form (a) allows subscripting of arrays and collections. The value of each array subscript expression must be in the declared range of the corresponding index type of the array. The number of array subscripts must be the same as the number of index ranges declared for the array. A collection must have exactly one subscript and this must be a pointer to the collection.

Form (a) also allows calls to functions. The number of expressions must be the same as the number of declared parameters of the function. Each expression must be assignable to the corresponding formal parameter of the function.

Form (b) allows field and tag selection for records and unions. (Fields of a record or variable and a union's tag are referenced using the dot operator).

A value of an enumerated type is a special case of form (b), namely, *enumeratedTypeId.id.* The final *id* must be one of the identifiers given in the **enum** type definition.

6.2 Expressions

An *expn* (expression) represents a calculation that returns a value. A *booleanExpn* is an *expn* whose value is **true** or **false**.

Turing is a strongly typed language, meaning that there are a number of constraints on the ways values can be used. The following sections explain how values are mapped by operators to produce new values.

An *expn* is one of the following:

    a.   *reference*
    b.   *explicitConstant*
    c.   [*moduleId*] *setTypeId* (*elementList*)
    d.   *substring*
    e.   *expn infixOperator expn*
    f.   *prefixOperator expn*
    g.   (*expn*)

Form (a) includes (1) references to constants and variables including subscripting and field and tag selection, (2) function calls and (3) values of enumerated types. See "References".

Form (b) includes explicit boolean, integer, real and string constants; see "Identifiers and Explicit Constants". Form (c) is a **set** constructor; see "Set Operators and Constructors". Form (d) is a substring; see "String Operators and Substrings".

An *infixOperator* is one of:

    a. +   (integer and real addition; set union; string catenation)
    b. −   (integer and real subtraction; set difference)
    c. *   (integer and real multiplication; set intersection)
    d. /   (real division)
    e. **div**   (truncating division)
    f. **mod**   (remainder)
    g. **   (integer and real exponentiation)
    h. <   (less than)
    i. >   (greater than)
    j. =   (equal)

> k. < =   (less than or equal; subset)
> l. > =   (greater than or equal; superset)
> m. **not =**   (not equal)
> n. **and**   (boolean intersection)
> o. **or**   (boolean inclusive or)
> p. − >   (boolean implication)
> q. **in**   (member of set)
> r. **not in** (not member of set)

A *prefixOperator* is one of:

> a. +
> b. −
> c. **not**

The order of precedence is among the following classes of the operators, in decreasing order of precedence:

> 1. **
> 2. prefix +, −
> 3. *, /, **div**, **mod**
> 4. infix +, −
> 5. <, >, =, < =, > =, **not =**, **in**, **not in**
> 6. **not**
> 7. **and**
> 8. **or**
> 9. − >

Expressions are evaluated according to precedence, left to right within precedence. Note that exponentiation is grouped from left to right.

6.3 Numeric Operators

The numeric (integer and real) operators are +, −, *, /, **div** (truncating division), **mod** (remainder) and ** (exponentiation).

The **div** operator is defined by:

$$x \, \textbf{div} \ y = trunc(a \div b)$$

where $\div$ means exact mathematical division and *trunc* truncates to the nearest integer in the direction of zero. The result is is of type **int**. The operands can be integer or real. Note that with real operands, **div** may produce an integer overflow.

The **mod** operator is defined by:

$$x \, \textbf{mod} \ y = x - y*(x \, \textbf{div} \ y)$$

If x and y are both integers, the result type is **int**, otherwise the result is real. Note that **mod** applied to real operands is useful for range reduction; for example, for $x > 0$, *sin(x)* can be computed as *sin(x* **mod** *2*pi)*. Note that **mod** with integer operands never produces an overflow, but with real operands, it may produce a real underflow. The / operator requires real operands and returns a real result.

Whenever a real value is required, an integer value is allowed and is converted to real by an implicit call to the *intreal* predefined function; see "Predefined Functions". Note that this rule implies the the / operator can accept two integer operands, but both will be converted real. The operators +, - (infix and prefix), * and ** require integer or real operands; if one or both operands are real, the result is real, else it is integer. The right operands of **div** and / must not be zero. If both operands of ** are integer values, the right operand must be non-negative. Examples:

$$7/2 = 3.5 \qquad\qquad -7/2 = -3.5$$
$$7 \text{ div } 2 = 3 \qquad\qquad -7 \text{ div } 2 = -3$$
$$7 \text{ mod } 2 = 1 \qquad\qquad -7 \text{ mod } 2 = -1$$
$$7 ** 2 = 49$$

A checking implementation is expected to detect division and **mod** by zero, zero to the zero power, integer overflow, and **real** overflow and underflow.

6.4 Comparison Operators

The comparison operators are $<$, $>$, $=$, $<=$, $>=$, and **not**$=$. These operators yield a boolean result. Operands of a comparison operator must have the same root type; see "Type Equivalence and Assignability". Only strings and scalars (values whose root type is integer, real, boolean, enumerated, set or pointer) can be compared. Arrays, records and unions cannot be compared. Booleans and pointers can be compared only for equality ($=$ and **not**$=$). See "String Operators and Substrings" for a description of string comparison.

6.5 Boolean Operators

The boolean operators are **and** (intersection), **or** (inclusive or), $->$ (implication) and **not**. These require boolean operands and return a boolean result. Note that $a ->b$ has the same meaning as (**not** a) **or** b. The boolean operators are conditional; that is, if the result of the operation is determined by the value of the left operand then the right operand is not evaluated. In the following, division by zero is avoided, because the right operand of **and** is executed only if the left operand is true:

if *count* **not** $= 0$ **and** *sum*/*count* > 60 **then**...

6.6 String Operators and Substrings

The only string operator is $+$ (catenation); it requires string operands and returns a string. An implementation may limit the allowed length of string values; this limit will be at least *255*.

The ordering of strings is determined by left to right comparison of pairs of corresponding characters until an end of string or a mismatch is found. See "Character Collating Sequence". The longer string is considered greater. The string with the greater of the mismatched characters is considered greater. Note that strings of differing lengths are never considered to be equal, and there is no implicit "blank padding" of the ends of strings. The following function recursively defines the "greater than" string relation in terms of comparison of strings of length one.

> **function** *GT(s,t:* **string** *): * **boolean**
>   **if** *length(s)* = *0* **or** *length(t)* = *0* **then result** *length(s)* > *length(t)*
>   **elsif** *s(1)* = *t(1)* **then result** *GT(s(2..*),t(2..*))*
>   **else result** *s(1)* > *t(1)*
>   **end if**
> **end** *GT*

The length predefined function returns the number of characters in a string value; see "Predefined Functions".

A *substring* is one of:

1. *reference (expn .. expn)*
2. *reference (expn .. *)*
3. *reference (expn)*

Form (1) takes a substring of the string reference from character L (L is the first expression) to character R (R is the second expression). Form (2) is similar, but R is taken to be the length of the original string. Form (3) is similar, but L and R are both taken to be equal to the expression; therefore, form (3) always returns a string of length one. The following restrictions apply to L and R: L >= 1 and R <= length(reference) and R-L+1>=0. Note that length(s(L..R)) = R-L+1. Note that for L>=1 and L<=length(s), s(L,L-1) is the null string, i.e., the string of length zero. A substring is an expression (not a variable), and it so cannot be assigned to.

6.7 Set Operators and Set Constructors

The set operators are + (set union), - (set difference), * (set intersection), <= and >= (set inclusion), and **in** and **not in** (membership). The set operators +, - and * take operands of equivalent set types and yield a result of the same type. The set operators <= and >= take operands of equivalent set types and yield a Boolean result. The operators **in** and **not in** take a set as right operand and an expression in the set's base type as left operand. They yield a Boolean result.

A *setConstructor* is:

> [*moduleId.*] *setTypeId* (*elementList*)

The *setTypeId* must be the name of a set type. The set constructor returns a set containing the specified elements.

An *elementList* is one of:

    a.   [*expn* {, *expn*}]
    b.   **all**

The element list is a (possibly empty) list of expressions in the base type of the set, or **all**. If **all** is specified, the constructor returns the complete set. If no elements are specified, the constructor returns the empty set.

6.8 Compile-Time Expressions

    A *compile-time expression* is an expression whose value is necessarily computed at compile time. The following are compile-time expressions:

1.   Explicit integer, real, boolean and string constants, as well as enumerated values
2.   Set constructors containing compile-time element values
3.   Compile-time named scalar constants
4.   The result of integer operator prefix $+$ and $-$, and infix $+$, $-$, $*$, **div** and **mod** when the operands are compile-time integer expressions
5.   The built-in functions chr and ord when the actual parameter is a compile-time expression
6.   The result of the catenate operator $(+)$ when both operands are compile-time string expressions

Expressions that are not necessarily computed at compile time are called *run-time* expressions.

6.9 Predefined Functions

    The following are pervasive, predefined functions.

eof(i: **int** *):* **boolean**

    Accepts a non-negative stream number (see description of **get** and **put** statements) and returns true *iff* there are no more characters in the stream. This function must not be applied to streams that are written to (via **put**). The parameter and parentheses can be omitted, in which case it is taken to be the default input stream.

pred(expn)

    Accepts an integer or an enumerated value and returns the integer minus one, or the previous value in the enumeration. Pred must not be applied to the first value of an enumeration.

succ(expn)

    Accepts an integer or an enumerated value and returns the integer plus one, or the next value in the enumeration. Succ must not be applied to the last value of an enumeration.

STRING FUNCTIONS

length(s: **string** *):* **int**

    Returns the number of characters in the string. The string must be initialized.

index(s,patt: **string***):* **int**

> If there exists an *i* such that *s(i..i+length(patt)-1)* = *patt*, then the smallest such *i* is returned, otherwise zero is returned. Note that 1 is returned if *patt* is the null string.

repeat(s: **string***, i:* **int***):* **string**

> If *i>0*, returns *i* copies of *s* catenated together, else returns the null string. Note that if *j> =0, length (repeat(t,j))* = *j*length(t).*

MATHEMATICAL FUNCTIONS

abs(expn)

> Accepts an integer or real value and returns the absolute value. The type of the result is integer if the *expn* is an integer; otherwise it is real.

max(expn,expn)

> Accepts two numeric (real or integer) values and returns their maximum. If both are integers, the result is an integer; otherwise it is real.

min(expn,expn)

> Accepts two numeric (real or integer) values and returns their minimum. If both are integers, the result is an integer; otherwise is is real.

sign(r: **real***): − 1..1*

> Returns − *1* if *r < 0*, *0* if *r = 0*, and *1* if *r > 0*.

sqrt(r: **real***):* **real**

> Returns the positive square root of *r*, where *r* is a non-negative value.

sin(r: **real***):* **real**

> Returns the sine of *r*, where *r* is an angle expressed in radians.

cos(r: **real***):* **real**

> Returns the cosine of *r*, where *r* is an angle expressed in radians.

arctan(r: **real***):* **real**

> Returns the arctangent (in radians) of *r*.

sind(r: **real***):* **real**

> Returns the sine of *r*, where *r* is an angle expressed in degrees.

cosd(r: **real***):* **real**

> Returns the cosine of *r*, where *r* is an angle expressed in degrees.

arctand(r: **real***):* **real**

> Returns the arctangent (in degrees) of *r*.

ln(r: **real** *):* **real**

> Returns the natural logarithm (base e) of *r*.

exp(r: **real** *):* **real**

> Returns the natural base *e* raised to the power *r*.

TYPE TRANSFER FUNCTIONS

floor(r: **real** *):* **int**

> Returns the largest integer less than or equal to *r*.

ceil(r: **real** *):* **int**

> Returns the smallest integer greater than or equal to *r*.

round(r: **real** *):* **int**

> Returns the nearest integer approximation to *r*. Rounds to nearest even value in case of tie.

intreal(i: **int** *):* **real**

> Returns the real value equivalent to *i*. No precision is lost in the conversion, so *floor(intreal(j))=ceil(intreal(j))=j*. To guarantee that these equalities hold, an implementation may limit the range of *i*.

chr(i: **int** *):* **string** *(1)*

> Returns a string of length *1*. The i-th character of the collating sequence is returned, where the first character corresponds to *0*, the second to *1*, etc. See "Character Collating Sequence". The selected character must not be *uninitchar* (a reserved character used to mark uninitialized strings) or *eos* (a reserved character used to mark the end of a string). See "Identifiers and Explicit Constants".

ord(expn)

> Accepts an enumerated value or a string of length 1 and returns the position of the value in the enumeration or of the character in the collating sequence. Values of an enumerated type are numbered left to right starting at zero. See "Character Collating Sequence".

intstr(i,width: **int** *):* **string**

> Returns a string equivalent to *i*, padded on the left with blanks as necessary to a length of *width*; for example, *intstr(14,4)="bb14"* where *b* represents a blank. The width parameter must be non-negative. If width is not large enough to represent the value of *i*, the length is automatically increased as needed. The string returned by *intstr* is of the form:
>
> > {blank}[-]digit{digits}
>
> The leftmost digit is non-zero, or else there is a single zero digit.

strint(s: **string** *):* **int**

Returns the integer equivalent to string *s*. String *s* must consist of a possibly null sequence of blanks, then an optional plus or minus sign, and finally a sequence of one or more digits. Note that for integer *i*, and for non-negative *w*, *strint(intstr(i, w)) = i.*

erealstr(r: **real***, width, fractionWidth, exponentWidth:* **int** *):* **string**

Returns a string (including exponent) approximating *r*, padded on the left with blanks as necessary to a length of *width*; for example, *erealstr(2.5E1, 9, 2, 2)* ="b2.50e+01" where b represents a blank. The *width* parameter must be non-negative. If the *width* parameter is not large enough to represent the value of *r*, the length is automatically increased as needed. The *fractionWidth* parameter is the non-negative number of fractional digits to be displayed. The displayed value is rounded to the nearest decimal equivalent with this accuracy, with ties leaving the rightmost displayed digit even. The *exponentWidth* parameter must be non-negative and gives the number of exponent digits to be displayed. If *exponentWidth* is not large enough to represent the exponent, more space is automatically used as needed. The string returned by erealstr is of the form:

{blank}[-]digit.{digit}E sign digit {digit}

where "sign" is a plus or minus sign. The leftmost digit is non-zero, unless all the digits are zeroes.

frealstr(r: **real***, width, fractionWidth:* **int** *):* **string**

Returns a string approximating *r*, padded on the left with blanks if necessary to a length of *width*. The number of digits of fraction to be displayed is given by *fractionWidth*; for example, *frealstr(2.5E1, 5, 1)* = "b25.0" where b represents a blank. The *width* parameter is as described under *erealstr*. The *fractionWidth* parameter must be non-negative. If *r = 0* or else *abs(r) < 1e6* and *abs(r) >= 1e−3*, no exponent is displayed, else *frealstr(r, w, fw)* is equal to *erealstr(r, w, fw, defaultew)*; *defaultew* is an implementation defined number of exponent digits to be displayed. For most implementations, *defaultew* will be 2. When no exponent is displayed, *frealstr* returns a string of the form:

{blank} [-] digit{digit}.{digit}

If the leftmost digit is zero, then it is the only digit to the left of the decimal point. The displayed value is rounded as described under *erealstr*.

realstr(r: **real***, width:* **int** *):* **string**

Returns a string approximating *r*, padded on the left with blanks if necessary to a length of *width*, for example, *realstr(2.5E1, 4)* = "bb25" where b represents a blank. The width parameter is as described under *erealstr*. The string *realstr(r,width)* is the same as the string *frealstr(r,width,defaultfw)*, where *defaultfw* is an implementation defined number of fractional digits to be displayed, with the following exceptions. With *realstr*, trailing fraction zeroes are omitted and if the entire fraction is zero, the decimal point is omitted. (These omissions take place even if the exponent part is printed.) If the entire fraction is omitted, then the decimal point is also omitted. If an exponent is printed, any plus sign and leading zeroes are omitted. Thus, whole number values are in general displayed as integers. For most implementations, *defaultfw* will be 6.

strreal(s: **string** *): * **real**

Returns a real approximation to string *s*. String *s* must consist of a possibly null sequence of blanks, then an optional plus or minus sign and finally an explicit unsigned real or integer constant.

6.10 Attributes

There are pervasive attributes that are properties of variables rather than properties of values. For example, the *upper* attribute of a string gives its maximum length. Note that assigning a value to a variable does not change the variable's attributes. Example:

> **var** *s:* **string** *(10)* := *"Eggs"*
> **var** *t:* **string** *(6)* := *"Bacon"*
> *s* := *t*

At all times, *upper(s)=10* and *upper(t)=6*. The available attributes are:

lower(reference [,dimension])

Accepts an array and returns the lower bound of the array.

upper(reference [,dimension])

Accepts an array and returns the upper bound of the array; also accepts a string and returns its maximum length.

In lower and upper, *dimension* is a compile-time integer expression, which can only be present if the *reference* is a multi-dimensional array. It specifies which dimension, where the first is 1, the second is 2 and so on. The *reference* does not need to be initialized.

nil(collectionId)

Accepts a collection and returns the collection's null pointer.

6.11 Predefined Procedures

The following procedures are pervasive and predefined.

rand(**var** *r:* **real** *)*

Sets *r* to the next value of a sequence of pseudo random real numbers that approximates a uniform distribution over the range *0 < r < 1*. Example:

```
% Randomly print a sequence of phrases
var r: real
loop
    rand(r)
    if r > 0.5 then
        put "Hi ho, hi ho "
    else
        put "It's off to work we go "
    end if
end loop
```

randint (**var** *i:* **int**, *low, high:* **int**)

Sets *i* to the next value of a sequence of pseudo random integers that approximate a uniform distribution over the range *low <= i* and *i <= high*. It is required that *low <= high*.

randomize

This is a procedure with no parameters that resets the sequences of pseudo random numbers produced by *rand* and *randint*, so different executions of the same program will produce different results.

randnext (**var** *v:* **real**, *seq: 1..10)*

This has the same effect on *r* as does *rand*, with the difference that *seq* specifies one of 10 independent and repeatable sequences of pseudo random real numbers.

randseed (*seed:* **int**, *seq: 1..10)*

This restarts one of the sequences generated by *randnext*. Each restart with the same seed causes *randnext* to produce the same sequence for the given sequence.

open (**var** *streamNumber:* **int**, *fileName:* **string**, *mode:* **string**)

The *fileName* gives the name of a file that is to be read from or written to. The *streamNumber* parameter is set to the stream number to be used for the file in **get** or **put**. The *mode* must be "*r* " (for *read*) or "*w* " (for *write*) indicating whether the stream is to be read from or written to. If the *open* fails, *streamNumber* is set to zero.

close (*streamNumber:* **int**)

This disassociates the stream number from the stream it is presently designating.

The predefined procedures (*rand, randint, randomize, randnext, randseed, open* and *close*) have side effects. As a result, functions are not allowed to contain them or to directly or indirectly call procedures that contain them.

6.12 Uninitialized Values

The value of a scalar, string or set that is not initialized must not be used (fetched) in evaluating an expression. For example, before any of the following are executed, variable x must have been assigned a value.

> **const** $c := x$
> $y := x + y$
> $P (x + y)$

A scalar, string or set need not be initialized before being passed to a **var** parameter, but must be initialized before being passed to a non-**var** parameter. These rules imply that once a particular scalar, string or set variable is initialized, it will stay initialized.

A variable that has been declared and not assigned to (and not initialized in its declaration) is considered to be uninitialized. When an element of a collection is created by the **new** statement, it is uninitialized. Fields of a union become uninitialized when the **tag** statement is applied to the union. Part or all of an array, record or union variable may become uninitialized when the variable is assigned to, according to the initialization of the value being assigned.

When conditional evaluation of an expression does not require a particular value, the value need not be initialized. For example, in the following, if $i=10$ then x need not be initialized:

> **exit when** $i = 10$ **or** $x = y$

A nonscalar that is not a string or set can be assigned, used as the value of a **const**, passed to a parameter (**var** or non-**var**) or returned as a function result without being initialized. Note: the nonscalars in question (i.e. nonscalars that are not strings or sets) are arrays, records and unions. Scalar, string or set components of nonscalar types must be initialized before being used (fetched). An initialized component of a nonscalar can become uninitialized due to assigning to the containing nonscalar variable or changing the tag of the containing union.

A checking implementation of Turing is expected to enforce these restrictions on the use of uninitialized values.

6.13 Character Collating Sequence

Certain Turing language features, notably string comparison and the chr predefined function, depend on the character *collating sequence*. This is the sequence that determines the ordering among character values. There are two widely used collating sequences: ASCII and EBCDIC. A Turing implementation is expected to use one of these, with preference given to ASCII. Note that a Turing program that is correct assuming one of these sequences is not necessarily correct assuming the other.

The *ord* function maps a character value to its corresponding ASCII or EBCDIC value, which will be in the range *0..255*. For standard ASCII characters, the range is limited to *0..127*. Therefore, subject to limits on the domain of succ:

For *c* in char: *chr(ord(c))* = *c* and
$$succ(c) = chr(ord(c) + 1)$$

The ASCII and EBCDIC sequences share the important property that digits are contiguous.

For *c* in "*0*".."*8*": *succ(c)* = *chr(ord(c) + 1)*

Therefore, if *s* is the string of length 1 corresponding to integer *i* then *ord(s)-ord("0")* = *i*, for example, *ord("3")-ord("0")* = *3*. In ASCII, letter characters are also contiguous:

$$ord("A") = ord("B") - 1 = ord("C") - 2... = ord("Z") - 25$$
$$ord("a") = ord("b") - 1 = ord("c") - 2... = ord("z") - 25$$

Unfortunately, in EBCDIC the letters are not contiguous; there are gaps between letters *I* and *J* and between *R* and *S*. The test to see if ASCII character c is a capital letter is:

$$c > = "A" \textbf{ and } c < = "Z"$$

But for EBCDIC character c, we must use:

$$(c > = "A" \textbf{ and } c < = "I") \textbf{ or }$$
$$(c > = "J" \textbf{ and } c < = "R") \textbf{ or }$$
$$(c > = "S" \textbf{ and } c < = "Z")$$

Consult standard definitions of ASCII and EBCDIC collating sequences for more details.

6.14 Source Inclusion Facility

Other source files may be included as part of a program using the **include** construct.

An *includeConstruct* is:

include *explicitString*

The *explicitString* gives the name of a source file to be included in the compilation. The **include** construct is *replaced* in the program source by the contents of the specified file.

Include constructs can appear anywhere in a program and can contain any valid source fragment. Included source files can themselves contain **include** constructs.

APPENDIX: Short Forms

The following forms can be used as alternatives for the syntax given in the language specification. These alternatives shorten frequently used constructs.

Long form   Short form

$v := v + (expn)$ $v += expn$
$v := v - (expn)$ $v - = expn$
$v := v * (expn)$ $v *= expn$

if *expn* **then** *statements*   [*expn*: *statements*
elsif *expn* **then** *statements* | *expn*: *statements*
else *statements* |: *statements*
end if   ]

case *expn* **of**   **case** *expn* **of**
   label *expns* : *statements* | *expns* : *statements*
    ...   ...
   label : *statements* |: *statements*
end case   **end case**

union *id: typeSpec* **of**   **union** *id: typeSpec* **of**
   label *expns* : *declarations* | *expns* : *declarations*
    ...   ...
   label : *declarations* |: *declarations*
end union   **end union**

loop   {
   statements   *statements*
end loop   }

exit   >>

exit when *expn*   >>: *expn*

return   >>>

result *expn*   >>>: *expn*

for *optionalId* : *expn..expn*   { + *optionalId* : *expn..expn*
   statements   *statements*
end for   }

for decreasing *optionalId* :
    expn..expn
    statements
end for
	{— *optionalId* : *expn..expn*
	
	    statements
	
	}

and	&
not	~
put	!
get	?
array *indexTypes* **of**	{ *indexTypes* }
procedure	**proc**
function	**fcn**
pervasive	*
import	:

Example using short forms.

Long form

```
function pervasive  GCD(i,j: int): int
    var x: int := i
    var y: int := j
    loop
        exit when x = y
        if x>y then
            x := x—y
        else
            y := y—x
        end if
    end loop
    result x
end  GCD
```

Short form

```
fcn *GCD(i,j: int): int
    var x := i
    var y := j
    {  >>· x=y
        [ x>y. x — = y
        |     : y — = x
        ]
    }
    >>>: x
end  GCD
```

APPENDIX: Keywords and Predefined Identifiers

Keywords of Turing

all	and	array	assert	begin
bind	body	boolean	case	collection
const	decreasing	div	else	elsif
end	enum	exit	export	false
fcn	for	forward	free	function
get	if	import	in	include
init	int	invariant	label	loop
mod	module	new	not	of
opaque	or	pervasive	pointer	post
pre	proc	procedure	put	real
record	result	return	set	skip
string	tag	then	to	true
type	union	var	when	

Predefined Identifiers of Turing

abs	*arctan*	*arctand*	*ceil*	*chr*
close	*cos*	*cosd*	*eof*	*erealstr*
exp	*floor*	*frealstr*	*index*	*intreal*
intstr	*length*	*ln*	*lower*	*max*
min	*nil*	*open*	*ord*	*pred*
rand	*randint*	*randnext*	*randomize*	*randseed*
realstr	*repeat*	*round*	*sign*	*sin*
sind	*sqrt*	*strint*	*strreal*	*succ*
upper				

APPENDIX:

Implementation Constraints on Integer, String, and Real Types

Ideally, there should be no implementation constraints on Turing programs (see description of *mathematical* and *implementation constraints* in "Terminology and Basic Concepts). If there are no implementation constraints, then we call the language *Ideal Turing*. In Ideal Turing, the **int** type has an infinite range of values, and the **real** type has infinite precision and infinite exponent range; that is, **int** and **real** correspond exactly to the mathematical concepts of the integers and the real numbers. Similarly, in Ideal Turing the type *string* (without an explicit length), comprises all sequences of characters, with no limit on length.

Programs written in Ideal Turing can be thought of as mathematical objects, rather than as instructions for a computer. For example:

function *factorial(i:* **int** *):* **int**
    pre *i* $> = 0$
    if *i* $= 0$ **then**
        result *1*
    else
        result *i* $*$ *factorial(i* $-$ *1)*
    end if
  end *factorial*

In Ideal Turing, this function gives a definition of "factorial" for all non-negative integers; but note that in a particular implementation of Turing, integer overflow will occur for large values of *i.*

In most practical implementations of Turing, **int** will be limited to a range of integers: *minint..maxint,* and string lengths will be limited to *strmax.* To support program portability, it is recommended that in all implementations, *minint* $< = -(2**31 - 1),$ *maxint* $> = 2**31 - 1,$ and *maxstr* $> = 255.$

In an implementation, each non-zero **real** *r* may be represented by a floating point number of the form:

$$r = f * radix ** e$$

where:

    f is the significant digits part,
    e is the exponent,
    radix is the number base of the representation.

It is assumed that *f* is *normalized,* i.e., if *f* is not zero then

$$1/radix < = abs(f) \textbf{ and } abs(f) < 1.0$$

If *f* is zero then *e* is also zero. The number of digits of precision of *f* (in the given radix) may be limited to *numdigits.*

In most practical implementations, the exponent *e* will be limited to the range *minexp..maxexp.* To support program portability, it is recommended that the equivalent base 10 range of exponents be at least $-38..38,$ i.e., that *minexp* $* ln(radix)/ln(10) < = -38$ and *maxexp* $* ln(radix)/ln(10)$ $> = +38.$

Floating point operators provide an approximate but repeatable result corresponding to the exact mathematical result. For operators $+, -, *$ and $/$ with operands *x* and *y,* let *F* be the floating point result and let *M* be the exact result. For non-zero *M* the relative *round off error* is defined as:

$$abs((M-F)/M)$$

(If *M* is exactly zero, *F* should also be zero.) Each implementation of Turing is to specify the value of *rreb* (relative round off error bound) such that the round-off error for $+$, $-$, $*$ and $/$ never exceeds *rreb*. To support program portability, it is recommended that *rreb* be at most *1e−14*.

For implementations using rounding floating point operators, such as the DEC VAX, *rreb* is:

$$rreb = .5*radix ** (- numdigits + 1)$$

For implementations using chopping floating point operators, such as the IBM 370, *rreb* can be given as:

$$rreb = radix ** (- numdigits + 1)$$

Unfortunately, there are some implementations of floating point in which neither rounding or chopping is consistently carried out; in this case, *rreb* is larger than would be calculated by these formulas.

Each implementation of Turing will provide a standard **include** file called *limits* which will contain definitions of *minint, maxint, maxstr, radix, minexp, maxexp, numdigits* and *rreb*. This **include** file will also contain the definition of functions that access and modify exponents of a floating point values:

getexp(r: **real** *):* **real**
>   Returns exponent *e* of *r*. If *r = 0*, then *e = 0*.

setexp(r: **real** *, e:* **int** *):* **real**
>   Returns value of *r* with the exponent changed to *e*. The value of *e* must be in the range *minexp..maxexp*.

APPENDIX: Collected Syntax of Turing

1. OVERVIEW

This collected syntax of the Turing language is given in the order in which language constructs are presented in the Turing Language Report. The following syntactic notation is used:

>   {item} means zero or more of the item
>   [item] means the item is optional

Be warned: although this notation uses braces {...} and brackets [...] as syntactic notation, another use of braces and brackets appears in the appendix "Short Forms". That appendix explains the use of braces and brackets as short forms for **loop** and **if** statements.

Keywords and special characters are given in **boldface**. Nonterminals, e.g., *typeSpecification*, are given in *italics*. The following abbreviations are used:

>   *id* for *identifier*
>   *expn* for *expression*
>   *typeSpec* for *typeSpecification*

2. PROGRAMS AND DECLARATIONS

A *program* is:

>*declarationsAndStatements*

DeclarationsAndStatements are:

>{*declarationOrStatement*}

A *declarationOrStatement* is one of:

>a. *declaration* [;]
>b. *statement* [;]

A *declaration* is one of the following:

>a.   *constantDeclaration*
>b.   *variableDeclaration*
>c.   *variableBinding*
>d.   *typeDeclaration*
>e.   *subprogramDeclaration*
>f.   *moduleDeclaration*

A *constantDeclaration* is one of:

>a.   **const** [**pervasive**] *id* [: *typeSpec*] := *expn*
>b.   **const** [**pervasive**] *id*: *typeSpec*
>   := **init** (*initializingValue* {, *initializingValue*})

An *initializingValue* is one of:

>a.   *compileTimeExpn*
>b.   **init** (*initializingValue* {, *initializingValue*})

A *variableDeclaration* is one of:

>a.   **var** *id* {, *id*}: *typeSpec* [:= *expn*]
>b.   **var** *id* {, *id*} := *expn*
>c.   **var** *id* {, *id*} : *typeSpec* := **init** (*initializingValue* {, *initializingValue*})
>d.   **var** *id* {, *id*}:
>   **array** *compileTimeExpn..expn* {, *compileTimeExpn..expn*} **of** *typeSpec*
>e.   **var** *id* {, *id*}: **collection of** *typeSpec*
>f.   **var** *id* {, *id*}: **collection of forward** *id*

A *variableBinding* is:

>**bind** [**var**] *id* **to** *variableReference* {, [**var**] *id* **to** *variableReference*}

Note: A collection declaration must not occur in a subprogram. A bind declaration must not occur as a module field.

3. TYPES

A *typeDeclaration* is:

>**type** [**pervasive**] *id* : *typeSpec*

A *typeSpec* is one of:

    a. *standardType*
    b. *compileTimeExpn* **..** *compileTimeExpn*
    c. **enum (** *id* {*, id*} **)**
    d. **array** *indexType* {*, indexType*} **of** *typeSpec*
    e. **set of** *baseType*
    f. *recordType*
    g. *unionType*
    h. *pointerType*
    i. *namedType*

The *standardTypes* are:

> **int**
> **real**
> **boolean**
> **string** [**(** *compileTimeExpn* **)**]

A *recordType* is:

> **record**
>> *id* {*, id*} **:** *typeSpec*
>> {*id* {*, id*} **:** *typeSpec*}
> **end record**

A *unionType* is:

> **union** [*id*]**:** *indexType* **of**
>> **label** *compileTimeExpn* {*, compileTimeExpn*} **:** {*id* {*, id*}**:** *typeSpec*}
>> {**label** *compileTimeExpn* {*, compileTimeExpn*} **:** {*id* {*, id*}**:** *typeSpec*} }
>> [**label :** {*id* {*, id*}**:** *typeSpec*}]
> **end union**

A *pointerType* is:

> **pointer to** *collectionId*

A *namedType* is:

> [*moduleId* **.**] *typeId*

An *indexType* is the *typeSpec* of an "index type" (see "Types and Type Declarations").

A *collectionId* is the *id* of a collection.

A *typeId* is the *id* of a type.

A *moduleId* is the *id* of a module.

4. SUBPROGRAMS AND MODULES

A *subprogramDeclaration* is one of:

    (a) *subprogramHeader*
        [*importList*]
        subprogramBody

    (b) **forward** *subprogramHeader*
        import ([[**var**] [**forward**] *id* {, [**var**] [**forward**] *id* }])

    (c) **body procedure** *id*
        subprogramBody

    (d) **body function** *id*
        subprogramBody

A *subprogramHeader* is one of:

    (a)**procedure** [**pervasive**] *id*
    [(*parameterDeclaration* {, *parameterDeclaration*})]

    (b)**function** [**pervasive**] *id*
    [(*parameterDeclaration* {,*parameterDeclaration*})] [*id*] : *typeSpec*

A *parameterDeclaration* is one of:

    a.   [**var**] *id* {, *id*} : *parameterType*
    b.   *subprogramHeader*

A *parameterType* is one of:

    a.   *typeSpec*
    b.   **array** *compileTimeExpn* .. * {, *compileTimeExpn* .. *} **of** *typeSpec*
    c.   [**array** *compileTimeExpn* .. * {, *compileTimeExpn* .. *} **of**] **string** (*)

An *importList* is:

    import ([[**var**] *id* {, [**var**] *id*}])

A *subprogramBody* is:

    [**pre** *booleanExpn*]
    [**init** *id* := *expn* {, *id* := *expn*}]
    [**post** *booleanExpn*]
    declarationsAndStatements
    end *id*

A *moduleDeclaration* is:

    module [**pervasive**] *id*
        [*importList*]
        [**export** ([**opaque**] *id* {, [**opaque**] *id*})]
        [**pre** *booleanExpression*]
        declarationsAndStatements

[**invariant** *booleanExpression*]
declarationsAndStatements
[**post** *booleanExpression*]
    end *id*

Note: A subprogram or module declaration must not occur inside a subprogram or statement.

5. STATEMENTS AND INPUT/OUTPUT

A *statement* is one of:

    a. *variableReference* := *expn*

    b. [*moduleId* .] *procedureId* [(*expn* {, *expn*})]

    c. **assert** *booleanExpn*

    d. **return**

    e. **result** *expn*

    f. **if** *booleanExpn* **then**
          declarationsAndStatements
      {**elsif** *booleanExpn* **then**
          declarationsAndStatements}
      [**else**
          declarationsAndStatements]
      end if

    g. **loop**
          [**invariant** *booleanExpn*]
          declarationsAndStatements
      end loop

    h. **exit** [**when** *booleanExpn*]

    i. **case** *expn* **of**
          label *compileTimeExpn* {, *compileTimeExpn*} : *declarationsAndStatements*
          {**label** *compileTimeExpn* {, *compileTimeExpn* : *declarationsAndStatements* }
          [**label** : *declarationsAndStatements*]
      end case

    j. **begin**
          declarationsAndStatements
      end

    k. **new** *collectionId, variableReference*

    l. **free** *collectionId, variableReference*

    m. **for** [**decreasing**] [*id*] : *expn..expn*
          declarationsAndStatements
          [**invariant** *booleanExpn*]
      end for

    n. **tag** *variableReference, expn*

    o. **put** [: *streamNumber*,] *putItem* {, *putItem*} [..]

    p. **get** [: *streamNumber*,] *getItem* {, *getItem* }

A *putItem* is one of:

    a.   *expn* [: *widthExpn* [: *fractionWidth* [: *exponentialWidth*]]]

    b. **skip**

A *getItem* is one of:

    a.   *variableReference*

    b. **skip**

    c.   *variableReference*: *

    d.   *variableReference*: *widthExpn*

A *procedureId* is the *id* of a procedure.

A *streamNumber, widthExpn, fractionWidth,* or *exponentWidth* is an *expn* with a non-negative integer value.

6. REFERENCES AND EXPRESSIONS

A *variableReference* is a *reference* denoting a variable.

A *reference* is:

    [*moduleId* **.**] *id* {*componentSelector*}

A *componentSelector* is one of:

    a.   (*expn* {, *expn*})

    b. **.** *id*

A *booleanExpn* is an *expn* whose value is **true** or **false**.

A *compileTimeExpn* is an *expn* whose value is necessarily computed at compile-time (see "Compile-Time Expressions").

An *expn* is one of the following:

    a.   *reference*

    b.   *explicitConstant*

    c.   [*moduleId*] *setTypeId* (*elementList*)

    d.   *substring*

    e.   *expn infixOperator expn*

    f.   *prefixOperator expn*

    g.   (*expn*)

An *infixOperator* is one of:

    a. +   (integer and real addition; set union; string catenation)

    b. −   (integer and real subtraction; set difference)

    c. *   (integer and real multiplication; set intersection)

    d. /   (real division)

    e. **div**   (truncating integer division)

    f. **mod**   (integer remainder)

    g. **   (integer and real exponentiation)

    h. <   (less than)

    i. >   (greater than)

      j. =   (equal)
      k. < =   (less than or equal; subset)
      l. > =   (greater than or equal; superset)
      m. **not** =   (not equal)
      n. **and**   (boolean intersection)
      o. **or**   (boolean inclusive or)
      p. ->   (boolean implication)
      q. **in**   (member of set)
      r. **not in**   (not member of set)

A *prefixOperator* is one of:

      a. +
      b. −
      c. **not**

The order of precedence is among the following classes of the operators, in decreasing order of precedence:

      1. **
      2. prefix +, −
      3. *, /, **div**, **mod**
      4. infix +, -
      5. <, >, =, < =, > =, **not** =, **in**, **not in**
      6. **not**
      7. **and**
      8. **or**
      9. − >

A *substring* is one of:

      1. *reference* (*expn* .. *expn*)
      2. *reference* (*expn* .. *)
      3. *reference* (*expn*)

A *setTypeId* is the *id* of a set type.

A *setConstructor* is:

      [*moduleId.*] *setTypeId* (*elementList*)

An *elementList* is one of:

      a. [*expn* {, *expn*}]
      b. **all**

INDEX